When You Walk

This book is dedicated to the memory of Shelagh Brown, writer, editor of *New Daylight*, and my friend, who died tragically in the year of its publication. Shelagh was an inspiration to myself and many others. She will be sadly missed.

When You Walk

Company and encouragement for ordinary followers of Jesus who sometimes find the going a bit tough

Adrian Plass

Published by
The Bible Reading Fellowship
Peter's Way, Sandy Lane West
Oxford OX4 5HG
ISBN 0 7459 3552 4

First edition 1997
10 9 8 7 6

Acknowledgments
The Revised Standard Version of the Bible (RSV) copyright © 1946, 1952, 1971 by the Division of Christian Education of the National Council of the Churches of Christ in the USA.

The New Revised Standard Version of the Bible (NRSV) copyright © 1989 by the Division of Christian Education of the National Council of the Churches of Christ in the USA.

The Holy Bible, New International Version (NIV), copyright © 1973, 1978, 1984 by International Bible Society. Used by permission of Hodder & Stoughton Ltd. All rights reserved. 'NIV' is a registered trademark of International Bible Society. UK trademark number 1448790.

Good News Bible (GNB) copyright © American Bible Society 1966, 1971 and 1976, published by the Bible Societies and Collins.

The New Jerusalem Bible (NJB) copyright © 1985 by Darton, Longman and Todd Ltd and Doubleday and Company, Inc.

A catalogue record for this book is
available from the British Library

Printed and bound in Great Britain
by Caledonian Book Manufacturing International,
Glasgow

Contents

	Introduction	7
1	The shape of the real world The Sermon on the Mount	9
2	Trailblazing heroes Some Old Testament figures	29
3	Theory or practice—talk or walk A nervous look at the letter of James	49
4	Travelling wisely Words of wisdom from Proverbs	69
5	Finding firm ground Reality in the Bible	89
6	Getting lost Search and recovery in the fifteenth chapter of Luke	109
7	Clear signposts The promises of God	125
8	Passionate parenting on the path to paradise Some reactions to Hosea	153
9	Unauthorized excursions The story of David and Bathsheba	175
10	New beginnings Chances to get up and go—again	193

11 Travelling two by two 211
The sexy Song of Songs

12 Gathering as we go 231
Harvest in the Bible

13 Story power—tales to travel by 243
Parables

14 Gaining fellow-travellers 267
The woman at the well

15 Obedience—aiming for the planned destination 281
The sticky, sulky, salutary story of Jonah

16 Heading for heaven—why did we leave in the first place? 299
1 Corinthians 15

17 Comfort for weary walkers 309
The Holy Spirit

18 Power to persevere 331
The miracle of resurrection

When you walk through a storm,
hold your head up high...

Oscar Hammerstein II

INTRODUCTION

Have you ever watched anyone arriving in heaven? I have. The person concerned was my youngest son, David, who was with me in Liverpool at the time. For most of his twelve years on earth, David had been a passionate supporter of Liverpool Football Club, to the extent that civil war invariably broke out in our house whenever Liverpool was drawn against Manchester United, the side supported with equal fervour by David's elder brother. Now we were in Liverpool itself, actually climbing the steps towards the family stand at Anfield, the footballing home of David's lifelong heroes. As we emerged into the basin-shaped arena with its neatly marked, bright green rectangular floor, I kept my eyes on David's face. No observer at healing or revivalist meetings can ever have witnessed more joy and wonder than I saw on my son's face at that moment. Anfield was real! It really, really did exist, and he, David Plass, was standing in it, breathing genuine Anfield air, waiting for eleven supermen to run from the tunnel over there on the opposite side of the stadium to play on the shimmering emerald carpet that lay below us. He was in heaven—especially as the right team won!

I have always felt that our journey to heaven (the one that isn't Anfield, I mean) will end in a very similar way. We shall be flooded with joy and relief when we discover that the place we dreamed of and worried about and tried to imagine, not only meets, but far exceeds our expectations. It will also, of course, be scheduled to last for a fair bit longer than ninety minutes. The death of Jesus has ensured that injury time will go on for ever.

In the meantime, we travel as hopefully as we can, and, in the process, find ourselves negotiating a variety of interesting obstacles and perilous pathways. We climb, we descend, we stumble, we stroll happily along the infrequent easy bits, and, if we've got any sense, we lean on each other and accept a helping hand from our brothers and sisters whenever things are just too tricky to manage on our own.

This book, a collection of Bible notes I have written for the Bible Reading Fellowship over the last few years, together with new and substantial introductions for each section, is a hand extended to those who travel the same narrow, bumpy road as me, and it is dedicated with sincere gratitude to all those kind people who have picked me up and dusted me down along the way.

Please join me. It does get tough at times, but if we travel side by side towards heaven, and Jesus himself leads us, we shall be like Liverpool Football Club and never walk alone.

A good, honest and painful sermon.

Samuel Pepys

THE SHAPE OF THE REAL WORLD

The Sermon on the Mount

How should I approach one of the greatest pieces of spiritual teaching that mankind has ever received? There is a strong temptation to cut and run. The Sermon on the Mount certainly doesn't need my flimsy footnotes to convey the depth and profundity that give it such central importance in the Christian faith. It feels like being asked to compose a limerick about Mount Everest. I can lose confidence very easily when faced with such a task. I was greatly helped on this occasion, however, by reading a comment by Red Smith, as quoted by Frederick Buechner. Smith said: 'Writing is really quite simple; all you have to do is sit down at your typewriter and open a vein.'

In other words, as Buechner points out, the aim is to effect—for better or worse—a transfusion from writer to reader. I can quite understand that this might sound affected and rather over the top, but it really does speak to me. I think that the idea of figuratively opening a vein makes a lot of sense, not just for writers, but for any of us who want to find within ourselves a true response to sections of scripture that are daunting or overfamiliar. Let me show you what I mean.

When I came to that part of this great discourse where Jesus talks about the broad way leading to destruction, and the narrow way leading to life that is only found by a few, I said to myself, 'Oh, yes, that's the bit that's always frightened me—now, what am I going to say about it?' I very nearly jettisoned my first, genuine, fearful response because it seemed too inward, inappropriate, personal and (ludicrously) trivial. But in fact the vein of fear was the vein that needed to be opened because that is where the life was flowing.

Forgive the violent change of metaphor, but, as we read the Bible, why should we not catch hold of those orphan responses, hanging about hopefully like ragged, starving children at a baker's window, and find out what they look like and what they're capable of when they're brought inside, fed, and warmed up a bit? God says that he will write his law on our hearts, and although others will certainly aid this process, it is essential that we do not simply think what we are told to think and believe what we are told to believe when it is not God who is doing the telling. We may be surprised at what we discover for ourselves.

This kind of approach is particularly important with the Sermon on the Mount because, broadly speaking, Jesus is challenging his listeners to make radical adjustments to the priorities instilled into them by a godless world, and to develop awareness of an eternal context for thoughts and actions and attitudes. It is not a game. It is a matter of life and death. If the way in which we react demands a little blood-letting—then, so be it. His example is before us.

Incidentally, the first of the following notes has become a particularly significant one for me because of a letter that I received in response to it.

I am very fortunate with my post, by the way. People write wonderful letters to me sometimes. Only this morning, for instance, a letter arrived with an Austrian postmark. It had been sent, as many letters are, via Harper Collins, who publish most of my books, but when I opened it I found the contents very puzzling. Inside the envelope was a piece of white paper folded twice. Nothing unusual about that, but when I unfolded this sheet it appeared to be completely blank. Why, I asked myself, has someone sent me a piece of unlined A4 sized white paper with nothing written on it? When I examined the paper more closely I discovered that it wasn't blank at all. There was just one word written in very small letters on the corner of one side of the page.

'*Danke*'.

That was the entire content of the letter, and it was quite enough, don't you think? However, I digress...

The response that I received to the first of these Sermon on the Mount notes was important to me because it further confirmed my belief that I had been right to offer God one of the weakest areas of my personality, that is, my disease of flippancy. I have suffered from this disease for as long as I can remember, and, as those readers who are fellow-sufferers will know, the major symptoms of this disorder are not always easily tolerated by the sufferer's nearest and dearest. In fact, incredibly, they seem to think that *they* are the sufferers! What can they possibly mean?

The trouble is that these symptoms can flare up at any time and in any place. I was at a dinner a couple of years ago, for instance, seated on the same table as a retired bishop and his wife. (I had been pledged to non-flippancy by my wife, who wasn't able to be there, but knows what I'm like.) The bishop, a truly charming, pleasantly old-fashioned man, was talking about the pleasures of retirement, and, in particular, the fresh opportunities that he and his wife had found to take up activities that had tended to fall by the wayside during their busy working lives.

'For example,' said the bishop, 'we have very much enjoyed the renewal of our interest in art.'

'Oh, that's good,' I replied, 'that must be very enjoyable.'

'Yes, indeed, it is most enjoyable. In fact, we now attend a regular class in which a different topic is covered on each occasion.'

'Well, that sounds very good,' I said, conscious that my conversation was somewhat lacking in sparkle. 'I should imagine that's, er, very good.' At least I wasn't being flippant.

'Yes, it is good,' confirmed the bishop. 'This week, for instance, we were looking at hue, tone and intensity.'

Oh, dear. I did try. I promise you I did. I fought against temptation, but I lost. I fell.

'Oh, yes,' I cried merrily, 'I went down the pub with them last Friday. Hugh and Ton', nice couple of lads, and Intensity's that rather stressy girl they hang around with.'

The bishop was a little taken aback at first, but once he'd realized that it was a case of 'Christians having fun' everything was fine. Christians are allowed to have 'fun'.

On the face of it this kind of silliness has very little worth, doesn't it? But it really is quite amazing what God can do with the loaves and fishes of what we are, as long as we actually get round to offering them to him. When I wrote my first Bible note on the Sermon on the Mount I was a little worried that some readers might consider the opening comments too light-hearted for such a serious subject. That's why it was lovely to get a letter from a lady called Margaret who wanted to tell me the following story. I have her permission to retell it for the benefit of others.

Margaret's husband, David, who has MS, got very edgy and bad-tempered during a course of steroids. One despairing Sunday Margaret reached the end of her tether. She had a good weep in the garden shed, then wondered back into the house and happened to pick up a copy of *New Daylight*, the periodical in which most of these notes originally appeared. In the note for that day, as you will see when you read on, I had bemoaned Jesus' strange oversight in omitting 'Blessed are the irritable for they shall be given claret' from the beatitudes. Remembering that claret was her husband's favourite tipple (hallelujah—we are one with you, brother David) Margaret hurried to the mini-supermarket and queued for the only remaining bottle of claret on the shelf. When she gave it to David and explained why she'd bought it they had a good laugh together, and, as Margaret herself put it, 'All the tension was released.' And that was before they drank the claret. Wonderful!

Don't kid yourself. The Jesus who made his comeback by cooking breakfast for his friends instead of organizing a sky-filling Speilburg spectacular is still in touch with the real world, and here, in the most famous sermon in history, he tells us what the shape of the real world should be.

Prayer

Father, as we approach this most significant of sermons, open our hearts and minds in such a way that we are prepared to receive ideas and teaching that may displace responses from the past. We pray that we may feel genuine excitement as we listen to these words, heavy with eternal significance. Help us to freely offer ourselves, our weaknesses and our strengths to you, so that, through us, you can do unexpected and miraculous things in the lives of others. Amen.

The poor sheep

Matthew 5:1–6 (NIV)

Now when [Jesus] saw the crowds, he went up on a mountainside and sat down. His disciples came to him, and he began to teach them, saying: 'Blessed are the poor in spirit, for theirs is the kingdom of heaven. Blessed are those who mourn, for they will be comforted. Blessed are the meek, for they will inherit the earth. Blessed are those who hunger and thirst for righteousness, for they will be filled.'

I have searched this passage in vain for a statement tailored to my baser weaknesses and appetites:

'Blessed are the irritable, for they shall be given claret.'

'Blessed are the taller than average, for they shall develop a forehand that would send Bjorn Borg diving for cover.'

'Blessed are the fundamentally lazy, for their Bible notes will be done for them by divine intervention.'

Jesus doesn't make any of these rather superficially attractive promises, but the promises he does make are, ultimately, far more significant and encouraging than any individually oriented indulgences could ever be. As I read these famous words yet again I knew that they reminded me of something very familiar, but I couldn't quite put my finger on it. Where was I accustomed to encountering groups of people who were poor in spirit, sorely in need of comfort, meek by nature and yearning from the bottom of their hearts to be good?

The answer of course, as even my feeble brain grasped in the end, was that Jesus was describing the Church—that is, the people who make up his body on earth—almost exactly as I have experienced it and them in the course of my travels from town to town, and country to country during the last few years. True, from time to time, I have encountered bold and vigorous spirits who don't appear to fit the pattern, but, in the main, they—or rather, we—are like sheep. And, whether we are High-Church mutton or house-church lamb, these extraordinary declarations invite us to rejoice in our weakness, because it is that very weakness, crying out for a shepherd, that brings Jesus to us.

A hunger and thirst for righteousness clearly implies a serious *lack* of righteousness. We are allowed to fail, as long as we genuinely yearn to succeed.

Prayer

Lord Jesus, you turned the world upside down with your teaching. Turn me now so that I am facing the truth.

A frightening promise **Matthew 5:7–12 (NIV)**

'Blessed are the merciful, for they will be shown mercy. Blessed are the pure in heart, for they will see God. Blessed are the peacemakers, for they will be called sons of God. Blessed are those who are persecuted because of righteousness, for theirs is the kingdom of heaven. Blessed are you when people insult you, persecute you and falsely say all kind of evil against you because of me. Rejoice and be glad, because great is your reward in heaven, for in the same way they persecuted the prophets who were before you.'

Have you noticed how aggressively some people react to followers of Jesus nowadays? Adherents to other religions and philosophies are, quite rightly, accorded the respect that is due to any sincere group of believers, but there seems to be something about the Christian faith that provokes irritation, intolerance, scorn and even rage in folk who are otherwise perfectly reasonable. This used to puzzle me, because that kind of response is not just about the inadequate way in which we represent God—it seems to go much deeper than that. As I absorb passages like the one above, however, I think I begin to understand why people get so cross with Jesus.

You see, he wants to take their lives away.

In exchange he offers new lives that make sense only in the context of the kingdom of God. The divine madness says that it is good to be persecuted, insulted and lied about if such things are suffered for Jesus' sake. Will mercy, purity and a yearning for peace take us very far in this world? A lot of people think not. No wonder they become fearful and angry. Christianity is not a plan to improve the quality of life—it is God calling to the very depths of our being. He is calling to tell us that we must no longer huddle defensively into the three score years and ten that is our tiny corner of eternity. He is calling us to understand that many of the things we have valued most are trash. He is calling out that death is by no means the greatest disaster of all. He is calling with passionate urgency to say that the real madness lies in trying to put sticking plaster over the gaping wound of sin that is slowly killing the world.

He wants to take our lives away, and yes—we are frightened.

Prayer

Open our eyes to eternity, Lord.

My light, *my* salt

Matthew 5:13–16 (NIV)

'You are the salt of the earth. But if salt loses its saltiness, how can it be made salty again? It is no longer good for anything, except to be thrown out and trampled by men. You are the light of the world. A city on a hill cannot be hidden. Neither do people light a lamp and put it under a bowl. Instead they put it on its stand, and it gives light to everyone in the house. In the same way, let your light shine before men, that they may see your good deeds and praise your Father in heaven.'

I wonder if the disciples found it hard to accept that they were the light of the world. I find it extremely difficult until I stop thinking about myself, and realize that any light I may shed was switched on, and is maintained, by God himself. We Christians are scared stiff of advertising God, in case people think we are drawing attention to ourselves. This is a shame, because it is in the dark vessels of our lives that the light of God will be most apparent. I'm certainly not suggesting that we should go around crassly shoving the flashlight of our good deeds into people's faces, but there is a form of false modesty that results in missed opportunities.

When I first began to write and broadcast, a number of people who had known me at a much earlier age were frankly incredulous about my claim that I was now a follower of Jesus. One man in particular, a Christian who had been at the same secondary school as me, found it very difficult to believe that the person he had known in the 1960s was capable of change. I'm afraid that his scepticism was perfectly reasonable. As a teenager I had developed a habit of withering sarcasm to hide profound insecurity, and must have hurt and infuriated many people when I wielded the only defensive weapon I had. Now, God had transfigured, or turned his light towards, that sarcasm, turning it into satire and (hopefully) using it in a constructive way for the benefit of the Church. It must have taken people like that ex-schoolmate of mine a long time to accept that the change was a genuine one. But once he and others were convinced, they had to praise God really, because there was no other explanation.

We must be salt and light in the world, and that's all right, as long as everyone remembers who owns the saltmine and pays the electricity bill.

Prayer

Father, you have given us the task of bringing flavour and illumination to this world. Teach us how to do it properly.

Lust and real life

Matthew 5:27–30 (NIV)

'You have heard that it was said, "Do not commit adultery." But I tell you that anyone who looks at a woman lustfully has already committed adultery with her in his heart. If your right eye causes you to sin, gouge it out and throw it away. It is better for you to lose one part of your body than for your whole body to be thrown into hell. And if your right hand causes you to sin, cut it off and throw it away. It is better for you to lose one part of your body than for your whole body to go to hell.'

My left earlobe might just about make it into heaven if I obey this command literally—but only if God stretches a point. Even my left earlobe has its seamier side. I'm afraid that the best of us is likely to enter heaven looking rather like Admiral Nelson.

When I was a very earnest young Christian we were taught that *all* sins and vices, including lust, can be overcome, and that failure to achieve such victories would constitute a denial of the efficacy of the resurrection power of Christ. This, as I am sure you will agree, is a very heavy thing to lay on a person of any age, let alone a teenager who has just awakened violently to the fact that the world is absolutely awash with desirable females. To make matters worse, my constant diet of testimony paperbacks included a book by some gleaming American Christian who actually claimed to have completely eradicated lust from his life. I can't remember the name of this paragon, or which part of himself he cut off to achieve such a spectacular result, but I do remember feeling utterly defeated by the contrast with my own puny efforts.

Honesty requires an acceptance of the fact that lust is a thorn in the flesh—or to use a more modern expression, a pain in the neck—for many, if not most of us. It really is a blinking nuisance, isn't it? But let's not all start gouging our flesh or cutting our heads off just yet. They tried that sort of thing in the distant past, and it never worked then.

I think Jesus is talking about the need to steer ourselves around publications, people, viewing matter and any other specific situations that we *know* are dangerous for us. Temptation is only the gateway to sin, but indulgence is a ski-slope.

Question

Do you think it's possible that we approach this whole area too lightly and *too seriously?*

The thirsty beggar **Matthew 5:38–42 (NIV)**

'You have heard that it was said, "Eye for eye, and tooth for tooth." But I tell you, Do not resist an evil person. If someone strikes you on the right cheek, turn to him the other also. And if someone wants to sue you and take your tunic, let him have your cloak as well. If someone forces you to go one mile, go with him two miles. Give to the one who asks you, and do not turn away from the one who wants to borrow from you.'

I was walking in Winchester late one cold evening with my friend, Ben. The street seemed deserted, until we were suddenly confronted by a shabby figure emerging from a shop doorway. With long matted hair, an overcoat tied with string, and terminally split shoes, he was what we used to call a 'tramp', although the loony political correctness of the present age would probably label him 'habitationally challenged'.

What was certain was that the poor chap was very cold and miserable. With considerable effort he cranked himself up to put the bite on these unexpected passers-by.

'Excuse me, Sir,' he embarked on a familiar script, 'could I speak to you as one man to another? I wondered if you might have some cash you could help me with.'

Now, I don't know about you, but I'm usually pathetic in these situations. I cringe and twist and dither about and perform theological triple somersaults in my head and go away wishing I'd done the thing I didn't do or that I'd not done the thing I did do. This occasion was different—thank God.

'Yes', I said briskly, 'I have.' I extended my hand towards him. 'I've got a five pound note here that I'm going to give you.'

My habitationally challenged friend was clearly taken aback. A new script! He managed to take the five pounds, though, and stood looking at it in a dazed fashion.

'I give you this money,' I continued, 'trusting that you will put it to the best possible use.'

'Well, actually,' he replied faintly, 'I was thinking of having a drink.'

'Precisely,' I said, 'that's exactly what we would have done with the money if I'd kept it. Goodnight to you.'

Prayer

Father, I can be such a patronizing hypocrite sometimes. Help me not to judge or condemn others because they count for less in the eyes of the world. Let me see them through your eyes and deal with them as equals.

Music in a new place **Matthew 5:43–48 (NIV)**

'You have heard that it was said, "Love your neighbour and hate your enemy." But I tell you: Love your enemies and pray for those who persecute you, that you may be sons of your Father in heaven. He causes his sun to rise on the evil and the good, and sends rain on the righteous and the unrighteous. If you love those who love you, what reward will you get? Are not even the tax collectors doing that? And if you greet only your brothers, what are you doing more than others? Do not even pagans do that? Be perfect, therefore, as your heavenly Father is perfect.'

My experience of loving enemies is very similar to my experience of moving pianos from one room to another on my own. It's crashingly hard work, halfway through you begin to wish you'd never started, but in the end you hear music in a place where you've never heard it before.

What makes this whole area so difficult is that the line between enemies and friends is not as clear as one might think. Friendship can move so easily into enemy mode, and it's at such times that we fail most miserably to uphold this principle which, Jesus tells his disciples, should distinguish them from pagans. These shifts in the nature of relationships happen an awful lot in families, don't they?

A friend told me of a conflict that developed between himself and his fourteen-year-old daughter, whom he actually loved very much. Having settled firmly into mega-sulkdom over some minor incident, she refused to communicate with her father (other than with the occasional grunt) for a period of more than two weeks. The levels of hurt and rage in my friend rose to such a height that just the thought of his 'little girl' made him grind his teeth and swear under his breath.

The crunch came one evening when she stormed up to her bedroom after being asked to perform the most undemanding of tasks. He thundered up in her wake with murder in his heart, and was about to crash into her room and pull her head off when something made him stop. My friend *is* a Christian and although he fails often he never gives up. Time for a little piano moving, he thought. My friend has become my enemy. With murder still crouching inside him he sat on the bed, spoke softly and lovingly, and held his arms out.

She responded! Tears—music in a new place. Just as well, or he'd have chucked her out of the window.

Thought

Loving enemies—you don't have to feel it. You have to do it.

Give me your heart **Matthew 6:19–21 (NIV)**

'Do not store up for yourselves treasures on earth, where moth and rust destroy, and where thieves break in and steal. For where your treasure is, there your heart will be also.'

Three people arrived outside the gate of heaven. One, a well dressed man, carried a large sack.

'In this bag', he explained, 'is the wealth of a lifetime.' He patted it. 'If this little lot, plus a spot of the old wheeler-dealer chat, doesn't get me through those gates, I shall be very surprised. And, just to cover the religious angle, I've popped my heart in too, so they can have the lot if they want. There!'

The second person was a pious-looking woman in simple threadbare garments. She carried a much smaller bag.

'I have not collected great wealth', she said, in a faint, burdened voice. 'Our Lord commanded us to store up treasure in heaven, and therefore my life has been spent in service to others.'

'What is in your bag?' questioned the rich man.

'Accounts,' she replied with modest pride. 'Notebooks, lists and ledgers recording every good deed and charitable act I have ever performed. I shall present them together with my heart, which, like you, I have placed inside in case it should be required.'

The third person, a weary looking fellow dressed only in a loin-cloth, and empty-handed, spoke nervously.

'I bring nothing,' he faltered. 'In life I neither accumulated wealth, nor did I pour myself out for others as selflessly as you, Madam. Most troubling of all, though, I have given away my heart—I fear I shall not enter heaven.'

The rich man and the pious woman walked ahead to the gates together, but returned very soon, faces dark with disappointment.

'No luggage allowed beyond the gates,' said the rich man sadly.

'And we are not allowed to leave our bags *outside* the gates,' sobbed the woman. 'We shall have them for ever!'

The man in the loin-cloth watched the pair walk slowly away, then approached heaven himself. True, he had no luggage, but his heart was lost. What hope for him?

The angel who opened the gates ushered him in with a sweeping bow, before placing into his hand something that shone and glittered like the most perfect diamond.

'Yours, I believe,' he said.

Prayer

Look after our hearts, Lord, until we come to you.

Worry or life?

Matthew 6:25–27 (NIV)

'Therefore I tell you, do not worry about your life, what you will eat or drink; or about your body, what you will wear. Is not life more important than food, and the body more important than clothes? Look at the birds of the air; they do not sow or reap or store away in barns, and yet your heavenly Father feeds them. Are you not much more valuable than they? Who of you by worrying can add a single hour to his life?'

A friend of mine who pastors a local fellowship told me once about a conversation with his five-year-old son.

'Dad,' said the little boy dolefully one morning, 'God's not answering my prayers any more.'

'I'm sorry to hear that, Tim,' said my friend, 'anything in particular?'

'I asked him to close the window,' replied Tim in scandalized tones, 'but he didn't!'

Tim's slight misconception of the role of God in his life illustrates the kind of problem that can arise from key scriptures like this. I know people who have used these verses as a stepping stone towards the condition known as 'living by faith'. They stop worrying about where the next meal is coming from, while whole teams of other people start worrying on their behalf. God will not feed the canary while I am on holiday, and he will not (on the whole) supply the needs created by idleness. I'm sure God *does* call some people to live by faith, but it has to be his decision, and even then, as we learn from Paul's experiences and accounts, material needs are not necessarily going to come first on the Holy Spirit's agenda. The thing we can say in this connection is that if God does authorize and initiate a task, he will supply whatever is needed to get it done, although his idea of what is needed and ours may differ quite dramatically.

So what is this passage saying to the Church generally? It seems to be expressing yet again the divine frustration (can God get frustrated?) with the persistent, petty, potentially disastrous preoccupation of human beings with things of the body. Most of us are not just arranging the chairs on the Titanic, we're planning next week's menu and getting up teams for deck-tennis.

There are boats leaving for the kingdom. Can you see them?

Prayer

Help us to trust you. Draw our eyes towards the cosmic vision.

It's not easy, Jesus

Matthew 6:31–33 (NIV)

'So do not worry, saying, "What shall we eat?" or "What shall we drink?" or "What shall we wear?" For the pagans run after all these things, and your heavenly Father knows that you need them. But seek first his kingdom and his righteousness, and all these things will be given to you as well.'

Dear Jesus,

Over the last few days I've been writing very positively about all the things you said to your disciples in this famous sermon (yes, I know—*big deal!*) but this morning I feel jaded, and now, as I read your exhortation to avoid worrying about the precise things that this society *trains* us to worry about, I am confused. A Christian friend has just lost his one-man business through no fault of his own, and although his church has been warmly generous, he and his wife and four children are *very* bothered about what they're going to eat, drink and wear. What is your message to them and us? Is it up to the rest of your wider family to provide practical support? Does that sometimes constitute the miracle of faith? I don't undervalue that kind of miracle at all—I think it's wonderful. But is that 'it'? We've read books where miraculous provision happens constantly, but it's the exception rather than the rule in most churches I know.

You never had a problem in this area, did you? When you needed to pay tax you sent old Peter off to catch a fish, and there was the cash in the creature's mouth. When you had five thousand people to feed, you just kept breaking bits off one small meal until everyone had more than enough to eat. As for drink—well, gallons of water turned into top-grade wine at a snap of your fingers.

But then, you'd been through that gruelling forty-days sorting-out period in the wilderness, hadn't you? During that time you refused to use your spiritual cashpoint card, because (just as you say in this passage) the kingdom has to come first. After that battle was won the rest was a piece of cake, or a piece of fish, or a gallon of wine, or whatever. That became the easy part.

I guess the answer to my question is that most of us just haven't been through that sorting-out process—not really, and until we do, until we break through into the clean air of kingdom priority, we're bound to be stuck in a fog of worry and need.

It's not easy, Lord Jesus. It's not easy. Help us to understand the challenge, and then to face it. We pray for all those who, like my friend, are feeling worried and confused.

Thank you.

Love, *Adrian*

Just look at him... **Matthew 7:1–5 (NIV)**

'Do not judge, or you too will be judged. For in the same way as you judge others, you will be judged, and with the measure you use it will be measured to you. Why do you look at the speck of sawdust in your brother's eye and pay no attention to the plank in your own eye? How can you say to your brother, "Let me take the speck out of your eye," when all the time there is a plank in your own eye? You hypocrite, first take the plank out of your own eye, and then you will see clearly to remove the speck from your brother's eye.'

How true, and I should know, because we have someone in our house group who does just what Jesus is talking about. This person (whose name begins with 'Z' and who has a significant role in the second-tier leadership of our church—all the more surprising, really, wouldn't you agree?) is constantly judging others, and generally being negative about the group. I've asked Stanley Morgan, our group leader, whether he intends to say anything to Z, but I'm afraid poor old Stanley is no more able to confront now than he ever was. When you consider he's allowed Eve thingy, who may or may *not* be a believer, to get away with something close to heresy for the whole year since she attached herself to us, it's clear not much can be expected in that quarter.

The pity of it is that Z's critical attitude and Stanley's weakness bring out the very worst in Jeanette, who, having paid her debt to society and been forgiven by God, is not going to benefit from having her anti-social proclivities stimulated, if you grasp my inference. That's leaving aside the fact that if Jeanette *does* give way to her subversive instincts we won't see Malcolm for dust, not that Malcolm (who's lived with his mother all his life and is a real Poirot of a—well, I was going to say 'man', but nobody's quite sure) would know dust if he saw it, him never having laid a finger on a Hoover in his life. I doubt if dear Malcolm's interested in *any* women, let alone Jeanette in full flow.

The only one who's not affected by Z's nastiness is Violet Stratton, but then she's not been affected by *anything* for as long as I can remember, poor soul. She'd win prizes for nodding and smiling, but there's no edge to her since her 'holiday', if you get my drift.

So, that's the situation. Pray that Z will see the light—and become like me.

Thought

Let's build a cabin with all these planks—then set fire to it.

Ask me... Matthew 7:7–12 (NIV)

'Ask and it will be given to you; seek and you will find; knock and the door will be opened to you. For everyone who asks receives; he who seeks finds; and to him who knocks the door will be opened. Which of you, if his son asks for bread, will give him a stone? Or if he asks for a fish will give him a snake? If you, then, though you are evil, know how to give good gifts to your children, how much more will your Father in heaven give good gifts to those who ask him! So in everything do to others what you would have them do to you, for this sums up the Law and the prophets.'

I want to be touched by affectionate eyes,
I want to be welcomed when welcome is rare,
I want to be held when my confidence sighs,
I want to find comfort in genuine care.

I want to be given untakeable things,
I want to be trusted with hearts that might break,
I want to fly dreaming on effortless wings,
I want to be smiled on when I awake.

I want to see sunsets with people who know,
I want to hear secrets that no-one should hear,
I want to be guarded wherever I go,
I want to be fought for when dangers appear.

I want to be chained to the lives of my friends,
I want to be wanted because and despite,
I want to link arms when the foolishness ends
I want to be safe in the raging night.

I want to be sheltered although I am wrong,
I want to be laughed at although I am right,
I want to be sung in the heavenly song,
I want to be loved—I want to be light.

Prayer

Father, I seem to find it awfully easy to assemble a list of things that I want from other people and from you. The problem comes when I turn the whole thing round and consider what it would cost me to give instead of to take. Please show me ways in which I can give pleasure to you and to the people I meet by doing for them the things I would want them to do for me. Thank you for your fatherly love. Teach me to see your hand in all the good things that happen to me.

It frightens me... **Matthew 7:13–14 (NIV)**

'Enter through the narrow gate. For wide is the gate and broad is the road that leads to destruction, and many enter through it. But small is the gate and narrow the road that leads to life, and only a few find it.'

These verses have always frightened me. The adult Adrian Plass, insubstantial, wraith-like creature though he is, does have a clean theological perspective on the question of faith and salvation. I am saved. I am going there. Oh, yes I am—hallelujah!

The other Adrian Plass however, more formless but more authentic, the skinny 1960s kid with the long grey shorts that never did up properly, and the pudding-basin haircut, and the permanently worried expression, is in a bit of a panic, and needs to talk to Jesus. He finds him sitting alone beside the Sea of Galilee, gazing out over the water.

Adrian: Excuse me, could I ask you something?

Jesus: *(smiles)* Anything.

Adrian: You know that bit about the little gate and the narrow road and only a few find it and all that?

Jesus: *(solemnly)* Yes, I think I know that bit.

Adrian: *(deep breath)* Well, it frightens me.

Jesus: *(nods thoughtfully)* I can understand that. Did you want to ask something in particular?

Adrian: You don't mind?

Jesus: I never mind questions. Do you mind answers?

Adrian: I don't know yet—the thing is, what *is* the narrow gate, what *is* the narrow road, and—well, am I one of the few?

Jesus: *(after a long silence)* Answers can be very complicated or very simple. What sort of answer would you like?

Adrian: *(in a very quiet voice)* Simple please, so that I understand.

Jesus: Okay, then my answer to all three questions is a question.

Adrian: I sort of knew it would be.

Jesus: If I got up now and walked away without telling you where I was going, or whether I would ever come back, or what I would be doing, or how it would all end—would you take my hand and come with me?

Adrian: *(throat suddenly dry)* Right now?

Jesus: Right now. Would you come?

Adrian: I... I think so...

Prayer

Jesus, you said that you are the Way, the Truth and the Life. Help us to take your hand.

What am I, Lord? **Matthew 7:15–20 (NIV)**

'Watch out for false prophets. They come to you in sheep's clothing, but inwardly they are ferocious wolves. By their fruit you will recognise them. Do people pick grapes from thornbushes, or figs from thistles? Likewise every good tree bears good fruit, but a bad tree bears bad fruit. A good tree cannot bear bad fruit, and a bad tree cannot bear good fruit. Every tree that does not bear good fruit is cut down and thrown into the fire. Thus, by their fruit you will recognise them.'

There is something deeply chilling about the idea of this unplanned, spiritual fancy-dress party, where in the midst of unsuspecting guests, ferocious wolves come as sheep, thistles dress up as figs, and thornbushes masquerade as vines. It's a horrible picture isn't it, but let's be clear about something. Jesus is talking here about deliberate, vicious deception, by people who have an appetite for harming others. Dressing up as a sheep among other sheep, when you are actually a ravening wolf looking for food, is not a minor departure from moral rectitude, nor could it ever be done by accident. It is the devil's own work, and if that scares us, then so it should.

I emphasize this point because many anxious people ask themselves whether *they* are actually thistles pretending to be grapevines. After all, they say worriedly to themselves, the fruit I produce is a pretty varied crop. If, as Jesus says, a good tree can't produce bad fruit, and some of the fruit I produce is bad, then, logically, I must be a bad tree, or even a ravening wolf, without even realizing it. *Help!*

Enough of this neurosis—I've been through it myself. Good trees certainly produce fruit that's variable in quality, because (we might as well labour the metaphor while we've got it) sometimes the rich soil of fellowship is lacking, or the life-giving water of prayer has dried up, or the warm climate of scripture has—oh, never mind, you get the picture, don't you? It's difficult enough to keep my Jesus-planted tree in reasonable order, without worrying that I might be the anti-christ in disguise as well.

We need to heed this warning that Jesus gives us. There are false prophets abroad, and, like wolves, they do seek to destroy (the devil does all his best work *inside* the church), but if our hearts are yearning for God, even though we fail sometimes, then that woolly stuff we find ourselves covered with is quite genuine.

Prayer

Baaaa!

God with us

Matthew 7:21–23 (NIV)

'Not everyone who says to me, "Lord, Lord," will enter the kingdom of heaven, but only he who does the will of my Father... Many will say to me on that day, "Lord, Lord, did we not prophesy in your name, and... drive out demons and perform many miracles?" Then I will tell them... "I never knew you. Away from me, you evildoers!"'

A few years ago Bridget and I met a lady whose husband had recently died after contracting one of those appalling diseases that cause almost total physical helplessness. Mary and Chris (not their real names) had enjoyed a very happy marriage and were devastated. Quite apart from the dread of death, there was the fact that everyday living was now very hard work for Mary, and terribly frustrating for Chris. Two things happened towards the end of Chris' life that have some bearing on today's passage.

First, Chris was taken by a well-meaning friend, in his wheelchair, to a local healing meeting. When he was returned later that evening Mary was horrified to discover that both of his knees were grazed and bleeding. The distraught friend explained that the 'healers' had lifted Chris out of his wheelchair two or three times, and after praying loudly for his healing on each occasion, had dropped him onto his knees, telling him that he was now able to walk. It was an unimaginably awful experience on every level.

The second thing was the arrival on the doorstep one day of another Christian friend, whom I shall call Eileen, to announce quietly that the Holy Spirit had sent her to help look after Chris for as long as was necessary. Eileen was married and had a family herself, but from that day she was as good as her word. The burden of work was halved, and Chris could stop worrying about his wife wearing herself out. Mary was even able to take a brief holiday.

After Chris' death Eileen continued to support Mary, and was in fact with her when we met at a holiday house-party in Devon.

'Not long after Chris died,' Mary told us, 'my son, Martin, said to me one day, "Mummy, wasn't it good how Auntie Eileen came to be God for us that day?"'

It was indeed good that a true follower of Jesus had heard a command and obeyed it. It was the tougher, more committed way, but it was what God wanted, and that's the point. Of course God does heal in miraculous ways, but if a desire for spiritual gymnastics overcomes the rule of love and obedience—we'd better watch out.

Prayer

Bind us to your will, Lord. Keep our eyes and ears on you.

A warning as well

Matthew 7:24–28 (NIV)

'Therefore everyone who hears these words of mine and puts them into practice is like a wise man who built his house on the rock. The rain came down, the streams rose, and the winds blew and beat against that house; yet it did not fall, because it had its foundation on the rock. But everyone who hears these words of mine and does not put them into practice is like a foolish man who built his house on sand. The rain came down, the streams rose, and the winds blew and beat against that house, and it fell with a great crash.' When Jesus had finished saying these things, the crowds were amazed at his teaching, because he taught as one who had authority, and not as their teachers of the law.

Christians often talk about the difficulty of persuading people who are happy and secure that they need God. It's popular in church circles to suggest that such people are actually not happy at all. Deep down, the legend goes, they are in misery and know that something extra is needed in their lives. Well, there are people like that—I know, because I've met them. But I've also met folk with no faith at all, who are far more consistently content and peaceful than I am (probably nicer than me as well) who, as far as one can tell, have no overt or concealed desire for anything extra at all, let alone God. This shouldn't really surprise us. In the dramatic parable of the two house builders (somewhat difficult to focus on clearly after a lifetime of Sunday School projects and jolly little songs), Jesus is telling us quite clearly that this is likely to be the case. Presumably, before the storms came, the two householders were equally happy—indeed, it may be that the man whose house was built on sand had picked a more attractive spot altogether. Why on earth (or sand) should he slave away like his neighbour to build a foundation that would never be needed in the balmy climate of contentment?

The answer, of course, is that he might alter his views if that same neighbour were to let him in on the secret that storms are coming, and that those storms will be wilder and more destructive than anything he has dreamed of in his wildest nightmares.

He might also benefit from hearing about a man called Jesus, filled with love and integrity, who stood on a mountainside two thousand years ago and, like the first real grown-up in the history of the world, told men and women how to find life and defeat death.

Prayer

Lord, may it be Jesus that we preach—may we be bold with his promises and his warnings.

A hero is one who knows how to hang on one minute longer.

Norwegian proverb

TRAILBLAZING HEROES

Some Old Testament figures

One wonders why it never occurs to any of the characters in long-running television soap operas to ask themselves why such strange things tend to happen in their small worlds.

Why, for instance, do all soap 'marriages' seem doomed to end in premature death, inexplicable parting after recent declarations of undying love, and strange disappearances that are only ever solved if the actor concerned gets sick of doing talk-shows and (if they're Australian) pantomimes in England, and returns to the nice little earner that supported him or her in the past?

Why on earth, they might further ask themselves, do individual characters suddenly produce behaviour that is wildly, irrationally untypical of the personality that they have developed over the months or years?

Why, in pubs and other crowded places, do only two people at a time speak in voices loud enough to be heard, and why do third parties never come into a room until the first and second parties have reached the end of their significant conversation, and drifted into a brief snatch of small talk?

Most puzzling of all perhaps is the fact that entire geographical areas become totally repopulated over periods of just a few years. A truly extraordinary social phenomenon! Where do all those lost people go?

Could it be that, in some strange, shadowy world, long-abandoned soap stars meet to discuss and reminisce about the good old days when they actually existed, albeit at the mercy of writers and pen-twiddling, paperclip-twisting members of story-development conferences? Let us hope that such encounters are well-policed. Some of those legendary soap stars were pretty strong characters, weren't they? Imagine Ena Sharples from 'Coronation Street', Dirty Den from 'EastEnders', and Paul Robinson from 'Neighbours' settling down in the corner of their local, a bizarre combination of the The Rovers Return, The Queen Vic and The Watering Hole, to discuss the rival merits of their individual contributions to soap history. The fictional fur would certainly fly, and it's not easy to judge who would emerge the winner of the argument. If you press me, though, I must admit that most of my money would be on Ena Sharples.

I mention this unlikely scenario because it strikes me that a somewhat similar encounter must have occurred between the Old Testament figures that you are about to meet in the following section. Obviously there are major differences. They are not soap characters, of course, although the telling of their stories in so many different ways over so many generations has, for many people, tended to give them that same aura of paste-board-like unreality. After watching four children grow up I have seen so many giants of the Old Testament coloured with crayons and cut out of cardboard with a little bit stuck on the back to make sure they stand up all right, that I have almost forgotten that they were real people.

Nor, I assume, will their meetings have taken place in a pub, although I suppose one can never be absolutely sure with God...

The other big difference is that Abraham and the rest of them must be retrospectively redeemed (unlike Ena, Den and Paul, who will have failed to qualify on the grounds that they don't actually exist) and will presumably get on pretty well.

Just imagine it, though—the whole crowd of them seated round a big circular table at lunchtime. There would be Jephthah, reunited with his daughter at last, and feeling more than a bit silly; Adam and Eve, politely refusing the fruit bowl every time it comes round, and effusively apologizing to everyone in sight; David, Uriah and Bathsheba having a bit of a laugh about the bad old days; Noah and Jonah, contrasting their very different experiences of being saved from drowning; Jacob and Esau sharing a bowl of soup; Samson showing off little strength tricks to Job, who is really only waiting for a chance to say some more about a really good treatment for boils that he's just come across; Joseph, closely attended by his brothers and wondering if there's any way he can claim royalties on the musical; Moses and Joshua selecting milk and honey as an ideal dessert experience; Daniel trying to talk the good-natured Zephaniah into adopting his highly successful and royally approved vegan diet, and, at the top of the table, Abraham himself, reunited for ever with his beloved son, Isaac, and beaming genially around at the assembled company.

Do you realize that we shall be with them one day?

On a more serious level, the stories that feature these great Old Testament figures are vital links in the chain of our understanding about how God deals and has dealt with those who claim him as their leader. The history of the Jewish people and their progress towards the time when it would be possible for God's law to be written on their hearts, offers countless parallels to the journey that we undertake today when we choose to follow Jesus, the new Adam, through a desert of earthly problems to the promised land of total unity with him. If we will accept them, there are lots of lessons to be learned.

And let us thank God that, as we take that journey, we are not like soap characters. Our authenticity will never be sacrificed to the needs of the plot, nor will we be 'dumped' out of existence because some more exciting idea has come along. We are real people who have been adopted into the real family of God, exactly the same family as that illustrious body whose members are seated around the heavenly table that I have just described.

Prayer

Father, help us to look more deeply into the lives of these people whose names have become so familiar that we are in danger of missing important aspects of their relationships with you and with each other. We understand that you have left a record of your dealings with them so that we can learn a little more of what it means to walk with Jesus in our own age. May the lessons go deep into our hearts, and enrich our spirits with their wisdom. Amen.

Abraham and Isaac

Genesis 22:9–10 (NIV)

Abraham built an altar there and arranged the wood on it. He bound his son Isaac and laid him on the altar, on top of the wood. Then he reached out his hand and took the knife to slay his son.

When our first child was born, I remember gazing through the glass wall of the 'baby ward' at this little scrunched-up person. I'd never experienced the kind of love I felt at that moment. It was different from anything I felt for family, friends or even my wife—not more, just different. It filled me with a determination to care endlessly for his welfare, a determination that, as most parents know, doesn't lessen with the years.

At the same time, I had been spiritually 'raised' in a climate of self-sacrifice and denial. God had to come first, and the setting aside of strong feelings for friends or family was regarded as a positive virtue. The story of Abraham being asked to sacrifice Isaac just made me feel sick. A shadow fell over my perception of the relationship I had with God, because I knew that I would never sacrifice Matthew, neither actually nor symbolically. How could I, when I loved him much more than I loved the creator of the world? Inwardly, I flirted with atheism, preferring the prospect of human relationships followed by oblivion, to the shift in priorities that God seemed to be demanding.

The journey from that state of mind to my present one is too long and eventful to describe here, but some things I now know to be true. First, God stood beside me outside that baby ward, excited like me about the arrival of someone who was as much a new son for him as for me. His commitment to caring for Matthew was and is endless too, in the literal sense. Secondly, my love for my son has changed. It's more about him and less about me. I *want* him to enjoy eternal life. I *want* him to walk through the streets of heaven with a brand-new, indestructible body. I want him to be a child of God above anything else. Thirdly, perhaps most importantly, I have come to understand a little better what I would, with great respect, call the 'sanity' of God. He knows me and my weaknesses and strengths, and has done since the day when he chuckled fondly outside the baby ward where *I* was born. He has been a good and very wise Father, and, as that fact becomes real to me, I come closer to loving him more than anyone in the world.

Prayer

Father, I'm a long way from trusting you as Abraham did. Help me to learn that trust is the best way for me, and thank you for sacrificing your own Son so that mine can live.

David

2 Samuel 12:19–20 (NIV)

David... realised that the child was dead. 'Is the child dead?' he asked. 'Yes,' they replied, 'he is dead.' Then David got up from the ground. After he had washed, put on lotions and changed his clothes, he went into the house of the Lord and worshipped. Then... he ate.

David's response to the death of the child conceived in his adulterous relationship with Bathsheba says something very profound about his understanding of God. He prayed and wept for seven days and nights, but when the child died, he accepted the judgment of the Lord. David loved God. His relationship was a *real* one. In crunch situations the reality of what we believe makes a demonstrable difference—or not, of course. A friend of mine, who was a traffic warden, recently died in hospital of cancer, amazing visitors with a new strength and authority as he approached his death. He really wanted to be healed, but he was ready to accept the will of the God he trusted. For his funeral service I wrote and read the following lines:

He stood at the crossroads of his own life
Directing the traffic of emotions, thoughts, events
Too watchful once, perhaps
For woe betide some maverick urge that tried to jump the queue
And overtake good common sense that ought to set the pace
He tried, he really tried to set his face against irregularity
Longed to see the day when all of life's unruly streams
Would be reorganized into an earthly paradise of dead straight lines
With no untidy tailbacks to upset him
Alas for all his dreams, his bosses wouldn't let him
He had three bosses
One in heaven, one in Hastings, one at home
The first and last of these instructed him in many things
They taught him that the waving through of tender thoughts
A blind eye turned when unashamed compassion
Does a sudden U-turn in the outside lane
Need not be crimes
That facts and feelings have to double-park sometimes
And in the end, in the main, love was flowing freely
Far too soon, far too soon for us, the traffic noises died

And on that soundless day
A chauffeur-driven certainty came softly in the morning
And carried him away.

Prayer

Father, may we develop the kind of trust in you that upheld these two men who worshipped the same God. We want it to be real, Lord.

Noah

Genesis 7:11–12 (NIV)

In the six hundredth year of Noah's life, on the seventeenth day of the second month—on that day all the springs of the great deep burst forth, and the floodgates of the heavens were opened.

A friend, whom I shall call Herbert, told me once about an encounter over coffee with someone whom I shall call Bertha. For some reason my name or one of my children's names came up in the conversation.

'Do you know the Plasses?' asked Bertha, settling into an I've-got-something-to-say sort of posture.

Herbert, who isn't a Christian but knows us very well, was quite unable to resist the temptation to find out what Bertha was going to say, and replied vaguely, 'Well—you know, I've come across them. Why do you ask?'

'You want to be very careful there,' replied Bertha darkly. 'Don't get more involved than you absolutely have to.'

Herbert was deeply intrigued to hear us talked about as though we were some sort of suspect political movement. 'Why do you say that?' he enquired innocently. 'Is there something wrong with them?'

'They're religious fanatics!' announced Bertha dramatically. 'They want to draw other people in, that's all they're interested in.'

'I didn't realize you knew them,' said Herbert.

'Oh, I've never spoken to them,' said Bertha, 'but it's common knowledge.'

Bertha wasn't very sure of her facts, but I found it interesting that 'common knowledge' held us to be fanatics—weirdos whose lives were centred on something not of this world. I would hate those who really know us to describe us in that way, but I guess it's inevitable that those who have heard and believed in the approach of a great disaster, and the possibility of great salvation, will seem slightly strange to the rest of the world. That's why nominal religion is such a crime. True Christianity might appear bizarre in some ways, but at least people notice it and wonder why it's there.

Few of us will be called upon to look quite as ridiculous as Noah must have appeared, but let's value our divine foolishness a little more than we have in the past. When the great rain of judgment comes, we won't look weird any more, and we might even have been able to hand out a few spiritual umbrellas in advance.

Prayer

Father, it's so hard to get the balance right between openness about what we believe, and normal contact with the world. Give us courage and good judgment.

'Men listened to me expectantly, waiting in silence for my counsel. After I had spoken, they spoke no more; my words fell gently on their ears. They waited for me as for showers and drank in my words as the spring rain. When I smiled at them, they scarcely believed it; the light of my face was precious to them.'

Job is one of my heroes, not just because his regard for God survived poverty, skin disease and extremely annoying friends, but because of the kind of man he was. The content of this passage, a description by Job himself of the way in which his counsel was received by others in pre-boil days, is the target at which I unsuccessfully aim in my writing and speaking. This servant of God clearly brought three things straight from the heart of God to all those who listened.

(I can't believe I'm about to make three points about something. Perhaps I should get out of the Anglican Church before it gets even worse.)

First, he says that his words fell 'gently' on their ears. Oh, for a few more gentle words in church. Many of the people I encounter have already been bruised by bawled accusation and crushed by echoing admonition. Jesus could be very tough, but he felt such compassion for the crowds. He still does, so let us all be gentle on his behalf, unless we're very specifically called to behave in some other way.

The second thing is about the showers and the spring rain. Job helped his listeners to feel refreshed and lightened in spirit. They would have felt *more* able to cope after hearing him, not less. Forgive me for repeating one of my constant bleats, but the blessing of God does not discourage and disable me, it makes me feel that I might be able to get somewhere after all.

The last bit is my favourite. When Job smiled at them they could hardly believe it. I cannot adequately express the sheer delight I have experienced on those few (too few) occasions when I have seen some frightened face suddenly illuminated by the awareness that God is actually *smiling* at his nervous, guilt-racked son or daughter. They can hardly believe it! God is nice! Why did no one ever tell them?

Prayer

Father, help our gentle words to bring the refreshment of your smile to those of your children who need it.

Adam and Eve

Genesis 3:16–19 (NIV)

To the woman he said, 'I will greatly increase your pains in child-bearing; with pain you will give birth to children. Your desire will be for your husband, and he will rule over you.' To Adam he said, 'Because you listened to your wife and ate from the tree... cursed is the ground because of you; and through painful toil you will eat of it all the days of your life... By the sweat of your brow you will eat your food until you return to the ground, since from it you were taken; for dust you are and to dust you will return.'

I'm not sure if it's legitimate to feel sorry for Adam and Eve, but I always have done. Imagine facing up to the fact that you and your spouse are entirely responsible for every single problem faced by each and every one of countless billions of people throughout the history of the world. Can't you just picture this fig-leafed couple waiting red-faced and awkward just inside the gates of heaven to greet each newcomer with an apology and, perhaps, an apple?

'Sorry,' they would say, as the line of saints winds slowly past them, 'we honestly and truly are *very* sorry. Yes, ha, ha, you've got it—Adam and Eve, that's right. Yes, yes, we did make a bit of a mess of it—well, not a *bit* of a mess, more of a total mess. Still, it all worked out okay in the end, didn't it? Well, it did for you, anyway. No thanks to us, that's right—sorry again, see you later. Good morning to you! I'm Adam, and this is my wife Eve—I beg your pardon? Err, no, no, not mythical guilt symbols at all. We wish! Much rather we hadn't existed ourselves, to be absolutely honest. Both world wars and every ingrowing toenail there ever was—down to us, I'm afraid. Deeply sorry. Have an apple? No, well, can't say I blame you... Good morning to you! This is Eve and I'm Adam—responsible for the Fall, that's right—spot on. Well, both of us really—you don't like to apportion blame, do you? You had what? A difficult time with your third one? We genuinely are most terribly sorry...'

Whether or not we subscribe to the view that there really was a real Adam and a real Eve, who transgressed with a real apple after being tempted by a real serpent, we would do well to focus on our own real contribution to the fallenness of this world. There is only one official scapegoat, and I am quite sure that he definitely existed. Let us acknowledge the apple-sampling rogue that lies within each of us, and thank God for Jesus, the new Adam.

Prayer

Thank you for Jesus, who fixed it for us.

Uriah the Hittite

2 Samuel 11:11 (NIV)

Uriah said to David, 'The ark and Israel and Judah are staying in tents, and my master Joab and my lord's men are camped in the open fields. How could I go to my house to eat and drink and lie with my wife? As surely as you live, I will not do such a thing!'

There are some memories that we fight to avoid, aren't there? In my own case, they are mainly recollections of those occasions when one of my children has been suddenly hurt or deeply upset about something, and especially when that hurt involved a significant erosion of their naturally optimistic view of the world. I hate it. When those memories surface, particularly late at night, my heart sinks and I pray that some bright distraction will soon lighten my darkness.

Other memories, however, are to do with my own misdoings. Even though God long ago forgave me for certain sins, I still experience a sickness in my spirit when I am forced for some reason to look at those dark things.

I am quite sure that the memory of Uriah's enthusiasm and loyalty haunted David for the rest of his life. He murdered that good man to cover up his own adultery. That's the trouble with sin committed by big-hearted people. Such folk throw themselves into wrongdoing with the same abandonment that is evident in their acts of generosity and goodness. Layer after layer of deceit is laid down until only an explosion of evil or an act of incredibly brave disclosure will change the situation. David managed (goodness knows how, when he knew God so well) to kid himself that he would get away with sin of the worst kind, simply because he had managed to hide his crimes from men. In the end, he had to face God, of course, through the prophet Nathan, and although he was forgiven, the consequences of his sin were appalling. I really do find it extremely difficult to read about David's agony of spirit over his son Absalom.

Please, if you are involved in wrongdoing that is bound to end up hurting people who are close to you, or the God who loves you more than you can imagine, *do* something about it now. Take the brave option rather than the evil one. Easy to say, I know, but we'll pray with you now.

Prayer

Father, some of the people who are reading this note today are getting themselves into a lot of trouble. A world of remorse lies ahead. Please give them the courage to battle their way out of the darkness and into the light. It will be very tough, but you will be with them, and so, in spirit, will we. Thank you, Father.

Jonah

Jonah 3:10; 4:1–3 (NIV)

[God]... had compassion and did not bring upon them the destruction he had threatened... But Jonah was greatly displeased and became angry... 'O Lord, is this not what I said when I was still at home? That is why I was so quick to flee to Tarshish. I knew that you are a gracious and compassionate God, slow to anger and abounding in love, a God who relents from sending calamity.'

Of all the characters in the Old Testament the one I would most like to meet once a week in the pub is Jonah. I just know that our conversation about God, the universe and everything would be about as seamless as is possible in this fallen world. God was as much of a reality in this awkward prophet's life as a loaf of bread. Only the truest of believers would actually see the need to run away from the object of their belief purely because they knew all too well how he was likely to behave in a given situation. As for going into a sulk like a five-year-old because the *nasty-wasty people in Nineveh didn't get deaded*—well, what greater sign of faith could there be? Jonah *knew* God was there.

The reason I mention this is that I've recently become very aware of the different ways in which people talk about God, depending on where they happen to be, and who's listening at the time. I'm sure I'm the same. In public meetings or services most of us tend to speak of our faith in definite, formal words and tones, as if doubt is a disease that very few Christians suffer from. In private, however, there is often a quite distinctly different approach to such matters, one that, in many cases, suggests that public expressions of belief might have been more optimistic and expedient than truthful.

It can be quite a shock to settle down quietly for a drink with someone only to discover that the depth of their devotion to God is as evident in their private conversation as it was in a more formal situation. I love it when it happens, but it doesn't happen very often. Very few people are as closely engaged with the person of the Father as Jonah was, whether in a positive or a negative way.

Sadly, such awareness is not as popular as one might think. The kind of true faith that has explored the whole mountain is an enormous challenge to those who have half-decided to settle for a lifetime of pottering about on the lower slopes. But it is these people, the ones who talk about God in the same breath as they talk about the price of beans, who are needed in this generation.

Prayer

Give us more prophets like Jonah, Lord, people who know you, and will argue with you, and speak for you.

Haggai

Haggai 1:3–8 (NIV)

Then the word of the Lord came through the prophet Haggai: 'Is it a time for you yourselves to be living in your panelled houses, while this house remains a ruin?... Give careful thought to your ways. You have planted much, but have harvested little. You eat, but never have enough. You drink, but never have your fill. You put on clothes, but are not warm. You earn wages, only to put them in a purse with holes in it.... Go up into the mountains and bring down timber and build the house, so that I may take pleasure in it and be honoured.'

When I get to heaven I shall go searching round the various mansions until I find the one with Haggai's name printed over the front porch. Then I shall knock on the door, and when Haggai opens it I shall hold out my copy of the Bible and ask him to autograph his book for me. This summary of the problems faced by a society that does not put God first is absolutely masterful. However much we have or get, in the end it's worth nothing without the one who gives.

Nowadays, we work very hard at avoiding this fact, but God has an old and experienced assistant in this area of work, and the name of that assistant is Death. In the case of people like myself, the process is as follows: A queue of worries, needs and concerns occupies most of our attention for most of the time. We work very hard at shortening this queue, not least because it really is possible to deal with some of the issues. Shortage of money, for instance, can be a real problem, but it is *possible* for hard work and a little luck to solve that problem, at least to the extent that we are comfortable. Next in the queue might be our failure to find a wife or a husband or perhaps just a good friend. Relationships can be tricky, but if we go to the right places and take a real interest in others—who knows?

Two down, 85 to go. Very few of us ever work our way through to the end of the queue, because so many difficulties and challenges are desperately hard, if not impossible, to deal with, and others tend to take their place as soon as they do disappear. Sometimes, though—just sometimes—we reach a place where, by some miracle, we find ourselves staring at the very last item on the list. Death waits quietly and confidently, the problem that cannot be solved—unless we are inhabited by the living God.

Prayer

Father, help us to make a priority of building a house for you in our hearts.

Jephthah

Judges 11:30–32, 34–35 (NIV)

Jephthah made a vow to the Lord: 'If you give the Ammonites into my hands, whatever comes out of the door of my house to meet me when I return... will be the Lord's, and I will sacrifice it as a burnt offering.' Then Jephthah went over to fight the Ammonites, and the Lord gave them into his hands... When Jephthah returned to his home in Mizpah, who should come out to meet him but his daughter, dancing to the sound of tambourines!... When he saw her, he tore his clothes and cried, 'Oh, My daughter! You have made me miserable and wretched, because I have made a vow to the Lord that I cannot break.'

This little-mentioned tale contrasts bizarrely with the story of Abraham and Isaac, doesn't it? What an absolutely appalling situation! The more you think about it, the worse it gets. All I find myself able to do is ask a series of very obvious questions.

First—why did Jephthah open his big mouth and make rash promises when he didn't have to? What was the matter with him? It wasn't as if God had asked him to do it. Wild vows are dangerous, to say the least.

Secondly, what did he think was going to meet him when he returned in triumph, an earwig? Or did he perhaps expect some more dispensable member of the household to present him or her self. If he'd asked me (granted, I wasn't around at the time) I could have told him that it's always daughters who run to greet fathers when they come home from work. He just didn't think it through, did he?

Thirdly, why didn't he break his vow and take the consequences like a man? I don't suppose he knew what those consequences were likely to be, but if he was as fond of his daughter as he appeared to be he might have decided to find out. Instead, he killed her!

Last, but not least, why didn't God say to him, 'Look, Jephthah, old chap, let's forget that silly vow you made the other day, and just celebrate your victory over the Ammonites. I don't want your daughter to be sacrificed to me as a burnt offering—what kind of God do you think I am, for goodness sake?'

There are my questions, and I know the answers are located somewhere in the region of the ongoing revelation of the nature of God (have I got that right?), but what a story!

Prayer

Father, help us to keep our mouths shut when we're overexcited, to think things through before we make a decision, and to go on searching for the truth about who and what you really are.

Samson

Judges 16:19–22 (NIV)

[Delilah] called a man to shave off the seven braids of his hair, and so began to subdue him. And his strength left him. Then she called, 'Samson, the Philistines are upon you!' He awoke from his sleep and thought, 'I'll go out as before and shake myself free.' But he did not know that the Lord had left him. Then the Philistines seized him, gouged out his eyes and took him down to Gaza. Binding him with bronze shackles, they set him to grinding in the prison. But the hair on his head began to grow again after it had been shaved.

Fortunately the Bible is full of good news for those who have failed. I've never been as powerful or as strong or as resourceful as Samson, but what I do have in common with him is the experience of giving in when the pressure becomes unbearable. This can apply at work or at home or in any situation where 'getting things right' requires consistent care and attention.

It can be so dispiriting. It's many years since I gave up smoking (I used to smoke sixty cigarettes a day and I enjoyed every single one), but I can still remember the attempts I made to stop when I was in my late twenties and early thirties. For some reason I got the idea into my head that God was going to 'get me' if I didn't stop smoking, so I was always worrying about it. Sometimes I'd manage to last for a week, a month, or even a couple of months, but then the pressure would become unbearable, especially if some other worry had become more dominant, and I'd fail again and feel a miserable failure. I didn't understand God at all in those days, so each time I was pretty sure I'd lose my salvation at the very least. Why would he want to be bothered with someone who had let the enemy batter him into submission?

But after each of these failures, and there were many, my hair began to grow again, as it were, just like Samson's. Some kind of divinely natural healing process restored both my belief that I was valued, and my intention to please God, and, in the end, I did give up smoking, although it was sheer agony for about six months.

Please don't think, by the way, that I'm getting at you if you're a smoker. God deals with each of us differently, and in my case, it was my experience that when people went on at me about giving up, there was only one thing I wanted to do—go and have a fag!

Prayer

Father, sometimes we give in under pressure, and it feels as if we will never be quite as close to you ever again. Restore the strength of our trust in you, Lord, and keep us close to you in future.

Daniel

Daniel 2:26, 29–30 (NIV)

The king asked Daniel (also called Belteshazzar), 'Are you able to tell me what I saw in my dream and interpret it?' Daniel replied, 'No wise man, enchanter, magician or diviner can explain to the king the mystery he has asked about, but there is a God in heaven who reveals mysteries. He has shown King Nebuchadnezzar what will happen in days to come. Your dream and the visions that passed through your mind... are these: As you were lying there, O king, your mind turned to things to come, and the revealer of mysteries showed you what is going to happen. As for me, this mystery has been revealed to me, not because I have greater wisdom than other living men, but so that you, O king, may know the interpretation and that you may understand what went through your mind.'

Do read the whole of Daniel as if it was a novel, if you have not done so before. It's a marvellous piece of storytelling (no, I'm not saying it didn't happen, just that it's a good read), and a very clear picture of the way in which God operates through a life that is genuinely dedicated to him. The impressive thing about Daniel, in all his dealings with the Babylonian kings, is his refusal to extract any personal glory from the situations in which God has given him special knowledge or protection. In this particular case he is at great pains to make it clear that it is God, not himself, who is the ultimate revealer of mysteries, and that his qualifications for passing on the wisdom of God do not include any extra or unusual wisdom of his own. The consistent purity of motivation shared by Daniel and his three famous friends, makes them very strong. No one can truly damage the most important part of you if your first priority is to serve God.

We could do with a few Daniels in church leadership today. It's so easy, when involved in spiritual ministry, to put on a bit of a self-advertising show, instead of simply passing on whatever God has told you to. The great sadness about this is that, for both Christians and non-Christians, the glorious sanity of God can be obscured by quite unnecessarily dramatic and bizarre role-playing on the part of those who have power over others. I hope and pray that the Church may be entering a new phase in this country, one that will see God speaking and working more clearly and more powerfully than ever before. I just hope that, when this happens, we'll be like Daniel, and get out of the way.

Thought

When the time comes to face the lions, relationship is going to be worth more than religion.

Joshua

Joshua 5:13–15 (NIV)

Now when Joshua was near Jericho, he looked up and saw a man standing in front of him with a drawn sword in his hand. Joshua went up to him and asked, 'Are you for us or for our enemies?' 'Neither,' he replied, 'but as commander of the army of the Lord I have now come.' Then Joshua fell face down to the ground in reverence, and asked him, 'What message does my Lord have for his servant?' The commander of the Lord's army replied, 'Take off your sandals, for the place where you are standing is holy.'

Thirty days after the death of Moses, Joshua, the new leader of the Israelites, was filled with the spirit of wisdom, which was just as well because he was going to need it. He must, in any case, have learned a great deal from his old master, described by the writer of Deuteronomy as the greatest prophet ever seen in Israel. Perhaps, in particular, he might have learned the folly of attempting to outguess God. And here's another good example.

Thank goodness he didn't rush bloodthirstily at this armed man and try to cut him to pieces. He might have done, mightn't he? Buoyed up by the reproach of Egypt having been lifted, and the experiences that year of eating from the produce of Canaan for the first time instead of being sustained by manna, Joshua must have been feeling pretty good. What an interesting answer the commander of the army of the Lord gave to his question. Why did he say 'neither'? Why didn't he say, 'Well, I'm for you of course'?

Perhaps Joshua needed a little reminder about who was actually in charge. Perhaps his question should have been: 'Are you for the Lord or for his enemies?' Perhaps it was essential that, like Moses, he should be humbled on holy ground, especially as the whole Jericho extravaganza was about to take place.

We can very easily find ourselves swept away by the excitement of doing things for God. But woe betide us if we lose touch with the roots of our excitement and begin to see the world in terms of those who are for *us* and those who are against *us*. We are not in charge of our own lives, and if we go around tackling our personal Jerichos without reference to the real commander, the walls are very unlikely to come down.

Prayer

Meet us on holy ground, Lord, and remind us that you are in charge.

Zephaniah

Zephaniah 3:18–20 (NIV)

'The sorrows for the appointed feasts I will remove from you; they are a burden and a reproach to you. At that time I will deal with all who oppressed you; I will rescue the lame and gather those who have been scattered. I will give them praise and honour in every land where they were put to shame. At that time I will gather you; at that time I will bring you home. I will give you honour and praise among all the peoples of the earth when I restore your fortunes before your very eyes.'

I used to think I was the only person in England who'd ever read Zephaniah, but there must be a few others, mustn't there?

This passage is very significant as far as I'm concerned, and I really hope it might be helpful to you as well. It became especially important to me when I was in the middle of a stress illness (yes, that's right—the same tedious old stress illness that I always seem to be bleating on about). I had arrived at just about the lowest point it was possible to reach, and I really could not see how I would ever achieve spiritual, emotional, or financial stability again. I had abdicated from work, church and proper family commitment to such an extent that I wasn't able to even look at the problems that I was facing.

God used a number of things to haul me out of that state, including friends, family and some specific experiences of his closeness, but this short passage from dear old Zeph, if I may call him that, was a small but key influence on my gradual return to normal lunacy. Don't ask me why some Bible verses stand out so vividly—I don't know how the Holy Spirit does it. What I do know is that the compassion and love expressed in these promises from God to his people became promises from him to me, like tickets for a Liverpool–Manchester match tucked away in my inside pocket. In particular, I loved the final line, as expressed in this translation. I sensed a delight in the heart of God about his plans magically to transform my fortunes.

I do hope that those of you who are in the same position as I was will also feel that delight, and tuck these promises away carefully so that you can take them out from time to time and draw a little strength from them.

Prayer

Father, thank you for illuminating your words when it's necessary. Be with all those who have reached the end of their tether. Do some magic in their lives.

Jacob and Esau

Genesis 33:1–4 (NIV)

Jacob looked up and there was Esau, coming with his four hundred men; so he... put the maidservants and their children in front... He himself went on ahead and bowed down to the ground seven times as he approached his brother. But Esau ran to meet Jacob and embraced him; he threw his arms around his neck and kissed him. And they wept.

The power of these Old Testament stories is quite extraordinary, isn't it? I've just read the section that leads up to this historic meeting, and when the two brothers wept, so did I. Do the same and you'll see why I ended up all gooey. Jacob was so *worried* that Esau's head would still be full of the dastardly trick played on him by his brother all those years ago when Jacob (famously 'a smooth man') got the blessing from Isaac instead of Esau. Jacob was quite brave though, wasn't he? He was determined to encounter his brother whatever the consequences, and I suppose that shows how much he'd changed since the days when he so easily outsmarted the slightly bovine Esau.

During the years that they'd been apart Jacob had met an even sharper con-man than himself—Laban, his father-in-law—and he'd wrestled with God and was still limping as a result. This was not the same Jacob, and perhaps he should have realized that Esau would also have moved on from the resentment of the past.

Reconciliation is often like this. Our fear of rejection or conflict can separate us for years from people whom we once loved, would still love if we felt sure that reconciliation was possible. When we do actually take the plunge, it is often the case that both parties experience a tremendous joy on rediscovering a relationship that was always greater and more valuable than the reason for its fracturing.

Jacob's courage (despite his fear) didn't just result in peace between the two brothers, important though that was. His return to the country of his birth was an essential step in the history and destiny of what was to be known as the Israelite nation.

My making-up with Auntie Ada over what she said about our Billy thirty-five years ago, when she'd had one sherry too many after Sunday dinner, might not seem to be in quite the same league as Jacob and Esau, but who knows? Shall we try?

Prayer

Father, some of us have some peacemaking to do. It's frightening. Give us courage and determination, and an awareness that it's part of your plan for the future.

Joseph

Genesis 45:4–8 (NIV)

Joseph said, 'I am your brother Joseph, the one you sold into Egypt... Do not be angry with yourselves for selling me here, because it was to save lives that God sent me ahead of you. For two years now there has been famine in the land... But God sent me ahead of you to preserve for you a remnant on earth and to save your lives... So then, it was not you who sent me here, but God. He made me... ruler of all Egypt.'

This is one of the greatest Old Testament stories of all, but do you think Joseph got this bit right? I mean—obviously he was bowled over by seeing his brothers again, but was it really God who did it all?

Was it God who initiated the idea of slinging Joseph into a cistern, and then somehow silently persuaded the brothers to sell him to traders, just so that Jacob and his family wouldn't starve years later? And what about the fact that these incidents led eventually to the suppression and oppression of the Jewish people by an Egyptian nation that grew to hate them? Is that what God was planning all along?

If that was the case, then shouldn't we feel free to do whatever we feel like doing, however harmful it may be to others, confident in the knowledge that God is really behind our actions, and that therefore we can put the responsibility onto him? An attractive way to look at things, perhaps.

Forget it! Seductive though that approach to Christian living may be, we have been privileged to hear the words and sense the personality and presence of Jesus, who came to show us what God is actually like.

These Old Testament accounts are marvellously entertaining and profoundly instructive on many levels (Jesus himself quoted them often in support of his own teaching), but we would do well to temper both the unacceptable and the attractive aspects of this part of our Bible with the knowledge we have gained through the revelation of God in Christ.

Jesus made it clear that we are responsible for our own actions. He also showed us the depth of the love of God for us by going to the cross, and he did that for the very good reason that not a single one of us will be able to make our actions match the holiness of God.

The Bible—all of it—is full of God, but Jesus *was* God.

Prayer

Father, we thank you for the passion and drama and humour and wisdom of the Old Testament. We wrestle with some of the nasty bits, but you've let them be there, so thank you for those as well (by faith!). Most of all we thank you for Jesus, who came to reveal you and save us.

The supreme misfortune is when theory outstrips performance.

Leonardo Da Vinci

THEORY AND PRACTICE —TALK OR WALK?

A nervous look at the letter of James

Some time ago I was speaking on the phone to a friend. The main part of what I wanted to say to him went something like this: 'The thing is, I've given Tony every chance in the past. No, I've done more than that—I've really worked hard at our relationship because I know how much it means to him. I've given him credit for things that he had hardly anything to do with, I've swallowed things he said and done my best to just put them to the back of my mind, I've spent hours talking through things he was worried about and I've forgiven him every time he messes something up and leaves me to sort the damage out afterwards. And now—after all that—I hear that he's run me down in a public meeting in front of people whose good will is important—no, crucial—to my future. So I've decided that enough is enough. I can't continue with our friendship on that basis, so I'm going to ring him and tell him that, as far as I'm concerned, I'd rather we didn't meet again.'

I waited for my friend to sigh and click his tongue and say that he would do exactly the same if he was me. Instead, there was silence for a few seconds.

'Right,' said the voice on the other end of the line at last, 'so I guess you'll be staying well away from the New Testament for a while, will you?'

'What?'

'I said, I guess you'll be staying away from—'

'Yes, I heard what you said, but what did you mean?'

'Oh, well, I suppose I was just thinking that Jesus said something or other about forgiving people seventy times seven times. Or have I got it wrong?'

'No, as you well know, you've got it right, but it doesn't matter because I've already forgiven Tony a lot more than four hundred and ninety times, so he's had his allocation and now I'm going to stop.'

Another silence. Sometimes silences are not golden, they are very, very annoying indeed.

'All right,' I conceded, 'I was only joking. I know it means that there's not supposed to be any limit on forgiveness, but I've just had enough. I've run out of charity as far as he's concerned. I've tried *so* hard. Don't you think you reach a point where you have to just—part company?'

'Don't you want to be forgiven yourself, then?' asked my soon-to-be-ex-friend.

'I'm sorry?'

'Well, I was just thinking of the bit in the Lord's Prayer about how God forgives our sins as long as we forgive others, and then there's that parable, isn't there, where the steward gets let off his debts and then doesn't let someone else off and ends up going to prison. And there's the thing Jesus said about—'

'Yes, all right, you don't have to go through the entire Bible. I think I've just about got the point. You're not going to help me out by colluding with me, and you think I should forgive Tony and start all over again, don't you?'

'Sorry, it's just that I thought you were a Christian. I must have got it all wrong—have I?'

'Don't you think sarcasm might be a sin as well?'

'Yes, probably, but I know you'll forgive me...'

The book of James is mainly about the fact that Christianity is not just an abstract concept, but a relationship that will, if it is genuine, produce works reflecting the teaching and attitudes of Jesus. We Western Christians have a tendency to become so obsessed with theory and theology and a sort of academic spirituality, that we forget how practical the Holy Spirit is wanting to be in caring for others through us. In Jesus' parable of the two sons who are asked to perform a task for their father, it is the one with, if you like, the poor doctrine, who is obedient, while the one who produces all the right words does nothing.

Actually being what Jesus wants us to be, as opposed to talking about it, can be very tough indeed. Everything in me said that I had a right to reject Tony, but, as my friend pointed out (and as I shall point out to him on the very first occasion that *he* slips into sin and needs a little spiritual counselling from *me*), our personal rights have been subsumed into the will of God, and that will involve doing the right thing *even when it hurts*.

My wife learned this lesson painfully a few months ago. One morning she was about to set off for a warmly anticipated trip to visit her parents, when an elderly friend rang to ask if it was possible for Bridget to drive her to hospital in Brighton, as she was nervous at the prospect of going on her own. Bridget worked out that if she went straight to the hospital and straight back it would still just about be possible to arrive at her parents' house at the time she had planned. But, of course, it wasn't like that. It never is, is it? The elderly friend couldn't just be dumped at the hospital. She needed to be accompanied to the ward, and reassured, and calmed down, and all the other things that people need when they are frightened and in an unfamiliar place. By the time Bridget got back to the house she was in tears of frustration because it had got so late and and it would be dark by the time she arrived in Norwich.

I feel quite sure that Jesus would be sympathetic towards all three of the main characters in this little drama (I seem to remember that he kept his own mother waiting at one point) but I also think it was his idea that Bridget should go to Brighton.

The letter of James is enormously challenging, combining Pythonesque humour with an almost Basil Fawlty-like rhetoric in places (try reading verses thirteen to fifteen of chapter five in Fawlty tones). The central message, that works are a natural by-product of faith, is probably the one that the modern Church most needs to hear.

Prayer

Father, help us to face up to the challenge of 'doing' as well as believing. Amen.

Pure joy

James 1:2–8 (NIV)

Consider it pure joy... whenever you face trials of many kinds, because you know that the testing of your faith develops perseverance. Perseverance must finish its work so that you may be mature and complete, not lacking anything. If any of you lacks wisdom, he should ask God, who gives generously to all without finding fault, and it will be given to him. But when he asks, he must believe and not doubt, because he who doubts is like a wave of the sea, blown and tossed by the wind. That man should not think he will receive anything from the Lord; he is a double-minded man, unstable in all he does.

A typical interchange in the Plass household:

Bridget: (*Entering euphorically*) You'll never guess what, Adrian!
Adrian: (*Filled with anticipatory pleasure*) What's that then, Bridget?
Bridget: Well, the car won't start and it looks as if the problem is a highly complex and expensive one.
Adrian: (*Clapping ecstatically*) That's really great, Bridget! Fancy that happening on the same morning that we get a huge electricity bill we can't possibly pay and the ceiling collapsing in the front room. I must say that I consider all these things pure joy, don't you?
Bridget: (*Almost dancing with delight*) Oh, yes! It's a wonderful opportunity for us to develop perseverance through the testing of our faith.
Adrian: (*With tears of sheer happiness in his eyes*) Yes, indeed! I should think we'll be as mature and complete as it's possible to be after this little lot, won't we?
Bridget: (*Excitedly*) Let's ask God for wisdom to deal with everything, shall we?
Adrian: (*Fascinated by such a novel idea*) Yes! After all, he does give generously without finding fault, doesn't he?
Bridget: (*Struck by yet another thought*) And let's not doubt!
Adrian: (*Amused at the very idea*) No, of course not, because then we would be like waves of the sea, blown and tossed by the wind. Then we shouldn't expect to receive anything, should we? (*They laugh heartily together*)
Bridget: *(Almost choking with merriment)* We don't want to be double-minded and unstable, do we? *(They collapse on the floor, laughing hysterically)*

Prayer

Let's face it, Father, the concept of regarding trials with pure joy is an impossible dream for many of us. We accept, though, that you set this standard before us, and we humbly ask your help in moving towards it. Amen.

✦ Is it possible for trials and troubles to be considered pure joy?

The crown of life

James 1:9–12, 16–18 (NIV)

The brother in humble circumstances ought to take pride in his high position. But the one who is rich should take pride in his low position, because he will pass away like a wild flower. For the sun rises with scorching heat and withers the plant; its blossom falls and its beauty is destroyed. In the same way, the rich man will fade away even while he goes about his business. Blessed is the man who perseveres under trial, because when he has stood the test, he will receive the crown of life that God has promised to those who love him... Don't be deceived, my dear brothers. Every good and perfect gift is from above, coming down from the Father of the heavenly lights, who does not change like shifting shadows. He chose to give us birth through the word of truth, that we might be a kind of first-fruits of all he created.

I thought about the crown of life at a friend's funeral. Stan was elderly and had suffered terribly from emphysema, as well as recently diagnosed cancer. Now, thank God, the physical discomfort had ended, but the family was devastated. Betty, Stan's wife, a genuinely good person, couldn't contain the spasms of grief that continually rocked her body, while Bob's married daughter, Jane, cried so copiously that the very shape of her face seemed to melt and change.

Vicky, the youngest grandchild, was one big frightened question mark. She watched, wide-eyed, as the coffin was lowered. Grandad—in that box? Grandad gone? No more Nana and Grandad? Just Nana...? Suddenly it was too much. She buried her face in her auntie's jumper and burst into tears. Her older brother, Sam, was being tough. Only when the graveside ritual was over and everyone moved away, did he walk quietly back to the edge of the grave and release his tears.

Grief is infectious. But even as I wept with them all, I seemed to hear Jesus, saying in a voice fired with sympathy and excitement, 'Don't be afraid—I really have overcome death!'

Prayer

Father, it's easy to forget that the crown of life—an eternity spent with you—is the reason that Jesus came and died and was raised to life again. Help us to get our priorities right. Amen.

✦ Do I want this crown of life, and how am I dealing with the inevitability of death?

The long climb

James 1:19–27 (NIV)

My dear brothers, take note of this: Everyone should be quick to listen, slow to speak and slow to become angry, for man's anger does not bring about the righteous life that God desires... Do not merely listen to the word, and so deceive yourselves. Do what it says. Anyone who listens to the word but does not do what it says is like a man who looks at his face in a mirror and, after looking at himself, goes away and immediately forgets what he looks like... If anyone considers himself religious and yet does not keep a tight rein on his tongue, he deceives himself and his religion is worthless. Religion that God our Father accepts as pure and faultless is this: to look after orphans and widows in their distress and to keep oneself from being polluted by the world.

I wondered, as a young Christian, why we never said much about the book of James. The reason, of course, is that it is about *doing* as opposed to theorizing.

Some years ago I wrote a book of short stories called *The Final Boundary*. (It was banned in some Christian circles and used as a basis for Bible study discussions in others—is it any wonder that I get confused?)

One story, 'A Letter to William', concerned a fictitious situation in which salvation by faith had been replaced by a new system stipulating that mankind could only be saved by climbing Snowdon, the Welsh mountain, three times every week. Talking about climbing didn't count, nor did the singing of climbing choruses, nor did constructing small models of Snowdon to be symbolically ascended and descended by the congregation each Sunday. Those physically unable to climb were still obliged to arrive at the foot of the mountain three times a week to be transported to the top by other means.

I've been asked many times about the exact meaning of the story, and usually produce long, complicated explanations. Not any more. I shall just say, 'Read the book of James.'

Prayer

Father, thank you so much for the reference to orphans and widows. I know this definition of pure religion isn't a popular one in some quarters, but it is with you, and that's what matters. Amen.

✦ If James is right in his definition of true religion, what are the implications for the Church?

Who's who?

James 2:2–9 (NIV)

Suppose a man comes into your meeting wearing a gold ring and fine clothes, and a poor man in shabby clothes also comes in. If you show special attention to the man wearing fine clothes and say, 'Here's a good seat for you,' but say to the poor man, 'You stand there' or 'Sit on the floor by my feet,' have you not discriminated among yourselves and become judges with evil thoughts? Listen, my dear brothers: Has not God chosen those who are poor in the eyes of the world to be rich in faith and to inherit the kingdom he promised those who love him?... If you really keep the royal law found in Scripture, 'Love your neighbour as yourself,' you are doing right. But if you show favouritism, you sin and are convicted by the law as law-breakers.

One day, on tour in South Africa with the family, we were offered a lift from one town to another by a man who had been at one of our meetings. At his (very large) house next morning he told us his gardener had asked for a lift. Was that all right with us?

Gardeners in South Africa are black, and despite miraculously peaceful political change, master/servant roles are still evident. As we clambered into the car the gardener, Michael, hovered uncertainly. Katy (eight) counted passengers and headed automatically for the back, assuming that, as usual, she'd be expected to fit into the luggage area. Our host soon nipped this in the bud, ushering Katy into the remaining seat-space while the gardener coiled his large frame into the place where dogs and suitcases usually fit. Later, we discovered that we'd all felt profound embarrassment at this treatment of a grown man.

I'm sure our host would have wanted to say that the gardener might have been just as embarrassed as us if he'd been given a seat in the car, and that things would probably change in future etc., etc. But the fact is—I don't think it even *occurred* to him that Michael might have equal rights with us.

Before we get too smug let's ask ourselves who *we* regard as lesser simply because that's how we've always seen them.

Questions

Are there people in my church, my work-place, my road, my bus-queue who are 'obviously' less important than anyone else? If I take another look at them, might I see Jesus?

✦ Am I a spiritual democrat?

Bickering

James 2:10–13 (NIV)

For whoever keeps the whole law and yet stumbles at just one point is guilty of breaking all of it… If you do not commit adultery but do commit murder, you have become a law-breaker. Speak and act as those who are going to be judged by the law that gives freedom, because judgment without mercy will be shown to anyone who has not been merciful. Mercy triumphs over judgment!

Do your children argue? My four have argued in the past, still argue in the present and will undoubtedly continue to argue in the future. They don't *all* argue *all* of the time, but for as long as I can remember there has been a permutation of two who simply cannot encounter each other without finding some molehill of disagreement to turn into a mountain of raging, bickering, infuriating conflict. The maddening thing is that you *know*—you just *know*, that you never brought them up to behave in such a mindless, primitive way. Someone must surely have been creeping in during the night without you knowing and influencing their behaviour in this negative way.

One of the most sickening aspects of this sickening experience is the flood of accusations and counter-accusations upon which we poor suffering mums and dads are called upon to adjudicate. In our innocent pre-parent days, we vowed, didn't we, that we would always conduct negotiations and discussions with our hypothetical offspring in a calm, adult, constructive manner? Now, more often than not, we are reduced to screaming:

'If you two don't SHUT UP I shall—I shall kill you both! You're just as bad as each other! Why can't you be kind to each other?'

This is God's basic message (though expressed rather less frenetically, perhaps!) to those of us, his children, who constantly blame and judge and condemn other members of the kingdom we all inhabit, a kingdom that accommodates sinners only by the power of his mercy and grace.

We've said it before, we shall say it again, let's say it now: THE DEAREST WISH OF GOD IS THAT WE SHOULD LOVE ONE ANOTHER.

Prayer

Father, we hurt and anger you with our negative treatment of each other. Forgive us for indulging attitudes of superiority or ill-feeling or resentment towards our brothers and sisters. We will try! Amen.

✦ What kind of people make me cross?

Dancing verses

James 2:14–19 (NIV)

What good is it… if a man claims to have faith but has no deeds? Can such faith save him? Suppose a brother or sister is without clothes and daily food. If one of you says to him, 'Go, I wish you well; keep warm and well fed,' but does nothing about his physical needs, what good is it? In the same way, faith by itself, if it is not accompanied by action, is dead. But someone will say, 'You have faith; I have deeds.' Show me your faith without deeds, and I will show you my faith by what I do. You believe that there is one God. Good! Even the demons believe that—and shudder.

It has been suggested that the man called James who wrote this book might have been the natural brother of Jesus, and possibly one of the most important early leaders of the Church. This little section in particular seems to me to support that view. Its two distinctly Pythonesque comments are strongly redolent of the type of dry wit that we find Jesus using to such good effect in the Gospel stories and dialogues. The first of these, the comment about wishing your starving brothers well without offering practical help, has been making me chuckle since I first looked at it thirty years ago, and James' sardonic congratulation to those who believe in God just as the demons do could have come straight out of one of our modern situation comedies (one of the few funny ones, I mean).

I can't help wondering if James pinched these one-liners from his brother. Effective humour is memorable, isn't it? Verses like these dance an endless little jig in the mind, thereby constantly calling attention to themselves. This is good and useful for two reasons.

First, the message of the words themselves is such an important one. Yet again, James is driving home the self-evident but no less neglected truth that belief without action is useless.

Secondly, and I suppose this appeals to me particularly because of the kind of work that I do, these verses remind me that God can be as Chestertonian as he can be solemn, and that I can look forward to a day when he and I will have a really good laugh together.

Thank you

Thank you for the rich complexity of your personality, your creation and your dealings with us. Thank you that you laugh and cry, smile and frown. We look forward to knowing you better. Amen.

✦ What makes God laugh? What makes him cry?

Words and actions

James 2:20–26 (NIV)

You foolish man, do you want evidence that faith without deeds is useless? Was not our ancestor Abraham considered righteous for what he did when he offered his son Isaac on the altar? You see that his faith and his actions were working together... And the scripture was fulfilled that says, 'Abraham believed God, and it was credited to him as righteousness'... You see that a person is justified by what he does and not by faith alone. In the same way, was not even Rahab the prostitute considered righteous for what she did when she gave lodging to the spies...? As the body without the spirit is dead, so faith without deeds is dead.

Do you remember a television quiz called *Runaround* (I think)? A general knowledge question was asked, then thirty or so children raced across an open space to line up under one of three possible answers, including the correct one, displayed high up on the opposite wall. When a hooter sounded, the children had seconds in which to change lines. Quite a lot did.

Let's imagine that entrance into heaven is similar. Having covered the space between earth and heaven people have formed lines outside the gates, all hoping that they've got the right answer. Let's look at just two lines.

The first is straight and confident, men and women with well-thumbed fat black Bibles under their arms, and a world of theology on their lips. They have perfected the art of worship and how to pray effectively. Some have been involved in healing and deliverance. The church was their lives. The second line is a bit of a mess, mainly because everyone is trying to not be at the front. Some of them have got Bibles as well, but they don't look very confident at all. A funny looking crowd altogether, in fact. To be honest, some of them seem downright inadequate. They've got just enough faith between them to stick around on the off-chance that they may be allowed in. These are the people who actually did things—the ones who got their hands dirty because, inadequate though they were in some ways, they sensed that the theory of love demands a practical response.

Now footsteps are heard on the other side of the gate. Those in the first line straighten up expectantly. The second line ceases to be a line altogether as its members hold on to each other nervously. A hooter sounds. Five seconds to change lines.

Prayer

Show us how to be your hands, Lord. Amen.

✦ What is the visible evidence of my faith?

Manipulation

James 3:1–6 (NIV)

We who teach will be judged more strictly... If anyone is never at fault in what he says, he is a perfect man, able to keep his whole body in check. When we put bits into the mouths of horses to make them obey us, we can turn the whole animal. Or take ships as an example. Although they are so large and are driven by strong winds, they are steered by a very small rudder wherever the pilot wants to go. Likewise the tongue is a small part of the body, but it makes great boasts. Consider what a great forest is set on fire by a small spark. The tongue also is a fire, a world of evil among the parts of the body. It corrupts the whole person, sets the whole course of his life on fire, and is itself set on fire by hell.

I don't think any of us would seriously argue with these comments about the potentially inflammatory nature of the tongue, but it's worth mentioning that, as well as the obvious problems, there are more subtle ones. Here's an example.

Working with children in care, as I did for many years, often involved case-conferences to discuss and decide on the next step in a child's life. Early in my career I would present my personal opinion passionately as soon after the beginning of the meeting as possible, only to find that it was lost or forgotten as the discussion continued and other attitudes were put forward. Eventually I learned that the most effective ploy was to let everybody talk themselves out, as it were, until mine was the only view unexpressed. One by one the other members of the conference would turn to me, vaguely assuming (quite erroneously) that as I'd said nothing so far, anything I *did* say must be worth hearing. Silence has an odd effect on people. Besides, as lunchtime approaches, any firm and apparently well-considered view is worth having.

My comment would begin with the words, 'Well, I've been listening carefully to everything that's been said, and I must say...' After that it was usually downhill, and I'm quite sure that on a number of occasions I was *completely wrong*.

Prayer

Father, protect us from the temptation to manipulate others. Often we do it without even realizing that it's become a habit, especially in our own families, and with close friends. Amen.

✦ Which kinds of talking are helpful, and which are not?

Salt and fresh water **James 3:7–12 (NIV)**

All kinds of animals, birds, reptiles and creatures of the sea are being tamed and have been tamed by man, but no man can tame the tongue... With the tongue we praise our Lord and Father, and with it we curse men, who have been made in God's likeness. Out of the same mouth come praise and cursing. My brothers, this should not be. Can both fresh water and salt water flow from the same spring? My brothers, can a fig-tree bear olives, or a grapevine bear figs? Neither can a salt spring produce fresh water.

Why is there such a contrast between the things that we say? Same mouth, same brain—what goes wrong? How can salt and fresh water flow from the same spring? Yet they do in most of us. These early Church chaps tend to be very black and white, but many of us struggle to retain a reasonable shade of grey.

Let's be honest, the most dramatic contrasts occur between the way we are with our nearest and dearest, and the way we present ourselves to the rest of the world, and there's a sense in which that's exactly as it should be. We've got to relax somewhere. But it isn't just that. Much as I love my wife, I've never been as angry with anyone as I've been with her, and vice versa, only less so. There can be a gap between public and private morality. Bridget and I have been amazed by the depth of darkness we have seen in the private lives of some who spend their time calling others to the light.

What to do? Do we work hard at being as unpleasant in public as we are in private? An intriguing thought, but I don't think God would bless that one, do you? Should we doggedly role-play polite warmth in private? Well, some of us could certainly offer a more natural courtesy to the people closest to us, but change has to be real or we shall quickly run out of steam and be back where we started.

No, there is little alternative to opening up the situation in four areas: honesty with ourselves, honesty with God, honesty with the people our behaviour affects most, and honesty with some trusted outsider in order to bridge the public/private gap. After that we shall have a job on our hands, but we shall have *started*, and we won't be alone.

Prayer

Father, stand in the gap and heal us. Amen.

✦ What difference would there be if I bridged the public/ private gap?

Personal filters

James 3:13–18 (NIV)

Who is wise...? Let him show it by his good life... But if you harbour bitter envy and selfish ambition in your hearts, do not boast about it or deny the truth... For where you have envy and selfish ambition, there you find disorder and every evil practice. But the wisdom that comes from heaven is first of all pure; then peace-loving, considerate, submissive, full of mercy and good fruit, impartial and sincere. Peacemakers who sow in peace raise a harvest of righteousness.

Speaking as one who, in the course of listening quite frequently to other people's problems, has developed a habit of nodding solemnly as though I am nurturing profound insights into whatever the situation happens to be, but rarely if ever actually has the faintest idea what to say or suggest, I really would welcome a little of the wisdom that James is talking about here.

In this context I find it particularly interesting that he names purity as the first and most essential component of wisdom that comes from heaven, because it is often our less-than-pure personal agendas that impede useful communication on these occasions. Both hearing and responding have to make their laborious way through all the political, social, sexual, religious and idiosyncratic filters that make us what we are. Interestingly enough, it's usually the religious filter that gives me the most trouble. I still find it very hard to break away from a rather rigid worldview that was inserted into me like an extra skeleton when I was a young Christian. Sometimes I simply have to ignore a worriedly narrow little voice that tells me I'm committing some gross heresy merely by listening to, or not arguing with, something that doesn't 'fit'.

At the bottom of the writer's list comes impartiality and sincerity, but I'm sure this is more of a summing-up than a relegation. These are the things that will set you and me free in our contacts with others, whatever the context may be. It might be useful to use this passage as an aid to prayer when we know that some tricky encounter is coming up. Wouldn't it be wonderful to feel that we had helped to raise a harvest of righteousness?

Prayer

Give us wisdom, Father, the kind of wisdom that is yours rather than ours, a wisdom that sets us free from ourselves and thereby frees others. Thank you. Amen.

✦ In which specific areas do I need wisdom today?

Surviving change

James 4:1–7 (NIV)

What causes fights and quarrels among you? Don't they come from your desires that battle within you? You want something but don't get it. You kill and covet, but you cannot have what you want. You quarrel and fight. You do not have, because you do not ask God. When you ask, you do not receive, because you ask with wrong motives, that you may spend what you get on your pleasures. You adulterous people, don't you know that friendship with the world is hatred towards God?... But he gives us more grace. That is why scripture says: 'God opposes the proud but gives grace to the humble.' Submit yourselves, then, to God. Resist the devil, and he will flee from you.

Meeting an old Christian friend called Tom in the pub, I found him very low. His problems concerned money, personal failure and God, all closely connected. Business collapse had left his family in a very difficult financial position, triggering feelings of inadequacy that have dogged Tom since childhood.

'It's not that I don't believe in God,' he said dolefully into his pint. 'That wouldn't be so bad in a way. What I can't understand is why he lets us carry on being miserable. If he's not interested in helping my family he must love them less than I do, and if that's the case—well, I'm not sure I like him very much.'

Basically, Tom's relationship with God had not survived the change in his material circumstances, but if you serve up raw truth like that you're likely to get it thrown back in your face. As I listened I wanted to say to Tom that 'friendship with the world', as James puts it, can be subtle. Tom's family has always had a siege mentality towards outsiders who are probably out to 'get them', and I suspect that God was only allowed a place at the table as long as he was paying his dues. Should I have said this to him, or just sympathized with his bad luck? What do you think?

What *did* I actually do, drawing on my vast reserves of wisdom, experience and skills of interpersonal communication? I bought him another pint.

Prayer

Father, give us insight into our relationship with you, and courage when something needs to be said to somebody else. Amen.

✦ How closely is my trust in God bound up with material security?

Spring cleaning

James 4:8–12 (NIV)

Come near to God and he will come near to you. Wash your hands, you sinners, and purify your hearts, you double-minded. Grieve, mourn and wail. Change your laughter to mourning and your joy to gloom. Humble yourselves before the Lord, and he will lift you up. Brothers, do not slander one another. Anyone who speaks against his brother or judges him speaks against the law and judges it. When you judge the law, you are not keeping it, but sitting in judgment on it. There is only one Lawgiver and Judge, the one who is able to save and destroy. But you—who are you to judge your neighbour?

There is no doubt that spiritual spring-cleaning needs to happen on a regular basis, particularly because of the way in which we continually slip back into being 'lifted up' by things and people other than God. In my own case it might be book sales or prospective speaking tours or food or alcohol or activities with the family or the pure joy of writing Bible notes or... well, all sorts of things. Not (I hasten to add, before 'Outraged of Plymouth' gets his pen out) that any of those things are bad or un-Christian. On the contrary, most of them are the things for which I am mainly accountable to God. One of the major purposes of repentance, though, is to remind us that the most important part of us, the part that will live eternally, can *only* be lifted up and kept alive by the grace and mercy of God. It will always be humbling to realize how utterly dependent on him we actually are, but repentance, which is supposed to be a joyful thing (read the prodigal son), might also help us to express gratitude for the life and death of Jesus, the supreme gift which made repentance possible. My friend, Tom, whom you met in the previous note, had temporarily lost sight of that eternal dimension.

The two paragraphs in this passage, which at first glance appear to be about different things, actually fit together very well. If we really do humble ourselves before God in the wholehearted way described here, we're going to find it extremely difficult to sit in judgment on anyone else. Whatever the type or degree of our personal sins, we have all been equally lost, and we are all equally saved.

Prayer

Father, we're back to the question of priorities again. Remind us that it is you who lifts us up. We have no reason to be proud. Amen.

✦ What lifts me up?

Neo-nomads

James 4:13–17 (NIV)

Now listen, you who say, 'Today or tomorrow we will go to this or that city, spend a year there, carry on business and make money.' Why, you do not even know what will happen tomorrow. What is your life? You are a mist that appears for a little while and then vanishes. Instead, you ought to say, 'If it is the Lord's will, we will live and do this or that.' As it is, you boast and brag. All such boasting is evil. Anyone, then, who knows the good he ought to do and doesn't do it, sins.

The opening words of this passage have an extraordinarily modern ring to them, don't they? We live in a neo-nomadic age, where many people move frequently in pursuit of better jobs or to be close to the school they want for their children or for a variety of other reasons. I don't think James is criticizing that tendency, but he is saying what Jesus said so many times—that everything except our relationship with God must be held provisionally. In the end the practical concerns of this world will be meaningless, and that end can happen very abruptly.

Some years ago my mother suddenly became ill and was rushed to hospital at Pembury, which is more than twenty miles away from us. Late that night I rang the ward where she'd been taken, and was told that it was unlikely that she would still be alive in the morning. A friend drove me to the hospital, where I found my mother very ill and confused, but able to recognize me. When I kissed her goodbye an hour later I was sure that I would never see her again in this world.

Travelling home in the car was dream-like. I reflected on the fact that death is so big and so little—big in the sense that it removes *one whole person* and results in such loss and grief for the living; small in the sense that it can happen so quickly and be physically disposed of so totally. I felt frightened suddenly by the thought of how many of these neo-nomads are ambushed by death, and how shocked they must subsequently be by the realization that they were quite unprepared for this, the most important journey of their lives.

My mother survived for another four years, thank God, and the lesson continues.

Prayer

Father, help us to turn our eyes upon Jesus, and to see all our decisions and plans in the context of his eternal gift to us.

✦ Where does my plan begin?

King Rat

James 5:1–6 (NIV)

Now listen, you rich people, weep and wail because of the misery that is coming upon you. Your wealth has rotted... Your gold and silver are corroded. Their corrosion will testify against you and eat your flesh like fire. You have boarded wealth in the last days. Look! The wages you failed to pay the workmen who mowed your fields are crying out against you... You have lived on earth in luxury and self-indulgence. You have fattened yourselves in the day of slaughter. You have condemned and murdered innocent men, who were not opposing you.

Have you ever seen the film *King Rat*, in which the main character, a Second World War American soldier, is brilliantly played by George Segal? Segal's anti-hero, a resourceful but amoral wheeler and dealer, finds himself incarcerated in a Japanese prisoner-of-war camp, and becomes the wealthiest man in the camp through buying and selling and scrounging and stealing. Unburdened by scruples (British officers buy rat meat from him, and cheerfully eat it believing it to be squirrel), he rapidly achieves a position of dominance, living in comparative luxury, dispensing or withholding favours according to the profit involved.

Particularly memorable is the scene where Segal fries eggs before someone who has something he wants. The staring, lip-licking agony of this man who hasn't *seen* an egg for two years is painful to behold.

There is no doubt that, as far as the small world of that camp is concerned, and the small group of henchmen who defend and assist him in exchange for whatever scraps he throws at them, he is King Rat, the richest, most powerful man in the community.

The eventual liberation of the camp by allied troops corresponds to the picture drawn by James in this passage. Suddenly, the carefully hoarded supplies of food and bargaining items are worthless. Those who followed the 'King' in return for crusts are anxious not to be associated with him, especially as there is a strong indication that Segal's uniquely well-fed, healthy physical condition will result in investigation and punishment. The film ends with 'King Rat' isolated at the centre of the compound that, only yesterday, he ruled. If he had helped others in that little world he might have been a hero in the next. Instead, he is an outcast.

Prayer

Father, whatever we are rich in, help us to share it. Amen.

✦ What do I have in abundance? Do I share it?

Patience

James 5:7–12 (NIV)

Be patient, then, brothers, until the Lord's coming. See how the farmer waits for the land to yield its valuable crop and how patient he is for the autumn and spring rains. You too, be patient and stand firm, because the Lord's coming is near. Don't grumble against each other, brothers, or you will be judged. The Judge is standing at the door!... You have heard of Job's perseverance and have seen what the Lord finally brought about. The Lord is full of compassion and mercy. Above all, my brothers, do not swear—not by heaven or by earth or by anything else. Let your 'Yes' be yes, and your 'No', no, or you will be condemned.

At a meeting that I attended in London, someone said, with a great tiredness in his voice, 'I'm so weary of being a Christian—I just want to be with Jesus.'

More recently, an acquaintance who is very active in the church had received some bad news, and phoned to ask if she could come round for a cup of tea and a chat. For a while we talked about what had happened, then, after a short silence, she suddenly burst into tears and cried out through her sobbing, 'All I want is to just know that God loves me—that's all I want!'

Another friend who has been used constantly for the comfort of others over a quarter of a century, reached a point where his faith simply drained away and the purpose of living seemed to have gone altogether. Unexpected weakness in pillars of strength is not popular, to say the least. I think my friend would have cheerfully opted for being swept off the face of the earth by the arms of God, and taken to a place where he didn't have to try any more. I know the feeling.

There are a lot of weary pilgrims around, folk who really *have* been patient for a long time as James says we should be, but are now at the point where they can't go on without a bit of help. If we need that kind of help, let's ask for it. If we find someone whose patience is all used up, let's not be Christians for them—let's be Jesus.

Prayer

Father, we want to persevere and be patient as you command, but we break down every now and then. Help us to look after each other. Amen.

✦ What breaks down patience? What builds it up?

Informal encounters

James 5:13–20 (NIV)

Is any one of you in trouble? He should pray. Is anyone happy? Let him sing songs of praise. Is any one of you sick? He should call the elders of the church to pray over him and anoint him with oil in the name of the Lord. And the prayer offered in faith will make the sick person well; the Lord will raise him up. If he has sinned, he will be forgiven. Therefore confess your sins to each other and pray for each other so that you may be healed. The prayer of a righteous man is powerful and effective... My brothers, if one of you should wander from the truth and someone should bring him back, remember this: Whoever turns a sinner from the error of his way will save him from death and cover over a multitude of sins.

Have you noticed how 'The Pub' creeps into my writings on a fairly regular basis? Perhaps some of you are praying that my obsession with such establishments will be healed eventually. Well, don't hold your breath. It's not impossible that I may go teetotal one day, but that would be a silly reason to abandon The Ferret's Armpit, or whichever hostelry I'm frequenting at the time. After all, I'm supposed to be following Jesus, aren't I?

Why did this passage make me think about pubs? Well, it's full of things that happen there. My closest friends and I really do confess our sins to each other in such situations, and there really is an exchange of the things in our lives that are causing us to praise God or pray for rescue and release. In addition, and not infrequently, the business described in the last two verses of this book is very much on the agenda of such divinely secular occasions. We have to talk the nonsense out of each other sometimes, and that can be quite a tough prospect.

Of course, it doesn't have to be a pub. It may be morning coffee with a friend, or a walk on the hills, or half an hour in a launderette. I know that, but please don't relegate the meeting of close friends in informal situations to some lower-level, non-spiritual league. Jesus didn't, nor does the Holy Spirit.

A thought

Jesus will be wherever two or three are gathered together.

✦ Where does my Christianity *really* happen?

The most certain sign of wisdom is a continual cheerfulness; her state is like that in the regions above the moon, always clear and serene.

Michael De Montaigne

TRAVELLING WISELY

Words of wisdom from Proverbs

Unfortunately, 'wisdom' is one of that increasingly long list of words that have been devalued and, in fact, totally redefined by the commercial ploys of twentieth-century advertising. Nowadays, if you were to tell someone that the exercise of wisdom will be rewarded with a taste of ambrosia, the received message will probably be that if you keep your teeth nice and clean you'll be given a bowl of creamed rice. Sad, isn't it? In an age when true wisdom is much more urgently needed than toothbrushes we are not even quite sure what the word means any more.

As far as the Church is concerned, the last thirty years has seen a plethora (excuse me while I just press the thesaurus button and check that) yes, a plethora of paperback books that offer a sort of bright easy-stage wisdom on just about every problem that your average evangelical Christian is likely to face.

My wife was given one of these books a few years ago, by someone who must have felt that she was not coming up to scratch in certain areas. This volume was all about how to become the ideal Christian woman, and it helpfully included, on the front cover, a photograph of just such an exemplary woman, so that readers would know exactly what to aim for. This perfect looking creature was gifted with long lustrous hair, beautiful, yet worn with dignified modesty. Her face was blessed with a near-perfect complexion, and it shone with charity, restraint, good will and potential (but strictly monogamous) passion. One sensed that she had agreed to be photographed for the cover only so that God might be glorified by her witness to the quality of his handiwork when, as in her case, he really puts his mind to it.

Inside, the book was divided into handy sections, each dealing with a different aspect of being an ideal Christian woman. These included advice on how to say, think and do acceptable things in a church context, how to dress so that God is honoured but men are not tempted, how to support your husband in a submissive but godly and assertive way, how to balance the sacred requirements of hospitality with the sacred requirements of family, how to find time for prayer amid a busy schedule, and how to practise good stewardship with the Lord's domestic provision.

Bridget always tries to take it seriously when people present her with these heavily pointed gifts (my father, who used to worry about the fact that *everyone* gave him soap, spent most of his waking life taking baths), but she said that after reading about three-quarters of the book she noted in herself a growing desire to dress temptingly, boss me about, shut the door on visitors, ignore the family, give up praying altogether, splurge the Lord's domestic provision on cream cakes and an afternoon's shopping in London and find the woman depicted on the cover with a view to tying her up and pelting her with knobbly vegetables until she agreed to wipe that soppy grin off her face and do something coarse and un-Christian.

This is the problem with so many of these easy-answer publications, isn't it? Each one seems to promise so much; whether it be the one that offers six simple steps to Prophetic Scuba-diving, or a beginner's guide to Knitting in the Spirit, or one of that plethora (I'm feeling quite confident about the use of this word now) of deeply depressing books that tell you exactly how to recover from depression. Just as the phrase 'Christian Counselling' has, in the past, sometimes tended to be a covering excuse for dangerously unskilled and untrained tinkering with people's lives, so these books of pop-wisdom can actually leave the reader feeling defeated and inferior because he or she stumbles over one of the six 'simple' steps and is unable to get up again without on-the-spot assistance.

Yes, I know that there are notable exceptions. I know because I have benefited from them myself, thank God, but I also know that a whole generation of believers has grown up with the notion that development as a Christian is rather like being in a junior-school classroom, where life is sliced up neatly into conveniently discreet subjects which can be learned quite easily as long as one pays proper attention to the teacher. In fact, of course, for most human beings, Christian or otherwise, life never is as simple as that, and the wisdom that we need on the most basic level is of a rather different kind.

Where have I found wisdom? There have been books that have helped, and also particular individuals who were obedient enough to say the right word at the right time, but the following come to mind as being the most reliable sources of wisdom.

First, I believe that a resolve to follow Jesus is the purest form of wisdom that any of us can aspire to. We may be foolish followers, or intermittently sinful followers, or inadequate followers, but if, like the disciples, we have made the simple decision to go with him, then no one and nothing can harm the part of us that will join him in paradise. We would be very foolish indeed to follow anyone or anything else. We fail as we follow, but we mustn't give up.

Secondly, I find wisdom (about me) in my friends, if I care to listen. Few things are as valuable as the counsel of close friends who really do know me, and are willing to tell me the truth, even when I get stroppy about it. They are a practical, spiritual resource, and I thank God for them.

Thirdly, I rely heavily on my wife, who, as well as knowing me infuriatingly well, makes suggestions from time to time that seem to me quite definitely to come from the heart of God. Much as I complain about this process sometimes, I thank God for this blessing more than almost any other.

Last, but very far from least, I find wisdom from the Holy Spirit as he speaks to me from the pages of the Bible, a wisdom that is both accessible, and yet far greater in depth than I shall ever reach to or understand.

We need the wisdom of scripture. That is why I have written all the Bible notes in this book, including the ones in this section, which, as even the most dense among you might possibly have gathered by now, are on the subject of 'Wisdom'.

Prayer

Father, we meet so many people and get involved in so many things. We need the wisdom of your Holy Spirit. Help us to be humble enough to accept counsel from him, from those who know us well, and from the pages of scripture that we are about to read. Amen.

True wisdom

Proverbs 1:1–7 (NRSV)

The proverbs of Solomon son of David, king of Israel: For learning about wisdom and instruction, for understanding words of insight, for gaining instruction in wise dealing, righteousness, justice, and equity; to teach shrewdness to the simple, knowledge and prudence to the young—Let the wise also hear and gain in learning, and the discerning acquire skill, to understand a proverb and a figure, the words of the wise and their riddles. The fear of the Lord is the beginning of knowledge; fools despise wisdom and instruction.

I wonder how Solomon the Wise is dealing with the news that his words of wisdom are to be commented on in 1997 by Adrian Plass. 'They should have asked a theologian,' he's probably complaining, 'or a trained moral philosopher, or *something*. The man is a rank amateur!' Well, hard cheese, Solly, old mate. You've been dead a long time, now it's my turn.

And that response of mine sums up, in a way, the attitude to wisdom in the nineties, doesn't it? Like food and travel and many other areas of our lives, so-called wisdom is packaged and labelled and made available, particularly on television, for independent selection by those who may well not be wise enough to do the selecting. In America we discovered with horror the lengths to which those 'audience participation' programmes will go to attract viewers.

'Do you suspect that your husband or wife is having an affair? If so, would you like to confront them with the evidence on national television without them having any previous warning?'

That's no exaggeration, and the morality of such broadcasting is justified by the argument that, in this instance, it will be helpful to other married couples who are facing problems. Thus, the ancient Romans might have claimed that the spectacle of Christians being eaten by lions was actually a practical examination of feline dietary problems.

Far from giving prudence to the simple, or instilling discipline where there is personal chaos, these events offer nothing but emotional cream-cakes to viewers, some of whom are desperately in need of a sensible diet.

Prayer

Father, we know that the fear of the Lord does not sell many licences or much advertising but it remains the beginning of wisdom, and we pray that the young, the simple and the wise will find their counsel in you.

Spiritual thoughts

Proverbs 1:20–23 (NRSV)

Wisdom cries out in the street... 'How long, O simple ones, will you love being simple? How long will scoffers delight in their scoffing and fools hate knowledge? Give heed to my reproof; I will pour out my thoughts to you; I will make my words known to you.'

This passage reminds me of my friend Rabbi Hugo Gryn, who was well known and greatly appreciated as a broadcaster. Sadly, Hugo died recently. For four or five years Bridget and I met this master storyteller almost every week in the Maidstone studios of TVS to make a late-night 'God-slot' programme called 'Company'. This regional programme catered mainly for insomniacs, taxi-drivers, publicans, nightwatchmen, and people who didn't manage to turn off the television quickly enough after the snooker finished, but it was fun to do, and we loved meeting people like Hugo.

In the course of many conversations we often discussed the differences, obvious and not so obvious, between Christianity and Judaism. One of the most interesting differences put forward by Hugo concerned knowledge and spirituality. In the Christian Church, he suggested, knowledge is generally supposed to be acquired through the development of spirituality, whereas in the Jewish faith the more knowledge and understanding you have, the closer you are likely to come to a relationship with God.

I'm sure that these general tendencies are sometimes taken to extreme lengths by adherents to both faiths. Over a decade ago I was struck by the anger with which a small minority of those who attended charismatic churches rejected any suggestion that an intellectual approach to Christianity could have real worth. There seemed to be a fear that thinking and spirituality were in some way mutually exclusive, ridiculous though such a notion obviously is. Happily, the balance has now largely been restored in these areas, but I still encounter the odd person who tells me that it is 'dangerous to think'.

As for Hugo—the interesting thing is that his first real experience of God was an emotional one. Seventeen years old, and hiding in a corner of a German concentration camp one day, he wept for himself and the Jewish race and the whole world, and felt, for the first time, the reality and 'otherness' of God.

I feel so sad that Hugo can't be here to argue the point out a little further, but the opportunity may well come.

Prayer

Father, teach us to know you and to love you.

Criticism

Proverbs 1:29–31 (NRSV)

Because they hated knowledge and did not choose the fear of the Lord, would have none of my counsel, and despised all my reproof, therefore they shall eat the fruit of their way and be sated with their own devices.

After reading this passage I asked myself how willing I really am to accept criticism or rebuke from man or God. On one level I can answer the question easily. I have always hated all criticism, especially the constructive variety, because you can't dismiss it scornfully. You have to do something about it!

Having said that, I am painfully aware of my need for helpful criticism, but it has to come from someone who provenly values me already. When my wife, Bridget, makes negative comments about something I've said or done or written I'm quite likely to get cross, but I will then take my crossness and her comments away into a corner for closer examination in private. More often than not I have to admit that she is absolutely right, and I do genuinely value her insights. I just wish that I did not have to go through this process of childish resentment each time, though.

On another level I think some things have changed. I now truly believe that we are qualified for God's service by our weaknesses rather than by our strengths (although my use of the word 'we' instead of 'I' might be significant).

Bridget and I worked for a time at Burrswood, the healing centre founded by Dorothy Kerin, who died in 1961, seven years before we joined the staff. One evening we were taken out to dinner by an elderly, very wise lady of Russian origin named Marina, who had been one of Dorothy Kerin's closest friends. During the meal Marina said something that I found very hard to take.

'Adrian,' she said, 'you are capable of great good and great evil. You are weak, but Bridget is strong.' Turning to Bridget, she said, 'You will have to protect him, my dear.'

This image of me as a sort of schizophrenic wimp didn't go down at all well at the time. I struggled desperately to maintain my heroic self- image. In fact, although I don't think I showed it, I was furious. As the years have gone by, though, I have truly learned to value and appreciate that little nugget of wisdom. I carry it in a little side-pocket of my consciousness and take it out now and then when choices have to be made. I still hate criticism, but I do thank God for it.

Prayer

Go on, say what you think—no, really, go on, say it. I don't mind...

Hidden treasure

Proverbs 2:1–9 (NRSV)

My child, if you accept my words and treasure up my commandments within you, making your ear attentive to wisdom and inclining your heart to understanding; if you indeed cry out for insight, and raise your voice for understanding; if you seek it like silver, and search for it as for hidden treasures—then you will understand the fear of the Lord and find the knowledge of God. For the Lord gives wisdom; from his mouth come knowledge and understanding; he stores up sound wisdom for the upright; he is a shield to those who walk blamelessly, guarding the paths of justice and preserving the way of his faithful ones. Then you will understand righteousness and justice and equity, every good path.

The idea of hunting for understanding in the same way that one might hunt for hidden treasure is a fascinating one. Ever since I was a child I have dreamed of discovering something old and precious in a place that has been undisturbed for generations. Even now (my children are tired of hearing me say this), I fantasize about being left a very old house whose cellars and attics have remained untouched and unexplored for years. I find myself positively drooling over the prospect of hunting through dusty boxes and cupboards in the search for long-forgotten books and objects and pictures. Marvellous!

As this is never likely to happen, I shall content myself with the Bible, which is itself a storehouse of treasure, albeit one that is not always immediately visible or recognizable. Over the generations the sparkling gems of truth that lie between the covers of this remarkable book have tended to be obscured by the dust of over-familiarity, poor teaching, even poorer reading-out-loud, denominational bias and sheer fear of the vivid, non-religious life that it offers.

There are times, not continually, but frequently enough to bring me back to the search again and again, when some old dry-as-dust verse cracks open quite unexpectedly and there before me is the pure, precious metal of God's truth, often in the last place I thought to find it. When that happens I want to rush around waving my arms in the air like one of those old-timers in the westerns who've been panning for gold, and suddenly come across a shining reason to rejoice.

Prayer

Thank you for this treasure chest. Guide us as we search through its contents.

The prize

Proverbs 2:12–22 (NRSV)

It will save you from the way of evil, from those who… delight in the perverseness of evil… You will be saved from the loose woman, from the adulteress with her smooth words, who forsakes the partner of her youth and forgets her sacred covenant; for her way leads down to death, and her paths to the shades; those who go to her never come back, nor do they regain the paths of life. Therefore walk in the way of the good… For the upright will abide in the land… and the treacherous will be rooted out of it.

I want to ask a question that will probably annoy some of my brothers and sisters in Christ because they think the answer is such an obvious one. And anyway, they will probably add, it's not the sort of question you *should* ask. Here it is.

What's in it for us?

Vulgar, eh? But I have a feeling that a lot of Christians secretly want to ask that question, and I also believe that God wants us to be able to answer it, not just for ourselves, but also for people we meet who are outside the faith. Why should we want to be saved from the paths of wicked men? They seem to have quite a good time on the whole. And then there's the adulteress. Some of us might quite like to get involved with the adulteress or her male equivalent. It can't be *less* fun than Sung Eucharist at 8.00 a.m. on a wet Sunday morning, can it? Why should we be good? Why should we opt to be on the Lord's side?

What *is* in it for us?

Well, forget the right and proper answers for a moment and think about the kind of reply Jesus might have offered (not a bad guide for answering most questions). In the previous note we were talking about the hidden treasure to be discovered in the Bible. Jesus spoke about treasure as well. He said that we should store up treasure in heaven rather than on earth, and I'm sure he meant exactly what he said. He used the image of treasure very deliberately, and was clearly saying that, in heaven, the currency is different, but just as valuable. We shall be rich in the best possible way—the eternal way. That richness is manufactured from the base metal of obedience and love, transmuted into the unfathomable joy of being with Jesus himself, a joy that is impossible to comprehend fully until we experience it in its fulness.

That's what's in it for us.

Prayer

Father, help us to keep our eyes on the true prize.

Health and wealth

Proverbs 3:1–8 (NRSV)

My child, do not forget my teaching, but let your heart keep my commandments; for length of days and years of life and abundant welfare they will give you. Do not let loyalty and faithfulness forsake you; bind them round your neck, write them on the tablet of your heart... Do not be wise in your own eyes; fear the Lord, and turn away from evil. It will be a healing for your flesh and a refreshment for your body.

Well, this is interesting, isn't it? Read verse 2 again and you might see what I mean. The writer appears to be saying quite clearly that conscientious application of his teaching and commandments will result in a long life and material gain.

When we were touring Australia in 1996 we found a growing interest in and adherence to what is commonly named the 'health and prosperity' movement. Those who embrace such teaching believe, as I'm sure you already know, that if Christians make the kingdom of God a priority in their lives, God will be more or less obliged to bless them with material wealth and physical good health. I presume that verses like the one just quoted would be used by followers of this doctrine to support their claims.

So, perhaps they're right. The Old Testament's full of people getting rich when God's pleased with them. What do you think? After all, there it is in black and white—many years and prosperity. Let's go for it!

Actually, I'm *not* going for it, if you don't mind. There are very serious problems with using the Old Testament as a source of doctrine unless it is read and considered in the light of what Jesus teaches us in the Gospels. Without going into too much detail, I'd just like us to imagine how Jesus would react on being informed that his followers feel pretty confident that they are entitled to a reasonable income and substantial health benefits. This man who said that we would suffer just as he had, only more so; who sent out his followers without so much as a pair of sandals; who said that the poor are blessed; who sorrowed over the problems rich people would have in entering the kingdom of heaven; how would he have reacted?

I'll tell you how I think he would have reacted. I think he would have laughed until he cried. Or, come to think of it, he might have just cried.

Prayer

Lord, how long will it be before your people know what being rich and healthy really means?

Discipline

Proverbs 3:11–14 (NRSV)

My child, do not despise the Lord's discipline or be weary of his reproof, for the Lord reproves the one he loves, as a father the son in whom he delights. Happy are those who find wisdom, and those who get understanding, for her income is better than silver, and her revenue better than gold.

A friend of mine was telling me about his divorce as we drove back from the north of England.

'We were married for a very long time,' he said, 'and hardly anyone knew there were problems in our relationship. When it reached the stage where divorce was looking like the only real option, my wife and I decided to send out a letter to quite a large number of people—close friends, of course, relatives, and some of the people at our church. It was easier than having to explain it a hundred times over.'

I nodded. 'And did they all write back?'

'Oh, yes, we had some wonderful replies—a lot of understanding and compassion. People were really warm in the way they responded.'

'Were there any replies you didn't like?'

'There was one,' he replied thoughtfully, 'I don't mean it was unpleasant. It wasn't. It was very friendly. The person who wrote it said that he was sure we were doing the right thing.'

'What's wrong with that?'

He tilted his head and sucked air through his teeth. 'I dunno, I suppose it was just that the person concerned didn't actually know me all that well, and he'd hardly ever met my wife, so it seemed a little bit—well, a bit unhelpful to sound so sure that divorce was the right way to go. By contrast,' he went on, 'the two replies I valued most were just as warm and supportive, but they included a firm but gentle question about whether there could be an alternative to divorce. In effect, they were asking if we'd properly thought and prayed through the issue before making such a serious decision. I really appreciated those two letters.'

Prayer

Father, thank you for the times when our friends show real godly love by not letting us easily get away with things that could be bad for us, as well as supporting us with compassion and warmth. Help us not to reject your discipline, given directly or through someone else, when that's exactly what we need.

Fear

Proverbs 3:19–21 (NRSV)

My child... keep sound wisdom and prudence, and they will be life for your soul and adornment for your neck... your foot will not stumble. If you sit down, you will not be afraid; when you lie down, your sleep will be sweet. Do not be afraid of sudden panic, or of the storm that strikes the wicked; for the Lord will be your confidence.

Here are some questions relating to this passage. Don't worry—I'm not putting these down to make you feel bad about yourself. I'm going to try to face up to my own answers. If your response is the same as I think mine is going to be, then we'll pray together. If it's not, you can pray for me and those like me.

When I sit down, am I afraid?

The answer to that question is 'Yes, I *am* afraid.' There is a gloom that has shadowed my heart since I was a very young child. This shadow was cast by difficult events that I had no control over during that period, and also by some very injudicious reading of frightening books as I moved towards my teens. I would dearly like to be free of that shadow.

When I lie down, is my sleep sweet?

Generally speaking, no, it is not sweet. I ought to say immediately that one substantial reason for this is my weight (too great), and my evening meal (too much and too late). Those aren't the only reasons, though. Sleep is still a fearful land for me, a place where you would be unwise to let yourself relax completely. I used to suffer from something called Sleep Paralysis, which didn't help. It comes back sometimes when I'm very tense. I would love to enjoy sweet sleep.

Do I have no fear of sudden disaster or of the ruin that overtakes the wicked?

This question is not so easy to answer. That same shadow of gloom I have already mentioned is sometimes inhabited by phantoms of inevitable doom and destruction at the worst possible times, but I have much greater confidence nowadays that I cannot be overtaken by the consequences of my sin. God loves me, and because of Jesus I am saved. I don't think I've ever written it as bluntly before. Perhaps I believe it more bluntly.

That still leaves the problems with night-time and shadows and sleep. Let's pray about them.

Prayer

Father, I know I'm not the only one who finds the nights difficult. Grant us judgment and discernment in dealing with the practical things that need changing, and give us your peace and wisdom to wear like ornaments around our necks at the moment when the shadows begin to fall.

Get wisdom

Proverbs 4:7–8 (NRSV)

The beginning of wisdom is this: Get wisdom, and whatever else you get, get insight. Prize her highly, and she will exalt you; she will honour you if you embrace her.

Do you remember an item of news many years ago about a young couple who auctioned off everything they owned, including their house and furniture, in order to raise money for starving refugees in a distant country? I was quite young at the time, probably around sixteen, and I had only just become a Christian. I wasn't at all sure what to think about this extravagant gesture (we found out what we thought about things by asking the clergy usually), but I think I veered from admiration of such a generous, wholehearted act of giving, to concern that the young couple concerned were not exercising their stewardship properly (stewardship was a term I'd heard of for the first time only recently). Another part of me, pre-Christian and probably saner than the parts of me that had produced the first two responses, thought there was something very silly about ending up with nothing and having to rely on others to give you the things that you couldn't have because you'd just given them away to someone else. Or something like that.

Could this be the kind of wildly expansive act that the writer of the above passage is talking about when he says that we should acquire understanding, whatever the cost? Is there really a way in which we can exchange riches of some kind for the supreme gift of wisdom? I suspect that there is a way, but I am absolutely sure that the cost is much greater than the loss of material belongings or the contents of a bank account.

The clue lies in the readiness with which Jesus' disciples followed him when they were called. It was a readiness, not just to physically follow him, but to place him at the very top of their individual lists of what was most important to them. In dropping their own rights to decision and destiny those men gained the reality of his wisdom and power in their lives, despite the fact that there was no magical transformation of their personalities at that time. It can still happen today, but I don't think it happens much.

Prayer

Father, show us individually what it means to put Jesus first in our lives. We can't actually follow him physically through Luton or Carlisle now. How should we do it?

Keep your heart

Proverbs 4:20–24 (NRSV)

My child, be attentive to my words; incline your ear to my sayings. Do not let them escape from your sight; keep them within your heart. For they are life to those who find them, and healing to all their flesh. Keep your heart with all vigilance, for from it flow the springs of life. Put away from you crooked speech, and put devious talk far from you.

This injunction to 'keep your heart... for from it flow the springs of life' offers a deceptively simple challenge and a warning that is quite alarming. The challenge is to look clearly at what is in my heart, and the warning is that whatever my heart contains will be apparent in my life through actions or words.

Kinda makes you wanna sit tight an' say nuthin', don' it?

Those of us who have mapped the geography of our selves know what a dispiriting exercise this can be. We start off okay, marching boldly towards the edge of our talent or our goodwill or our patience or our generosity, and are suddenly brought up short by a precipice, usually at a point where it seemed as if the firm ground might go on for ever. Setting off in a different direction we discover that exactly the same thing happens. In fact, it happens again and again and again, until we start learning the shape and limits of what we are. For some this is a very welcome piece of learning—settle down and get on with it, they would say. For others, those with the blood of explorers in their veins, it is a kind of prison.

This is how many of us feel about the contents of our hearts. We look for enough compassion to care truly about the world and find a pathetically limited ability to place our arms around the suffering of others. We search for the strength of will and forgiveness to set ourselves and those we hate free from chains of resentment and bitterness, only to find weakness and a cherishing of hurts. We hunt within our hearts for the courage to fight when everything in us wants to lie down, and to wait quietly when we want to fight, but discover instead a self-indulgence that *will have* what it is greedy for.

We stand on the shore of our own lives, calling out to God that we can go no farther unless he provides a way.

Prayer

Father, we know that we are weak and limited and that our hearts are not clean, but Jesus told us that he is The Way by which we shall find life and power. We ask that he should inhabit the throne of our hearts and live his righteousness through us.

Sex

Proverbs 5:15–20 (NRSV)

Drink water from your own cistern, flowing water from your own well… Let your fountain be blessed, and rejoice in the wife of your youth, a lovely deer, a graceful doe. May her breasts satisfy you at all times; may you be intoxicated always by her love. Why should you be intoxicated, my son, by another woman and embrace the bosom of an adulteress?

A young man called Steve said to me, 'Is it normal to fancy other women after you're married?' He was one of those clear-eyed individuals who spend the first part of their lives expecting, and generally speaking discovering, that life is a good, wholesome, rewarding sort of affair.

He and his wife, Samantha, had fallen head-over-heels in love when they were twenty, and enjoyed a fairy-tale wedding. Now she was pregnant, and Steve was dismayed to find his young wife's hugely inflated body not attracting him as it had done. Indeed, his eyes were straying lustfully in the direction of other, slimmer females who were—well, not Samantha.

For Steve, this was a shadow over his life, a profound failure in his relationship with Sam and with God. He felt somehow mucky and diminished by the experiences he was having.

'I keep thinking,' said Steve, 'about Jesus saying that if you just *look* at another woman with desire you're already committing adultery. That means I've already committed adultery fifteen times since I got up today.'

I think my friend might have been a little taken aback by the matter-of-fact way I responded to his problem.

'Consider these points, Steve,' I said. 'One, there may be some men who haven't fancied other women after getting married, but if you got them all together they'd fit quite easily into a large wardrobe.

'Two, Jesus wasn't silly or unrealistic. He knew what human beings are like. He was one. He never compromised the truth, but he knew all about temptation, and he's more interested in helping you deal with that, than organizing thunderbolts because you're fantasizing about Bessie next door.

'Third, sex is a crucial part of being married, but real love is a complex, maturing thing. It takes a lot of time and work, but you can end up with something rich and right and priceless. The sex'll get sorted out, you'll see. Don't give up before you've started, mate. The best is yet to come.'

Prayer

Father, marriages are falling apart all around us. Help us to be strong and wise in our relationships, and to depend on you like children.

Better than gold

Proverbs 8:1–5, 10–11 (NRSV)

Does not wisdom call, and does not understanding raise her voice? On the heights, beside the way, at the crossroads she takes her stand; beside the gates in front of the town, at the entrance of the portals she cries out: 'To you, O people, I call, and my cry is to all that live. O simple ones, learn prudence; acquire intelligence, you who lack it… Take my instruction instead of silver, and knowledge rather than choice gold; for wisdom is better than jewels, and all that you may desire cannot compare with her.

Why *don't* people choose wisdom instead of silver or gold? Why are the very things that attract us to other people, whether they be kindness, gentleness or quiet wisdom, the last things we want for ourselves? Strange, isn't it?

I have seen this phenomenon very clearly in the lives of my own children as they've grown up. They have always loved and instinctively wanted to be close to people who had the qualities I've just described, but, certainly through their teenage years, for themselves they wanted something tougher and more brassily impressive to show off than these unselfish talents. I suppose most children pass through this phase, but some of us never come out the other side.

Take me, for instance. Even now, when I'm well into my forties, and ought to know better, I occasionally find myself carefully setting out to impress another person with some pathetic achievement or other. Almost invariably this other person will be one of these truly nice people who really, really do seem to want to hear me mouthing off vainly about myself. Even as I speak, I find myself looking at the person opposite and wishing that he or she could see in me the qualities of receptivity and kindness that I see in them.

When this happens I get quite disturbed, and I pray sincerely to God that I will eventually lose my obsession with myself and the way in which the rest of the world sees me. In the end, I would like to be so genuinely interested in other people that their image of me doesn't concern me any more.

An interesting thought occurs to me. *If* this miraculous change ever occurs—I won't know it's happened, will I? So, perhaps it's happened! No, I don't think so either...

Prayer

Father, lots of us want the applause without the rehearsal. Help us to value the qualities that are truly attractive and to keep our mouths shut until we gain some of them.

Wise notes

Proverbs 8:22–26 (NRSV)

The Lord created me at the beginning of his work, the first of his acts of long ago. Ages ago I was set up, at the first, before the beginning of the earth. When there were no depths I was brought forth, when there were no springs abounding with water. Before the mountains had been shaped, before the hills, I was brought forth—when he had not yet made earth and fields, or the world's first bits of soil.

Wisdom is a recurring tune in the symphony of creation, running on for ever, whatever else fails.

Have you ever written any music? Until about ten years ago I had never even thought about writing serious songs. Working in a succession of residential establishments we did have a go at putting together lyrics for songs to be performed in pantomimes and revues, but we always relied on the nearest keyboard wizard to supply the actual music.

Then, during a period of enforced idleness, as I was just beginning to find out how invigorating it could be to tell the truth, I suddenly wanted to write songs more than anything else. I felt terribly frustrated because I didn't know how to do it. I had an old guitar that I swear tried to hide in corners when it saw me coming, but I was somewhat limited by the fact that I could only play three chords with any confidence. The dull, throbbing, strumming noise that I produced with my right hand was equally uninspiring, and I was beginning to feel a bit discouraged when a friend suggested that I should just write the words and the tune of each song and then he'd 'turn them into music'.

The joy of it!

I shall never forget the first occasion that he turned up with a tape and put it on my cassette player. MY TUNE came out of those speakers sounding so splendid that I hardly recognized it. It was sung by someone who could really sing, and it was accompanied by drums and guitars and a keyboard and goodness knows what else. My little tune had been turned into music!

It was a small parable, applying not just to my miserably unproductive life at that time, but to the lives of many people who feel it's hardly worth offering God the unsophisticated melody of time, effort or talent that they possess.

My advice is—offer it! You'll be amazed what an expert can do with a simple tune.

Prayer

Father, make beautiful music with our lives.

Being there

Proverbs 8:27–31 (NRSV)

When he established the heavens, I was there, when he drew a circle on the face of the deep, when he made firm the skies above... when he assigned to the sea its limit... when he marked out the foundations of the earth, then I was beside him, like a master worker; and I was daily his delight, rejoicing before him always, rejoicing in his inhabited world and delighting in the human race.

I feel rather jealous of Wisdom in this passage, don't you? Fancy having been there! Just imagine being present when God was drawing up the blueprints for creation at the beginning of time, and watching as those plans were carried out on such an awe-inspiring scale. Nothing that Hollywood has ever produced comes close to the reality of what happened then. I love the thought of Wisdom being filled with delight as each day brought yet another amazing spectacle. In fact, I feel very sad that I won't ever see it, and this brings me to a little private fantasy that I'd like to share with you.

I've arrived in heaven, right? Some kind of conference-centre-managing-type angel has shown me to my mansion, no doubt situated right next door to someone I was sure would never make it, and I'm just flicking through the Heaven brochures before taking a stroll around. I learn to my surprise that there's a video shop just up the golden street, and I decide to pay it an immediate visit. When I get there I discover to my unutterable joy that the videos on offer cover every period of history from the beginning of time to the moment when I shuffled off my own particular mortal coil.

Incredible prospect, eh? Just think—on my heavenly Friday nights I can take out 'The Battle of Waterloo' and 'The Invention of the Wheel', or I might decide to settle down and watch 'Henry the Eighth'. Or perhaps I'd decide to get out a tape called 'The Jurassic Era', and enjoy footage of dinosaurs that would make Speilberg's efforts look pale by comparison. I might get a few friends together and spend the whole of one week watching 'Genesis', followed on Sunday by 'Exodus', starring the real Moses, who will almost certainly look nothing like Charlton Heston. Come to think of it, I could get Moses to come over and watch it with me—fill me in on all the details. Yes, that's what I'll do...

Prayer

Father, forgive my silliness, but I would love us all to warm up to the idea of heaven, and particularly to the idea of experiencing the joy described in this passage, simply because we are in your presence.

Beginnings

Proverbs 9:10–12 (NRSV)

The fear of the Lord is the beginning of wisdom, and the knowledge of the Holy One is insight. For by me your days will be multiplied, and years will be added to your life. If you are wise, you are wise for yourself; if you scoff, you alone will bear it.

I wish I could remember who said this and that about various things. I sound like P.G. Wodehouse on a bad day, don't I? I've been trying to recall who said something like, 'Give me the child for the first seven years of his life, and I will give you the man.' I think it might have been the Jesuits, but, there again, it might not.

Whoever did say it was right. During the years when I worked with children in trouble of various kinds, I saw, again and again, how experiences of early childhood produced patterns and attitudes that were probably there for life. Some teenagers were fighting an intense and essential battle to replace longstanding, negative ideas about themselves with more balanced and practically useful self-images.

Raymond, for instance, had already come through the trauma of his mother's divorce, and was subsequently rejected by his mother and her new husband for reasons that had more to do with making their own nest more cosy than anything Raymond had done. I remember playing snooker with Ray after he heard that he would not be going home, and listening as he poured out the feelings of guilt and failure that he had lived with all his life. Raymond blamed himself for *everything*, and is probably spending the rest of his life dealing with that very damaging illusion.

What does all this have to do with the passage? Well, I think it might be worth reflecting, as we read these familiar words about the fear of the Lord being the beginning of wisdom, that some Christians have had an equally unfortunate journey through the early years of their adoption into the family of God. Because of such problems as poor teaching, overheavy pastoring, unfortunate encounters with enthusiastic but wrong people and various other difficulties, a lot of the believers that I meet have a very low opinion of themselves (not the same thing as humility), and need a lot of help in regaining a balanced view of their worth in the eyes of God. Let's pray for them.

Prayer

Father, some of your children have had very unfortunate spiritual childhoods because of the mistakes of others. Help them to understand that you see them as they really are, and that, after a new beginning, they will find wisdom of their own.

We are but shadows till the heart be touched. That touch creates us–then we begin to be– thereby we are beings of reality and inheritors of eternity.

Nathaniel Hawthorne

FINDING FIRM GROUND

Reality in the Bible

There's a lot of talk about reality in the Church nowadays, and I'm sure most of us would reckon that's a very good thing. Certainly, I could hardly say otherwise, as I've made a fair bit of noise about it myself. And yet, how hard it is to pin down what is real and unchangeable with total confidence, not just in spiritual things, but in all sorts of areas. Let me give you one or two examples. The first one concerns our oldest son, Matthew. It may seem a minor and unimportant thing to you, but it amazed me.

Matthew was always a tea fanatic. Ignoring the trivial fact that Bridget and I had been making what we thought to be perfectly adequate pots of tea for forty years or so, he would, from time to time, lecture us sternly on the correct procedure for producing the perfect cup of tea. We had, he pointed out kindly but firmly, totally misunderstood the proportions, sequence and timing with which the essential components of this wonderful beverage should be brought into contact with each other. He generously donated substantial periods of his time, free of charge, to the task of ensuring that our education in this area should be completed. This removed our confidence altogether, of course. We became jitteringly nervous about preparing tea for him in case it should fail to meet with his approval and high standards—he being a sort of high priest of the tea-worshipping fraternity.

The rest of the fraternity, Matthew's friends that is, were similarly addicted to the hot brown stuff. The very mention of the word 'coffee' (a drink which we loved, but almost felt obliged to drink in dark corners where our shameful apostasy could not be witnessed) seemed to be regarded as a shocking heresy. They gathered like some loony sect in our kitchen, fussing and fiddling and muttering over their boiling and brewing and sugaring and adding of milk before bearing the sacred vessels on the sacred tray aloft to the high priest's chaotic Holy of Holies at the top of the house. Unfortunately, the ensuing ceremony rarely seemed automatically to conclude with a ritual return and cleansing of the sacred vessels. We humble, coffee-drinking acolytes were clearly more suited to that particular role.

This obsession with tea persisted throughout the whole of Matthew's school career, and was unabated as he began his degree course at Exeter University. This and his equally violent loathing for just about every vegetable under the sun were two of the most fixed and reliable facts in our universe. They were reality.

Then, one day, not long before finishing his course, Matthew arrived home for a weekend and offered to cook the dinner for that evening. Bridget, always open to new experiences, accepted the offer with alacrity, and watched with interest to see what was going to be on the menu. It was when Matthew started to throw all manner of vegetables into a large saucepan that the world began to rock on its axis, but it was when he lightly declared, 'Think I'll make myself a nice cup of coffee while I'm waiting for that lot to boil up,' that she had to sit down quite abruptly on the nearest kitchen chair.

'B-b-b-but, Matthew,' she stammered, 'you don't drink coffee. You've *never* drunk coffee! And what are you doing with those vegetables? You *hate* vegetables!'

At first, Matthew stared at Bridget as if she had gone mad, then a reflective look appeared on his face. Brows furrowed, he stared down the long tunnel of his past seeking some basis for what his mother had said. His face cleared at last.

'Ah, well, yes, that's right, I was a bit off vegetables, wasn't I? I like 'em now.' He looked at the cup in his hand. 'I always drink coffee now—can't stand tea. It's so insipid, don't you think?'

I know it sounds absurd, but Matthew's defection from the tea-drinking, non-vegetable-consuming community was as surprising as anything else that's ever happened to me. And it gives hope for all sorts of people and situations where what we have believed to be reality really might be able to alter. How well God can use such a propensity for change.

Some adjustments of reality are just as surprising but very much more worrying. I think in particular of those occasions when a person recreates his or her own past in a form that coheres more easily with present needs, biases and circumstances. This can often happen on a level that is not even quite conscious. I'm terrified that I've done it myself, especially as I probably wouldn't know it had happened unless someone else told me, and then I might not accept what they said. It occurs to me that you might not know what I'm talking about, so I'll give you an example.

I once found myself being driven from one meeting to another (for the benefit of those who don't know—I am a proud non-driver) by a lady named Vera who obviously had something on her mind. I knew that I'd met her before, actually, but for a long time I couldn't for the life of me remember where this meeting had taken place. Then, quite suddenly, it came back to me.

'Weren't you at that church down on the west coast where I came to speak a couple of years ago?' I asked.

She nodded vigorously. Bingo! I was right, and this recollection was obviously what she'd been waiting for.

'I've left there now,' she said, pressing her lips firmly together and shaking her head as if trying to rid herself of some dark and terrible memory.

I took my cue obediently.

'Something go wrong, did it? I seem to remember that your pastor down there was a good sort of guy. Phil, wasn't it?'

'I'd rather not talk about him if you don't mind.'

'Fine.' I nodded understandingly, settled back and waited patiently for her to talk about him.

Seconds passed.

'Only, you see, he's the reason I left the church and then moved up here.'

'I see—look,' I said, rather unkindly, 'you don't have to talk about it if you'd rather not, you know.'

'No, no,' she reassured me hurriedly, 'it's all right, I don't mind telling you. You see, I had to leave because Phil accused me of being a child of the devil.' Turning her head and glancing momentarily at me to gauge my reaction, she paused to allow the enormity of the offence to register, then fixed her eyes on the road again. 'I mean, I don't object to being told off if I do something wrong, but that's right over the top, don't you think? I couldn't stay after that, could I?'

I made a vague noise that might have indicated agreement or otherwise, but as we continued our drive I pondered on what Vera had said. I remembered Phil quite well. He'd struck me as being a very good man, committed to the people in his church and certainly not the sort of person who was likely to make the kind of statement that I'd just heard. We arrived soon after that, but every now and then, in the course of the evening meeting, and during the period when we all had coffee and biscuits afterwards, I went over those words in my head:

'He accused me of being a child of the devil.'

No! I shook my head as I got into the same car to make the return journey. I couldn't imagine Phil saying that unless he had some truly exceptional reason. As we travelled towards home I decided to bring up the subject once more. I didn't want to very much. After all, it was none of my business, was it? On the other hand, I really had thought Phil was a nice bloke.

'Vera,' I said, 'just going back to what Phil said to you for a moment—'

'Yes,' said Vera, more than willing to return to the subject, 'he said I was a child of the devil. That's why I had to—'

'Let's just get this straight. He actually said that, did he? He said those words—"Vera, you are a child of the devil"—just like that?'

'Well...'

I could see Vera's eyes in the driving mirror. A funny little jump happened in them, as though an inner adjustment had been made. She looked almost surprised.

'Well,' she continued slowly and much less confidently, 'he didn't actually use those exact words, but, I mean, that's what he meant—that's what he implied.' Her eyes had a worried, hunted look in them now.

I moved in for the kill.

'So what were his exact words?'

Vera swallowed hard. 'Well, err, what he actually said was that the way I was behaving wasn't what he'd expect from a child of God. But, surely, that means...'

Her voice trailed away as she realized that the implied step from one statement to the other was an impossibly large one. The rest of the journey was not very comfortable for either of us.

The interesting thing about this incident is that I am quite sure Vera had repeated her 'child of the devil' story so often that she had temporarily forgotten the words that Phil had actually used, and that little jump of the eyes had signalled the moment when she was forced back to a truth that had been too threatening for her to face in its genuine, original form.

I wondered how many people had been told what Phil 'said' in the year or two since he didn't say it?

Before we get too critical of old Vera, it's worth asking ourselves whether we have 'reconstructed' the truth in one or two areas of our lives. We might be surprised!

So, what *is* real? Let's explore.

Prayer

Father, as we begin to look at the issue of reality, help us to be honest about ourselves, our past, present and future. Amen.

Reality

John 8:32 (RSV)

And you will know the truth, and the truth will make you free.

A few years ago I travelled up to London for an evening discussion. It was a very hot summer night, and the upstairs meeting room was packed solid.

Sitting on the floor with my knees jammed under my chin, hot and uncomfortable, I was thanking God that the meeting was drawing to a close, when I suddenly realized that the man sitting three feet away from me on a chair was a very well known Christian speaker and Bible scholar. He was the sort of man whose reputation for spiritual insight sometimes causes people to gabble hysterically about how well their walk with the Lord is going, or emit shrill cries of 'Hallelujah!' and 'Praise the Lord!' to indicate soundness. How awful it would be, I thought, if he 'saw' something I did in 1972, just by looking into my face. Just then he took a piece of paper from his pocket and began to write something on it. He then folded the paper and, to my abject horror, leaned over and handed it to me. I unfolded it with trembling fingers and was about to read it when—the lights when out!

Sitting in the darkness, holding my piece of paper with 1972 scrawled over it for all I knew, I just wanted to die. When power was restored I saw that the man had written: 'Can you give me a few moments afterwards?' A few minutes later I followed him down the stairs like a little doggy to a small room, where he further alarmed me by announcing that he was in the habit of having visions, and that one of his recent visions involved me. It had nothing (I was thankful to hear) to do with 1972—not that I *did* anything in 1972, I hasten to add. Oh, the relief!

As we stood up to leave I couldn't help wondering if he'd read my books. He must have known what I was thinking. 'I've read your books,' he said, 'and I'd like you to know that the verse that's usually translated "The truth will make you free", can also be translated "*Reality* will make you free".'

It was a confirmation and an assurance, and it has been at the centre of everything I've thought, written and spoken about since that day.

A question

Can I handle reality?

The funny bike

John 3:1–3 (RSV)

Now there was a man of the Pharisees, named Nicodemus, a ruler of the Jews. This man came to Jesus by night and said to him, 'Rabbi, we know that you are a teacher come from God; for no one can do these signs that you do, unless God is with him.' Jesus answered him, 'Truly, truly, I say to you, unless one is born anew, he cannot see the kingdom of God.'

The reality of what we refer to casually as 'the Christian life' is quite different from the reality of life outside the kingdom of God. I hope that doesn't sound too airy-fairy or abstract, because the spiritual life is, in fact, more practical and gritty than any other. Read again about the carpenter who got involved in mass-catering and ended up nailed to a piece of wood, if you don't believe me. Jesus was telling Nicodemus that the whole axis of his life needed to change if he wanted to enter the kingdom. Being born again means a new context, a new perspective, new priorities and new behaviours.

My wife and I once went to a summer fair at the junior school where Katy is a pupil. One of the outdoor attractions was a bicycle that steers the wrong way. You've probably seen them—most annoying contraptions. When you turn the handlebars to the left the front wheel turns to the right, and vice-versa. The owners of this awkward vehicle were offering a prize of one pound to anyone who could ride the bicycle for six yards without putting a foot on the ground. It cost twenty pence for each attempt, and they were making lots of money because not a single person was able to adjust mentally and physically to this change in cause and effect. It was very funny to watch them trying.

Following Jesus involves a rather similar revolution in our steering habits, and many people fall by the wayside because of poor teaching in this area. 'Love your enemies.' How about that one? The world steers to the right, but we are called to do the opposite. My heart fails me sometimes when I look at the commitment that's required, but I want to live in the kingdom of God, so I shall go on practising, however many times I fall off.

Prayer

Teach me to steer, Lord.

Straight talking

Matthew 16:21–24 (RSV)

From that time Jesus began to show his disciples that he must go to Jerusalem and suffer many things from the elders and chief priests and scribes, and be killed, and on the third day be raised. And Peter took him and began to rebuke him saying, 'God forbid, Lord! This shall never happen to you.' But he turned and said to Peter, 'Get behind me, Satan! You are a hindrance to me; for you not on the side of God, but of men.' Then Jesus told his disciples, 'If any man would come after me, let him deny himself and take up his cross and follow me...'

There is a dearth of healthy confrontation in the Church nowadays. Here we see Jesus reacting with explosive anger to Peter's inappropriate and obstructive heroics. Immense, eternal issues were under discussion, and there was Peter trying to lob a very worldly spanner into the cosmic machinery. The cross was a price that Jesus was willing to pay so that men and women could inherit eternal life, and he had no intention of being distracted by sentimental assertions.

I used to feel that Peter was rather unfairly battered by Jesus on this occasion, but when I think about my own dealings with people I'm not so sure. I was infected, very early in my Christian life, with the politeness disease. Everything I said had to be expressed 'nicely', and if I did have anything negative to say it had to be done 'in love', which meant that I had approached the point in such a circumlocutory way that the recipient of my wonderful wisdom found it very difficult to know what I was talking about. I'm all for courtesy and love, but I think I have often used them as excuses for not being direct when it's necessary.

It's a matter of reality again. For a long time I saw one particular man every week for two or three hours. After months of nervously skirting around the issue I finally told him what I thought about his situation. 'Why didn't you say that before?' he asked. Exactly.

A question

How can we develop a proper assertiveness?

Standing firm

Daniel 1:11–16 (RSV)

Then Daniel said to the steward whom the chief of the eunuchs had appointed over Daniel, Hananiah, Mishael and Azariah; 'Test your servants for ten days; let us be given vegetables to eat and water to drink. Then let our appearance and the appearance of the youths who eat the king's rich food be observed by you, and according to what you see deal with your servants.' So he harkened to them in this matter, and tested them for ten days. At the end of ten days it was seen that they were better in appearance and fatter in flesh than all the youths who ate the king's rich food. So the steward took away their rich food and the wine they were to drink, and gave them vegetables.

Here's a chap who understood the 'funny bike' principle. As far as we know, Daniel never once compromised his religious principles, no matter which Babylonian king he happened to be dealing with at the time. This was his first challenge, and he came through it with flying colours. After ten days he and his companions were fitter and stronger than those who had eaten the rich court food. What a fortune he would have made nowadays. Daniel the Israelite's low-fat, vegetable only, hip 'n' thigh diet would have hit the bestseller list within a fortnight. Daniel's only interest was in doing the will of his God, his reward—the discovery that he would receive divine support if he stood up for what he believed in.

This unwavering attitude of Daniel's makes us feel quite threatened. I'd like to be him *after* his brave stance was endorsed by God, but I suspect that when faced with the original dilemma I would have said in sensible, no-nonsense tones: 'Look, I honestly think that fanaticism is a poor witness. I reckon it takes more courage to eat the king's food—I honestly do...' For Daniel, though, it was the thin end of the wedge. From now on it could only get easier to do the right thing and make the right decisions. By the time he arrived (as an old man) at the famous lion sketch he must have had a profound understanding of the principle that our most crucial needs are met and satisfied by doing what we are told.

A prayer

Lord, I am not brave, but I want to be.

The eyes of a child

Matthew 18:2–3 (RSV)

And calling to him a child, he put him in the midst of them, and said, 'Truly, I say to you, unless you turn and become like children you will never enter the kingdom of heaven.'

Jesus seems to be saying here that the reality of heavenly things is more apparent to childlike eyes than to the eyes of sophistication and 'grown-upness'.

Some time ago we took our bicycles down to Newhaven, crossed on the ferry to northern France, and spent a few very enjoyable days pedalling from town to town along the river valleys. Our last day was set aside to explore the port of Dieppe before recrossing the Channel that evening.

Just after lunch we entered the cool interior of a big church near the centre of town. I lost touch with the others for a while, but after a few minutes I discovered Katy, aged four at the time, staring silently at a life-size sculpture of Mary, the mother of Jesus, holding her son's dead body in her arms, and looking into his face with an expression of real pain and loss. Katy turned and saw me.

'Daddy,' she asked, 'why has Jesus got a hole in his side?' Stumblingly, I explained that a Roman spear had been responsible. Katy was horrified. She studied the sculpture again. 'Daddy, he's got holes in his feet. Why's he got holes in his feet?'

'Look.' I pointed to a small crucifix on the wall above us. 'They nailed his feet to that piece of wood called a cross, and those are the holes where the nails were.' 'Nailed his feet?!' She turned to look at the stone figures again. Her voice broke a little as she spoke. 'Daddy, he's got holes in his hands as well. They didn't nail his hands as well, did they?' Sadly, I explained. Katy moved closer to the sculpture, put her arm around Jesus and rested her face down on his knee.

Suddenly I longed to go back to the time when I first understood that Jesus died for me and it really hurt, before I covered my faith in words and worries. I wanted to be like a child again.

A prayer

Father, give me the eyes of a child.

What is your name? John 3:16 (RSV)

For God so loved the world that he gave his only Son, that whoever believes in him should not perish but have eternal life.

I've had a love/hate relationship with this verse since I was converted (whatever that means) at the age of sixteen. It expresses, of course, the greatest reality of all, but back in the 1960s it seemed to be used almost as a talisman by the young evangelicals who thought that the Bible might be the fourth person of the Trinity. I swallowed my hate for John 3:16 years ago. Now I love it, because it encapsulates the great truth that God is crackers about us. It ought to make us feel glad and proud (in the best sense) but an awful lot of Christians feel neither of those things. Many of us have a very poor self-image, a phenomenon that has little or nothing to do with pride and humility.

I remember a woman I met when I was signing books after a meeting one evening at some church in the north of England. She held a book out for me to sign and I asked, as I always do, for her name, so that I could write a dedication to her on the title page.

'Oh,' she said, shaking her head uncertainly, 'I'm not anybody really. Just sign it...'

'Go on, tell me your name,' I coaxed. 'You must be somebody.'

She blushed slightly.

'Oh, well, I'm just Sarah...'

God so loved just Sarah that he gave his only beloved son, that if just Sarah believes in him, she will not perish but have everlasting life. Why doesn't she believe that? There could be all sorts of reasons, but perhaps one might be that the Church puts far less value on Sarah than God does. The last couple of decades have seen an increased emphasis on individual spiritual achievement in certain areas. Getting and gaining from God in all sorts of quick-fix ways has tended to obscure and replace the kind of long-term care and valuing of individuals that should characterize the body of Christ. God loved the person who sits beside me in church enough to send Jesus. There aren't any nonentities.

A prayer

Father, teach us to value each other and ourselves. Thank you for sending Jesus just for me.

Blessings and troubles **Luke 1:26–30 (GNB)**

In the sixth month of Elizabeth's pregnancy God sent the angel Gabriel to a town in Galilee named Nazareth. He had a message for a young woman promised in marriage to a man named Joseph, who was a descendant of King David. Her name was Mary. The angel came to her and said, 'Peace be with you! The Lord is with you and has greatly blessed you!' Mary was deeply troubled by the angel's message, and she wondered what his words meant. The angel said to her, 'Don't be afraid, Mary; God has been gracious to you...'

Mary is one of my all-time heroes, or heroines, or heroic persons, and this particular passage contains a clue to the reason why I hold her in such high regard. She was a realist, a good servant, and a very puzzled lady. Mary is told by the angel that she is 'greatly blessed'. She is immediately 'deeply troubled'. For the rest of her life Mary continues to be greatly blessed and deeply troubled as she observes the development of her extraordinary son's ministry, his appalling death and subsequent resurrection.

Mary's example should have a freeing effect on folk like myself who have somehow got the idea that the 'greatly blessed' mode is the only legitimate one. Nearly all of the Christians that I know well have passed through, are passing through, and certainly will pass through periods of being deeply troubled. How could it be otherwise? This is a wild, fallen world, and we are weak, vulnerable people with widely differing backgrounds and personalities, but sharing the same hope as Mary, that we have life and ultimate healing in Jesus.

How important it is that we accept this reality in each other without offering inappropriate ministry or implicit condemnation. Share blessings, share troubles, and, above all, share Jesus. We'll get by.

A prayer

Father, help us to look after each other without unreal expectations or unhelpful responses. Thank you for Mary who was obedient and genuine.

Back to basics

Luke 24:13–17 (RSV)

That very day two of them were going to a village named Emmaus, about seven miles from Jerusalem, and talking with each other about all these things that had happened. While they were talking and discussing together, Jesus himself drew near and went with them. But their eyes were kept from recognizing him. And he said to them, 'What is this conversation which you are holding with each other as you walk?' And they stood still, looking sad.

A rich mix of troubles and blessings is one thing, but a long desert-like experience of spiritual loneliness is quite another. As I travel around the country I am quite often faced with the fact that some folk have felt neglected by God for a very long time. I know a free-church minister in the north-east, for example, who simply cannot understand why there has been little or no spiritual development in the church that he leads. He's a talented, caring man who seems to have done all the right things, but, like the two fellows in this passage, he has ended up 'standing still, looking sad' because Jesus seems to have disappeared and the future is pointless. This man (and many others like him) are yearning to feel their hearts burn within them again, so that they too can tell others, with the deep wild excitement they once knew, that 'The Lord is risen indeed!'

There are no universal solutions to the problem of spiritual depression (I once bought a 'universal' roof-rack that fitted every model of car in the cosmos except the one that we had) but the experience of these two travellers is interesting. First, they received a metaphorical clip round the ear for being silly, but it didn't put them off—Jesus gets that sort of thing right. Then they were taken back to first principles via the scriptures. Finally they received blessed bread from the stranger who turned out to be Jesus. *Then* their hearts burned!

It's worth a try. No-holds-barred repentance, followed by a quiet return to Bible-basics, leading to warm and intimate communion with the person who was with us all the time, even when we were standing still and looking sad.

A prayer

We want to burn with life, Lord. Meet us, teach us and eat with us, please.

Burglars

Luke 21:34–36 (RSV)

'But take heed to yourselves lest your hearts be weighed down with dissipation and drunkenness and cares of this life, and that day come upon you suddenly like a snare; for it will come upon all who dwell upon the face of the whole earth. But watch at all times, praying that you may have strength to escape all these things that will take place, and to stand before the Son of man.'

The Bible is a strange book. There's always a bit you never noticed, usually right in the middle of a very familiar passage. Take this extract from Luke, for instance. When I tell people that Jesus mentioned three areas of worldly distraction that weigh the heart down, and that these include drunkenness, they usually look very surprised and demand to know exactly where the quote appears. The situation is not helped by the fact that I almost invariably forget the chapter and verse and have to leaf feverishly through the New Testament searching for evidence.

Dissipation, drunkenness and cares of this life. In my time I've had a paddle in the first, got out of my depth in the second, but jolly nearly drowned in the third. Some of us who are in the 'standing still, looking sad' bracket may have to face the reality that we are hanging on to concerns and preoccupations so ponderous that they cast a perpetual shadow of gloom over all other aspects of life. The habit of *worry* can be a crippling one.

No burglars came again last night
Just as they failed to come the night before
And for as many nights as I remember
No burglars yet again
Although I listened, as I always do, for them.
They did not come
They were not here again last night
And what if they should never come?
A waste of nights—I might have slept
But if I had, I feel quite sure
They would have come—those burglars,
Yes, they would have come.

A prayer

Lord, our worries cling to us like poultices. Sometimes we pray about them and they seem to go away for a while. Then they come back and we are close to despair. Help us, Lord, we don't want to be distracted from you.

The failed father? **Luke 15:11 (RSV)**

And he said, 'There was a man who had two sons...'

If the story of the prodigal son had been told for the first time in this age, it would undoubtedly have been called 'The parable of the failed father'. After all, neither of his sons turned out very well, did they? One left home and spent all his money on riotous living and harlots, while the other grew up to be a sulky, po-faced individual who had no idea how to enjoy life. Something wrong with the parenting there, wouldn't you say?

Of course, Jesus was making a different point altogether and views on individual responsibility were very different at that time, and in that society. However, if we are trying to deal with reality, let's face the fact that very many people outside the Church, and not a few inside, have a big problem with this 'other view' of God's dealings with men and women. It's an old question, but here it comes again: If the creator really is omniscient and omnipotent, why did he produce creatures who were going to fail and rebel and experience suffering and pain as a result? Why doesn't he take responsibility for his own poor handiwork and planning? Doesn't he owe us a slice of heaven?

My evangelical training pops up answers to these questions with Pavlovian ease: God didn't want robots so he gave us free will. He is the potter and we are the clay, so we have no right to object. Our finite minds are incapable of comprehending his infinite and eternal purposes.

These arguments may or may not have virtue, but I can only say that they've never satisfactorily solved the problem for me. I wouldn't be a Christian now if my faith depended on an acceptance of the logic of creation and the fall. It doesn't depend on that—it depends on Jesus. Right at the centre of my chaotic, shifting, strangely-shaped religious belief lies the person of Jesus and the relationship that exists between us. He is the still point from which all references are taken and I have gradually learned that he is reliable.

I can't solve the problem of the 'failed' father, but Jesus knows the truth and I trust him. In the end—that is my answer.

A prayer

Father, there are lots of things I don't understand. Help me not to pretend I do when I don't. Thank you again for Jesus.

Time out

Matthew 14:6–14 (RSV)

But when Herod's birthday came, the daughter of Herodias danced before the company, and pleased Herod, so that he promised with an oath to give her whatever she might ask. Prompted by her mother, she said, 'Give me the head of John the Baptist here on a platter.' And the king was sorry; but because of his oaths and his guests he commanded it to be given; he sent and had John beheaded in the prison and his head was brought on a platter and given to the girl, and she brought it to her mother. And his disciples came and took the body and buried it; and they went and told Jesus. Now when Jesus heard this, he withdrew from there in a boat to a lonely place apart. But when the crowds heard it, they followed him on foot from the towns. As he went ashore he saw a great throng; and he had compassion on them, and healed their sick.

There was a time when even Jesus became still and sad. He was a real man, so it isn't surprising. Jesus and his cousin must have been very close. Their parents knew each other, they were the same age, and they lived within a day's journey of each other. Even before they were born John had leaped in his mother's womb when the excited Mary hurried to Elizabeth's hill-country home to describe her encounter with an angel. I may be wrong, but I've always felt that Jesus' impassioned outburst about John in the seventh chapter of Luke's Gospel contains a very personal note as well as a logical argument.

Now, on hearing that John is dead, he tries to find a place to be alone, a place to grieve, but the crowds are like baby birds, knowing only their own hunger, and as he sets foot on the shore they all are waiting for him. Business as usual. No more time for grief.

A prayer

Thank you, Father, for this special view of one of your son's very personal moments. I'm sorry he was made so sad by his cousin's death, and I want to thank you that he got on with the job so determinedly after drawing apart for a while. It gives me permission to do the same.

God of the gaps

Zephaniah 3:15–20 (RSV)

Do not fear, O Zion; let not your hands grow weak. The Lord, your God, is in your midst, a warrior who gives victory; he will rejoice over you with gladness, he will renew you in his love; he will exult over you with loud singing as on a day of festival. 'I will remove disaster from you, so that you will not bear reproach for it. Behold, at that time I will deal with all your oppressors. And I will save the lame and gather the outcast, and I will change their shame into praise and renown in all the earth. At that time I will bring you home, at that time when I gather you together; yea, I will make you renowned and praised among all the peoples of the earth, when I restore your fortunes before your eyes,' says the Lord.

This passage, and the last sentence in particular, became very important to me twelve years ago when I retreated from my normal responsibilities and activities because of a stress-related illness. One thing that assisted my recovery was the daily discipline of writing, a completely new occupation for me. There was something very therapeutic about taking feelings and memories from inside and placing them outside, on a sheet of paper. Gradually, the notion of becoming a full-time writer began to form in my mind. My family were very supportive, but most other people displayed a thinly-veiled scepticism when I described what I intended. I can hardly blame them. I had a mortgage, three children and a dog to support. How was I going to provide for them? Then, one morning, I read the final part of Zephaniah, and those last few words stood out like divine Braille, relieving the spiritual blindness that I was suffering at the time. God was going to restore my fortunes before my eyes, and although it was difficult to picture how it would happen, I felt sure that writing would be involved somehow. Soon after that I sent a selection of written pieces to the American writer, Elizabeth Sherrill, who, with her husband John, had been responsible for a string of best-selling books, including *The Cross and the Switchblade*. Elizabeth replied with the kind of letter raw beginners dream of. Armed with her generous encouragement I continued to wear out biros and tear up rejection slips from publishers informing me that 'our readers would not approve of our Lord Jesus Christ being written about in that fashion...'

But God kept his promise.

A question

Are we too quick to plug 'gaps'?

Long live love

1 Corinthians 13:8–10 (RSV)

Love never ends; as for prophecies, they will pass away; as for tongues, they will cease; as for knowledge, it will pass away. For our knowledge is imperfect and our prophecy is imperfect; but when the perfect comes, the imperfect will pass away.

Most people are fond of this passage, but there is nothing sentimental about what Paul is saying. All of the spiritual gifts will pass away, but love will remain. We are not saved by tongues, prophecy, words of knowledge, or any of the other useful pots and pans that equip the Christian kitchen. God is love and we are saved by the power of love. The other things are good but imperfect.

I have a friend who is a Jewish rabbi in the reformed movement. We have often looked for common ground. He is a very spiritual man and I am an Anglican. When David came to tea with his wife one day I put the following scenario to him.

'I arrive in heaven, right?' David nodded. 'And God says to me, "I'm awfully sorry, Adrian, but Jesus *wasn't* the Son of God. The Jews got it right and you didn't. But will you trust me anyway?"'

'Yes,' smiled David, 'I can imagine that quite easily.'

'Hold on,' I said, 'I haven't finished yet. While I'm chewing over what God's said to me—you roll up.'

'Oh,' said the rabbi, his smile fading a little.

'"Hello, David," says God, "I'm awfully sorry, but Jesus *was* the Son of God. You missed out on the Messiah. But will you trust me anyway?"'

'And what happens then?' asked David.

'Well, I guess you and I talk it over just outside heaven's gate, then we go to God arm in arm and say that as long as the three of us can be together nothing else matters.'

'Hmmm,' said David thoughtfully.

Don't throw scriptural thunderbolts at me. I *do* believe that Jesus is exactly who and what he said he was, but I also believe that the love between David and me is as real and as lasting as anything else.

Reflect

John Lennon was right. 'Love is real...'

Coming last

Micah 4:6–7 (RSV)

In that day, says the Lord, I will assemble the lame and gather those who have been driven away and those whom I have afflicted; and the lame I will make the remnant; and those who were cast off, a strong nation; and the Lord will reign over them in Mount Zion from this time forth and for evermore.

A friend and I took some members of the local youth club to Wales. I was a little nervous because I knew that the weekend itinerary included the climbing of a very high mountain, and I seriously doubted that I was fit enough to manage it. No rock-climbing was involved, just walking and clambering forever. I was sure my lungs and legs would rebel long before I reached the top.

Because of this apprehension I set off like an express train when we started, anxious to put failure or success behind me as quickly as possible. Some of the kids kept pace with my frenetic attack on the hillside, while others—the plump, the wrongly-shod, the frail and the disinclined—dribbled slowly along at the rear. It wasn't until I was about three-quarters of the way to the top and I stopped to admire the view (I claimed) that I took any notice of what was happening to the stragglers. Far, far below me, I could see a little line of bent figures toiling laboriously up the slope, and, right at the back, my friend and co-leader, Michael, who was much fitter than me and could easily have been further on than I was by now. As I watched, he stopped to encourage the smaller figure in front of him who seemed to have given up temporarily. I reached the top long before Michael. It took him hours to shepherd his reluctant lambs to the summit.

Sometimes it can look as if the elevated, front-running, high profile Christians are the significant, successful ones, but it is not so. Those who are carrying out the commission implied by these verses in Micah are the winners in God's eyes, for their example and their inspiration is Jesus himself.

A prayer

Father, give us patience and pleasure in helping those who are having trouble making it.

Serious fun

John 10:10 (RSV)

The thief comes only to steal and kill and destroy; I came that they may have life, and have it abundantly.

I was speaking at a very lively youth festival on the east coast. The young people seemed to be enjoying themselves enormously.

'I think it makes it easier for them to take in the serious things when they're having fun like this.'

It was one of the organizers who made this comment as we stood together and watched a laughing, scuffling, happy queue of teenagers waiting to enter a large tent where a popular band was due to perform. I agreed at the time largely because I suffer from chronic nodding-itis. Later, when I thought about what the chap had said, I remembered all the church youth-group leaders who have expressed to me their bewilderment about conflicting behaviours by the young people they are responsible for. They couldn't understand why decent, arm-raising, praise-emitting Sunday teenagers could change into such monstrous beings on some 'secular' occasions. Actually, this is merely the nature of the beast, broadly speaking, and it's probably a healthier attitude to life than the one taken by many repressed adult church-goers. Healthy teenagers look for life, and then enter it.

What could be more serious for the youngsters at that festival than to have fun? What more could one ask than that they learn to associate guiltless and exuberant living with the institution of the Church? Perhaps we should be hoping that our young people will grow up to be like King David, who was wholehearted in sorrow and repentance. Jesus promised us life in abundance—not emotional restraint and eternal moderation.

Consider this—God thought it worthwhile to send his Son to die for us so that we could enjoy eternal life. What will this life be? I don't know the answer to that question any more than you do, but I do know that it will contain the essence of everything that is bright and strong and beautiful and satisfying and peaceful and dynamic and real.

A prayer

Father, help us to accept your gift of abundant life and avoid preventing anyone else from finding it. Thank you in advance.

Cut your losses and let your profits run.

American proverb

GETTING LOST

Search and recovery in the fifteenth chapter of Luke

For as long as I can remember I have identified and empathized with people and things that are lost and damaged. In this connection I would like to tell you about two paintings that mean a great deal to me.

In our sitting room at home hangs a picture that used to be in the centre of the longer wall that faces you as you walk in through the door. It has now been relegated to a corner position on the opposite side, somewhat obscured by the opened door, where it waits, like one of those plain daughters in Victorian fiction, to be noticed by somebody. This relegation is not, I can assure you, a sign of any diminished appreciation on my part, but rather a mildly defensive reaction to the responses of some of our visitors. I have seen so many of them regarding it with bemused stares, rocking back on their heels and pursing their lips as they try to think of something to say. As a matter of fact, I can feel myself delaying an explanation of the actual content of this picture in case you also frown and shake your head in a puzzled, pitying sort of way, and secretly ask yourself if that man who was so good and patient with your sadly afflicted second cousin might be able to offer me a similarly helpful course of treatment.

Oh, all right, I'll tell you—it's a picture of a car.

'Well, what's wrong with that?' I hear many of you say. 'Lots of people develop an interest in transport of various kinds, and whilst we may not actually share that particular interest we fully understand why, in your own home, you would want to hang a—'

No—hold on, you don't understand. This isn't one of those meticulously executed, full-colour representations of an XP47 Cougar Vincenzo with streamlined triple-vaning and double overhead camshaft—I can't imagine anything more boring—no, this is something quite different. This is a broken-down, abandoned small vehicle of the Mini Traveller type, the sort with wooden frames around the windows, and it appears to have been dumped at the edge of a field. In fact, it must have been there for some time, because the undergrowth has crept up around the wheels and lower chassis, and the back doors are open and hanging crazily from twisted hinges. In the background an ominously dark wood seems to be waiting to swallow up the remains of what might once have been someone's pride and joy. It is a very sad little car indeed.

The unspoken, and occasionally spoken, question from a number of our guests has been: 'Why? Why on earth do you want a picture of a dead car on your wall, a car that will certainly remain unmended, a useless heap of metal and wood that will never again fulfil its original function?'

Ah, but that's exactly the point, you see. Having been in a broken down state myself, and having worked for many years with children who had been abandoned and despaired of, and having encountered a God who specializes in taking lost, broken things and miraculously restoring them to working order, I find my picture immensely inspiring. It's a bit like having a picture of Jesus on the cross, only less oppressive. That old car (and it is a brilliantly executed piece of work, by the way) is a constant reminder to me that nothing and nobody is beyond rescue and redemption in the kingdom of God.

I feel a bit guilty about bowing to the pressure of opinion as far as the position of my picture is concerned, but you should see what I've hung on that long wall in its place! As visitors enter now they are confronted by a large charcoal drawing of Jacqueline Du Pré, a shining talent who, as a result of illness and depression, became as lost and broken as the Mini Traveller that humbly awaits a little attention on the wall behind my sitting-room door.

The second picture—well, just thinking about the second picture brings back feelings of great excitement and anticipation. It isn't hanging anywhere in our house as I write, because we're going to take it into town to be valued as soon as we get a bit of spare time, but I'd love to see it on our bedroom wall, for instance, once that's been done. This is the story that lies behind it.

After my mother died at the end of 1996 my brothers and I set about the dismal task of disposing of all her belongings, including various items that must have been lying around in the loft for years. This collection included three or four dusty old religious pictures of the bleeding-heart variety, a genre which I have personally always found vaguely repellent. One or two of them were encased in quite impressive frames, but the general feeling was that they should be dumped, and because Bridget and I offered to do the dumping, they all ended up at our house, victims, as the days went by, of the chronic Plass inability to get things done with any urgency.

One evening, sitting in the kitchen on my own, I found myself idly wondering whether it might be worth removing the pictures and hanging on to the frames. Picking up one of the largest, I tore off the backing paper and found, to my intense interest, that a second, smaller picture had been used as a support for the picture that actually appeared behind the glass. Examining my discovery, I found that it was a photograph of rocks and sea, probably cut from a magazine many years ago and stuck onto a piece of card. Valueless, no doubt, but you can imagine the eagerness with which I picked up the next example of religious excess and ripped away the backing to see if anything interesting might be concealed underneath. Nor was I disappointed. This time I pulled out a print, dated just after the turn of the century, mass-produced and, again, probably worthless, but you can imagine how excited I was by now. I felt as though I had walked unexpectedly into an Aladdin's cave. Who could tell what I might come across next?

The third picture was smaller than the other two, but it looked older, and was, if anything, even more representative of that depressingly grim style of religious art that abounded in the Victorian age. This time I savoured each step in the process, slitting the crackling, fragile old brown paper carefully around the edge of the frame before bending back each of the nails that had held the picture in place for so many years. Holding my breath, I lifted out the sheet of card that formed the next layer and turned it over. There in front of me, in its own card frame, was an enchanting little original painting of a seaside scene, done in what my uneducated eye took to be water-colours. Looking more closely at the corner of the painting I saw that the artist had written the date 1879, and that the setting was Bournemouth. There was no signature. More than a century ago someone, feeling that this small picture was dispensable, had sealed it up inside the larger one, and mine were the first eyes to see it since then.

Whether or not this jewel of a find turns out to have any monetary value, I shall always love the fact that something so precious and attractive was hidden for so long behind such a garishly distorted portrayal of the Christian faith. Do forgive the obvious parallel, but it seems such a clear picture of how the sweet, strong reality of Jesus continues to be itself, however many mistakes the Church as an institution might make. And it is also a reminder to all of us that Jesus hides the most important part of what we are within himself, ready to be revealed to his Father when the right moment comes.

Our God is the God of the damaged and the lost.

Prayer

Father, as we walk with you, we pray for all those people who have become lost and hurt along the way. We all know some people like that, Lord. Some of us are *those people. Thankfully, you know where the lost ones have got to and what's happening to them, so we ask that, if there are ways in which we can be helpful in bringing them back to the right path or healing their hurts, we won't chicken out of making uninviting detours, nor make religious excuses for avoiding heavenly tasks.*

Thank you so much, Lord Jesus, that you have hidden each one of us, your valuable works of art, safely within yourself. Sometimes we wonder how the public face of your Church can possibly represent the person that you are, but we know that you are always working from inside to change things for the better. Help us to be courageous and faithful in helping you to accomplish this. Amen.

But we're Christians! **Luke 15:1–3 (NJB)**

The tax collectors and sinners, however, were all crowding round to listen to him, and the Pharisees and Scribes complained saying, 'This man welcomes sinners and eats with them.'

When I do an evening of 'funny stuff' for a church or group of churches, the event is usually well attended, I'm pleased to say. People love to laugh, and if there's a serious thought or two thrown in as well, they seem to accept that quite happily. When, however, I have been involved in concerns to raise money or consciousness for AIDS sufferers, or Prison Fellowship, or Third World poverty, the attendance has been considerably lower.

The material I use is exactly the same, but there seems to be a reluctance to come close to these sorts of issues, even in such an indirect way. Some folk have quite openly expressed their distaste for any Christian activity connected with AIDS, and Prison Fellowship is consistently underfunded and poorly supported, despite the fact that they do some marvellous work.

Not many Christians want to get their hands dirty, but those who do see miracles sometimes. Jesus didn't stay at the Jewish Hilton and make evangelistic visits to sinners. He was *with* them—eating with them, making real friends with them, telling stories, answering questions, untainted but fully involved. The Scribes and Pharisees couldn't stand it, just as some people still can't stand it nowadays.

Recently, a friend of mind came out of prison and was looking for lodgings in a nearby town. We found an establishment listed in the local directory as a 'Christian hotel'. When I phoned the number and explained what was needed the lady on the other end of the line said, 'Well, I'm not sure. We do have to be very careful who we take, because we are a *Christian* hotel, you see...'

God help us as a church, if we're saying, 'We do have to be very careful who we take, because we are a *Christian* church, you see...'

Think

Do we make real friends with those we don't approve of? Are we ready to get our hands dirty in God's service? Read Matthew 25:31–46.

Shepherds or policemen? **Luke 15:4 (NJB)**

'Which one of you with a hundred sheep, if he lost one, would fail to leave the ninety-nine in the desert and go after the missing one till he found it?'

Here, Jesus is asking the Scribes and Pharisees to take a 180 degree turn in their attitude to sinners. From scolding to caring; from abandoning to searching out; from indifference to love.

Some years ago one of our major universities undertook studies into the nature and components of successful counselling. After much research, observation and discussion, three major factors were identified as essential characteristics of an effective counsellor. They were as follows:

(1) The effective counsellor must be willing to enter the world of his client.
(2) He must not be condemnatory of the person he is counselling.
(3) He must value that person demonstrably.

A little reflection might have saved that university an awful lot of time and trouble. Two thousand years ago Jesus (who is sometimes called the Mighty Counsellor) entered our world, not to condemn us, but to show how much he valued us by dying on that horrible cross.

I wonder how the Scribes and Pharisees coped with a suggestion that they should be shepherds rather than policemen; that it was worth an enormous expenditure of time and effort to seek out just one of those grubby little sinners and save him from the consequences of his separation from God.

Some years ago I was a lost sheep myself, despite the fact that I had been a Christian for more than twenty years. Emotionally distraught, out of work, and no longer attending a church, I said to my wife one day that if there was a God who loved me he could come and help, and if there wasn't, it didn't matter anyway. The good shepherd heard my bleat and came, particularly through certain friends who worked for the shepherd, rather than the religious police force.

A prayer

Thank you for coming into our world, Jesus. I'd like to help you in your search. Show me something specific that I can do.

Searching with tears **Luke 15:5–7 (NJB)**

'And when he found it, would he not joyfully take it on his shoulders and then, when he got home, call together his friends and neighbours saying to them, "Rejoice with me, I have found my sheep that was lost." In the same way, I tell you, there will be more rejoicing in heaven over one sinner repenting than over ninety-nine upright people who have no need of repentance.'

When my youngest son, David, was a little boy, we went to Cornwall for a family holiday. One afternoon we decided to spend some time on the beach at Newquay. After an hour or so of sandcastle building, paddling and ice-cream consumption, we realized that David was missing. An hour later, after searching every square yard of the beach, we could still find no trace of him. Bridget, my wife, was pacing aimlessly up and down the beach, tears in her eyes, desperately hoping that the small figure would appear.

Meanwhile, I made my way to the lifeguard point and asked the young man on duty to call David over the public address system. That didn't work either. A great darkness began to settle over my heart. My mouth had dried up and I was unable to keep my eyes from the thin white line where the sea met the shore. I was terrified. It must have been half an hour later when the friend who was with us on the beach found David playing quietly on the sand two hundred yards or so from where we had last seen him. The relief and joy in our little party was palpable. I hoisted David up onto my shoulders and carried him back to the car.

Jesus wanted his listeners to understand that his search for the lost—the shepherd's search for his sheep—is conducted with even more passion and urgency than our desperate hunt for David on that summer day. No wonder they rejoice in heaven when one sinner repents. God is crackers about us.

Reflect

Jesus searches for us with tears in his eyes. When he finds us the whole of heaven goes bonkers with happiness.

Sharing sorrow and joy **Luke 15:8–10 (NJB)**

'Or again, what woman with ten drachmas would not, if she lost one, light a lamp and sweep out the house and search thoroughly till she found it? And then, when she had found it, call together her friends and neighbours, saying to them, "Rejoice with me, I have found the drachma I lost." In the same way, I tell you, there is rejoicing among the angels of God over one repentant sinner.'

This story (presumably told so that contemporary ladies could get the point of the sheep story) reminds me of the occasion when Bridget lost all our holiday money when she was pushing one of the children round the shops at Hailsham. She rang me at work to pass on the bad news and was clearly astonished by the calm and muted manner with which I responded.

'Okay, Bridget,' I purred soothingly, 'not to worry—I'll sort it out somehow. It's only money...' Little did Bridget know that this warm act of forgiveness and understanding was solely attributable to the fact that I was surrounded by a little circle of child-care trainees who had been enduring my views on the need for warmth and forgiveness in dealing with kids in care. When I arrived home later I discovered that the money had been found and returned to Bridget, so I was able to perpetuate the myth of my tolerance and generosity of spirit.

We certainly rejoiced together over the return of that cash, but we didn't invite any neighbours in to share our joy. Perhaps that is one of the lessons of this little parable. We are not very good at inviting others into the centre of our joys and our tragedies. Births, weddings, house-warmings and deaths tend to be the only occasions when this happens in grey old England. But we are the body of Christ, and we belong to each other. Some of the warmest and most memorable moments in the history of the little house-group that Bridget and I lead have been the times when individuals have made a gift to the rest of us of quite small joys and sorrows. This kind of sharing often requires an act of the will.

A prayer

Father, I'm not really very good at giving my life to other people. Please help me to be more generous and courageous.

A story of God **Luke 15:11–13 (NJB)**

Then he said, 'There was a man who had two sons. The younger one said to his Father, "Father, let me have the share of the estate that will come to me." So the father divided the property between them. A few days later, the younger son got together everything he had and left for a distant country where he squandered his money on a life of debauchery.'

The Bible tells us that Jesus used stories all the time in his contacts with the crowds who flocked to hear him. Now, I happen to know, as a feeble but committed storyteller myself, that the best stories are the ones that are based on fact—things that have really happened to me or to people I know. This famous story has the same ring of truth about it. During that invaluable period of sixteen years or so, when he was (presumably) a working carpenter, Jesus must have put together a sizeable mental portfolio of memories and anecdotes. This is probably one of them. I wish there was more storytelling and less preaching in the Church these days.

I have often wondered why the prodigal left home so deliberately. Unlike sheep and drachmas, he didn't get lost—he went. Perhaps he looked at his elder brother, po-faced, aridly virtuous and miserable, and decided anything was better than ending up like that. It seems more likely, though, that he made the common mistake of separating the gifts from the giver. It can take a long time to realize that we have lost touch with the springs of our own joy and pleasure, and the process can be a subtle one. Some Christians, convinced that they are working for God, arrange religious activities that seem quite laudable, but if those activities don't have their roots in the will of God they are going to bloom once, then die.

The prodigal is incapable, at this stage, of realizing that as the good things flow away from him, nothing else will flow in to replace them—not as long as he is away from home, that is. The principle holds good for all of us.

Reflect

Jesus took his life, rolled it up in a ball and gave it to us. He lost the life he loved, so that we would never be hungry. Maybe it's best to work from home...

Stuck in a pigsty

Luke 15:14–16a (NJB)

'When he had spent it all, that country experienced a severe famine, and now he began to feel the pinch; so he hired himself out to one of the local inhabitants who put him on his farm to feed the pigs. And he would willingly have filled himself with the husks the pigs were eating but no one would let him have them.'

Much of my early working life was spent caring for children in trouble. Some of them came from appalling backgrounds, and, inevitably, I came into contact with many of the parents of these confused teenagers. I met wives who had endured continual battering from their husbands, and men who had served frequent sentences in prison as a result of their consistently inexpert criminal activities. The children themselves were often locked into patterns of behaviour that had never brought them anything but negative responses.

Again and again I was struck by the apparent inability of unhappy people to explore alternatives in lifestyle or behaviour that would immediately make a difference. Why stay with a man who beats you up every other day? Why persist in acts of petty crime when the police catch you every time? It was only when I reached a point of intolerable pain and had to make an involuntary withdrawal from work and church that I realized I was exactly the same. I had completely ignored the need to tackle some very obvious problems in my own life.

The prodigal son in this story is exactly the same. His descent from riches and riotous living to the ignominy of the pigs must have been a relatively gradual one. He could have made the decision to go home at any stage, but he seems to have been unaware of this option until he reached a point where his need was so great that he *had* to consider any alternative.

Lots of us are blinkered to obvious needs in our lives, and others usually see where we are heading long before we come to our senses. Prayer, sensitivity and practical help could prevent a few of us from hitting rock-bottom.

A prayer

Father, take the blinkers away so that we can see the changes that need to be made in our lives. If there are people known to us who are heading for disaster, give us the sensitivity and wisdom to help them.

At least I'll eat... Luke 15:16b–19 (NJB)

'Then he came to his senses and said, "How many of my father's hired men have all the food they want and more, and here am I dying of hunger! I will leave this place and go to my father and say: 'Father, I have sinned against heaven and against you; I no longer deserve to be called your son; treat me as one of your hired men.'" So he left the place and went back to his father.'

Let's not get too sentimental about this lad. No doubt he has some very warm and nostalgic memories of home. But his primary motivation for returning is an eminently sane and practical one. He wants some food. He is hungry. He is lacking the fuel that sustains life at its most basic level. Sin isn't much fun when you're dying of starvation.

Coming to our senses in a spiritual sense is a very similar experience. When worldly distractions lose their potency and props are snapped or fatally weakened, men and women know suddenly that their spirits are thin and emaciated. Only the bread of life can make any difference to this sort of terminal malnutrition.

It is worth mentioning, though, to those who are dithering about whether to leave the pigs or not, that this God who is offering sustenance is the one who created kites, and sex, and good wine, and spring flowers, and children's eyes. Coming home to him will not just be survival—it could turn out to be an awful lot of fun.

I can easily picture this 'oik' of a prodigal—a sort of New Testament Baldrick—crawling up the road towards home, rehearsing his little set speech over and over again, boldly perhaps, and then with cringing humility, hoping to strike a note that will be effective with a potentially furious parent. Most of us expect very little from God, especially if, like myself, we have been encouraged at an early stage to look at ourselves as miserable, crawling, verminous little creatures, tolerated by God, but only when he holds his nose and averts his eyes. The prodigal wasn't expecting much, but he was in for a shock.

A prayer

For those who are thinking of starting the journey back to the Father, we pray for courage. If there's anything we can do to help, please show us clearly, so that we don't mess things up.

A hurricane of love **Luke 15:20–21 (NJB)**

'While he was still a long way off, his father saw him and was moved with pity. He ran to the boy, clasped him in his arms and kissed him. Then his son said, "Father, I have sinned against heaven and against you. I no longer deserve to be called your son."'

I have annoyed some of my evangelical friends occasionally by telling them of an acquaintance who came to his Christian faith as a result of attending classes in Buddhism. After obediently emptying his mind of almost everything that normally occupied it, he found that Jesus filled the mental vacuum that remained. Eventually he cancelled the Buddhist classes, joined a local church and made a commitment to Christ.

The same thing happens to the prodigal son in this story. He is a 'long way off' when his father spots him (probably from an upstairs window) and can hardly have expected such an early response. Too often the attitude of Christians to their non-believing acquaintances reminds me of the old joke about a country yokel who is asked for directions by a traveller.

'Well,' says the yokel, 'Oi wouldn't start from 'ere if I was you...'

God knows where people are and when he should meet them. Sometimes they come along very strange roads indeed.

Here we see the dear old prodigal hit by a hurricane as he lopes along, learning his little speech by heart as he goes. The hurricane is his father, of course, overjoyed to see the son he has always loved so much, and not ashamed to sprint down the road, holding his robes up with one hand. What an extraordinarily vulnerable picture of God that is.

With his father's arms wrapped round his head, the surprised prodigal manages to bleat out a muffled version of the set speech he's been rehearsing. His repentance is embraced with joy. Repentance and forgiveness are not opposite ends of the spectrum. They are parts of the same joyful experience.

Reflect

We know nothing about how and when God will call and meet people. Our job is to be obedient and carry out orders, however strange they may seem sometimes.

So happy you're home! **Luke 15:22–24 (NJB)**

'But the father said to his servants, "Quick! Bring out the best robe and put it on him; put a ring on his finger and sandals on his feet. Bring the calf we have been fattening, and kill it; we will celebrate by having a feast, because this son of mine was dead and has come back to life; he was lost and is found." And they began to celebrate.'

Having children of my own has taught me more about the fatherhood of God than anything else. When one of my children is naughty I feel an intensity of love towards him or her that yearns for a resolution of the problem. I don't mean that I never lose my temper or act irrationally (such a claim would qualify me for a degree in hypocrisy). But I do greet them, when they stumble through the apology barrier, as if they had never done anything wrong. It's so nice to have them back!

What a surprise for the prodigal. He would have settled for three meals a day and a bed in the barn. Instead he's covered with gifts and told that there's going to be a party to celebrate his return. The fragile little pose that he'd prepared for this first big encounter would hardly have been proof against such extravagant, limitless generosity. The face would have crumpled, a tear or two would have appeared—Daddy really wanted him back.

I met a modern prodigal in Australia once, a man who ran away from home when he was fourteen, and didn't return until he was nearly twenty. He planned to drive home in style to surprise his Dad. But on the way his car broke down. He had to ring his parents for help. The stylish return lost some of its dignity as the young man was towed home in a lifeless vehicle by his beaming father. Lots of people break down on their way back to God. Don't worry if it happens to you—he'll come and get you.

A prayer

Thank you for loving us so much when we are naughty. I wish I really knew how much you like to be with me. I still break down from time to time. Please rescue me when it happens.

Furious! **Luke 15:25–28a (NJB)**

'Now the elder son was out in the fields, and on his way back, as he drew near the house, he could hear music and dancing. Calling one of the servants he asked what it was all about. The servant told him, "Your brother has come, and your father has killed the calf we had been fattening because he has got him back safe and sound." He was angry then and refused to go in...'

People often ask me if the characters in my books are based on real individuals. They are particularly interested in a couple called Stenneth and Victoria Flushpool, self-appointed moral watchdogs in the imaginary church community that we encounter in *The Sacred Diary of Adrian Plass*. Do they really exist? I refuse to answer that question on the grounds that it may incriminate me, but I can tell you that people from different places all over the country claim that I must have visited *their* church before writing the book, because the Flushpools (under another name) are definitely members of their congregation.

One thing is sure; no one has ever openly identified himself or herself with any negative character of the Flushpool variety. Perhaps some defensive mechanism prevents such recognition. I wonder if the Pharisees and Scribes recognized themselves in the elder brother of the prodigal story? These ancient Jewish Flushpools hated to see sinners relaxing with Jesus. Like the prodigal's miserable sibling, they had never taken the trouble to discover the true nature of the God whom they claimed to serve. They could have had a party if they'd wanted—they never asked.

Watch out for Flushpools in the Church. They coax people into conversion, then tell them off afterwards because they're not perfect immediately; they elevate man-made activities onto a sacred level; they mistrust laughter and relaxation; they are stern and unhappy.

We must pray for them—especially if we *are* them...

A prayer

We pray for relaxation and joy throughout your Church, Father. Forgive us for allowing religious activities to atrophy and become meaningless. Help us to be shepherds rather than policemen.

Come to the party! Luke 28b–30 (NJB)

'And his father came out and began to urge him to come in; but he retorted to his father, "All these years I have slaved for you and never once disobeyed any orders of yours, yet you never offered me so much as a kid for me to celebrate with my friends. But, for this son of yours, when he comes back after swallowing up your property—he and his loose women—you kill the calf we had been fattening."'

Do you sulk? I do. It is recorded elsewhere that I am a master of the shuddering sigh, the kind that indicates profound suffering, bravely borne. The whole point of a sulk is that you advertise your misery, and then refuse comfort or help when it's offered. My wife ruins my best sulks by tickling me.

Here we see the elder brother locked into a monster sulk. Hanging about outside the life and light of his brother's party he is clearly hoping that his father will come and plead with him to come in. That will give him the opportunity to refuse. Sure enough, out comes Dad, anxious that his other son should share the fun, the joy, and the fatted calf. The resentful lad pours out his anger and hurt at this point, unable to contain himself any longer.

Many Christians would be able to identify with this deep, stress-filled anger towards God. I met a bank manager once who, years ago, prayed for his younger brother to be healed from a terminal illness. The brother died, and the resulting disappointment and fury remained unexpressed for decades.

Strange as it may sound, many of us need to forgive God for what he has done to us, or failed to do for us. Of course, we know that he can't really have got it wrong, but that doesn't take the hurt away. Let's climb up on his lap and cry out our frustration and pain. Let's beat our fists against his chest like small children and let him see our confused passion.

He can handle it. He will put his arms round us until our anger dissolves in tears, and we realize that he loves us after all, and always did.

A prayer

Father, if there are unresolved issues between us, I'd like to face them and sort them out. It's very hard to argue with someone who's perfect, but I do feel angry with you sometimes. Help me to express my feelings to you and trust your response.

Getting it right

Luke 15:31–32 (NJB)

'The father said, "My son, you are with me always and all I have is yours. But it was only right we should celebrate and rejoice, because your brother here was dead and has come to life; he was lost and is found."'

The elder brother has the same problem as many Christians in this age. He simply cannot understand that families at their best operate on the same principle as the three musketeers—'all for one and one for all'. When one is happy everyone rejoices, and when one mourns, the rest mourn with him or her.

The apostle Paul (who never read Dumas, but must have met him by now) put it rather differently. He said that each of us is part of Christ's body on earth, and that all parts, including the unusual ones, are vital to the function of the whole.

I used to belong to a Bible-study group which included a lady who made superb cakes, and a man who had a deep understanding and appreciation of God's forgiveness. We shared the cake and the forgiveness with equal enthusiasm, and we did not insist that the cake-maker should have hands laid on her to increase her sense of forgiveness. Nor did we send the man off for an intensive course in cake-making. Over the past couple of decades there has been a lot of emphasis on individual spiritual success. Articles entitled 'Washing up the Christian Way' and 'Carpet-laying in the Spirit' have implied that every aspect of life must be victoriously and overtly claimed for God. Perhaps there is some truth in that, but how much more important it is that we share, value and appropriate each other's talents and blessings, and that we add our strength to the carrying of each other's burdens.

The elder brother got it wrong. The Scribes and Pharisees got it wrong. Perhaps we could have a shot at getting it right.

Reflect

Perhaps we have undervalued some people because their gifts or perceptions do not come high on our list of priorities. Perhaps we hug what we have and are to ourselves, instead of letting it belong to the body. Let's take a fresh look at the people around us.

A promise is a kind of debt.

Moroccan proverb

CLEAR SIGNPOSTS

The promises of God

I have been asking myself the following question.

In which circumstances do I feel most confident that the general promise of God will be kept? I mean, I suppose, the promise that he is what he says he is, that we will become what he says we will become, and that the whole happy-ever-after potential of the Gospel narratives will one day be fully realized in our lives.

I know some people feel that such questioning indicates a lack of respect, but it is important to grasp the fact that those of us who do question in such a way are actually dealing with our own weakness and doubt, not with the trustworthiness or otherwise of God. One of the greatest and most helpful revelations in my largely revelationless life has been the knowledge that God is God and I am me. I am sure you will be gasping in wonder at the banality of this statement, but, however silly it sounds, that simple separation does mean a great deal to me. God will continue to be who and what he is despite me, while I, relieved beyond measure that he continues to love me even when I am in the most frightful messes, will continue to be me, and pray for change as farmers pray for rain in a drought.

So, where do I feel confident in the promise of God? There are a number of answers to this question, but, for the moment, I want to talk about just one.

I see the promise of God being fulfilled in the lives and spirits of my friends.

One night I was having a quiet drink and a bowl of chips with my friend Ben Ecclestone. Ben and I worked together on *Learning to Fly*, a book of poems and pictures charting the journey of our friendship over the last decade or so. Fortunately we no longer need to pretend anything to each other concerning what we feel and believe about our common faith. Last night we were discussing the problems we have both encountered with doubt and assurance.

'Sometimes,' said Ben, 'I've found myself feeling that deep down I know it's all a load of nonsense, and it's just lack of courage that stops me from admitting it to myself.'

'I know what you mean,' I replied, dipping a chip in his tomato sauce because I'd finished mine, 'I sometimes think it would take a lot more courage for us to give up our faith than to hang on to it. Imagine all the fuss and palaver if we told everyone that we'd decided we weren't Christians after all. I couldn't be a Christian writer any more, unless I joined A.N. Wilson firing on the retreat, and you'd have to give up being an elder, wouldn't you? Hassle all the way, eh? Besides, I reckon there's an even deeper level where you know that it *is* all true. Uncovering that would be a problem—you wouldn't have anything left to worry about then, would you?'

'Maybe it's a matter of temperament,' suggested Ben. 'There's a chap I know in a church near ours who wouldn't even know what we were talking about if he was sitting here now. Everything's black and white in his world. No problems about doctrine or faith or doubt or anything like that—all completely straightforward. But I reckon he's always been like that. It's just the way he's made. He's not like us. He doesn't have to keep taking his entrails out and studying them miserably to see if they're all right, he just lives his life. Sometimes I really wish I was like him. I'd be a lot more use if I was.'

'No you wouldn't,' I said, 'I know the bloke you're talking about. He's got about four things to say, and if someone comes along with a problem that doesn't fit one of them he's lost without even knowing that he's lost. You've helped loads of people because you don't pretend to know all the answers. Besides,' I dipped another chip deep into Ben's ketchup and studied the bright red sauce for a moment before popping it into my mouth, 'I rather like entrails.'

I have sat over so many bowls of chips and bottles of wine with Ben, 'finally' sorting out our own difficulties and the problems faced by the Church, formulating radical solutions that we alone are able to understand and offer. I'm sure we talk an awful load of rubbish at times, but as I looked at Ben last night, I sensed, as I have sensed so many times in the past, the profound love that God feels for this son of his who has done so much for so many people in the name of

Jesus, but has never quite been able to make the final step into a real assurance that he is truly valued and loved by his heavenly Father.

I know for a fact that Ben's worst nightmare involves an encounter with an angel holding a clipboard at the gates of heaven. The angel runs his finger down a list and shakes his head unemotionally. 'No Ecclestone here, I'm afraid,' he says, and the gates clang shut behind Ben as he trudges off towards Hades to consume soggy chips and vinegary wine with me for ever.

My faith *for* Ben is unshakeable—I just know that the person he is, the person who is complex, artistic, stubborn, loyal, fretful, self-effacing and fearful of rejection is as safely held in the palm of the hand of God as any man or woman ever was or ever will be. As a matter of interest I think he probably feels as confident about my eternal future as I do about his. And that, in a nutshell, is why Christians need Christians. For it is in each other that we see the promise of God coming to fruition.

You see, as I've just said, I have no doubt about Ben's salvation, but if you ask me about mine—well, I'm really not quite as sure...

Prayer

Father, thank you so much for our friends, and the assurance of salvation that we see so clearly in them. Help us to love them and pray for them.

Fishers of men (part one)

Matthew 4:18–20 (NIV)

As Jesus was walking beside the sea of Galilee, he saw two brothers, Simon called Peter and his brother Andrew. They were casting a net into the lake, for they were fishermen. 'Come, follow me,' Jesus said, 'I will make you fishers of men.' At once they left their nets and followed him.

The fishing record of my immediate family is far from distinguished. My youngest son did once catch a moderately sized fish off a pier in Australia, but I ruined the moment when, in a sudden fit of compassion, I threw it back before he had a chance to take a photo.

My middle son has never caught a fish, but he did once catch *me*. With a metal imitation minnow on the end of his line he drove one of the three large hooks into my right ear. Walking into a nearby health-centre with this bizarre decoration dangling from my earlobe was not one of the high spots in my life.

This same son never did quite perfect the art of casting. On one occasion, bravely putting behind him a series of miserably unsuccessful attempts and applying every available ounce of concentration to one last try, he hurled himself bodily into the water, leaving his rod and line lying neatly on the bank.

My own attempts at angling have been equally useless.

Jesus promises that we will become fishers of men, but I have to confess that most of my attempts at one-to-one evangelism are sadly reminiscent of the Plass family's angling exploits. I think that, through my books, I can sometimes be the simplest sort of signpost, pointing people towards Jesus, but when it comes to the people next door I'm absolutely useless at talking about what I believe. This doesn't trouble me as it used to.

As a young Christian I got the idea that everyone ought to be evangelizing in just about every situation all the time, and an automatic pang of guilt hit me every time I bought a piece of cod in the fish shop and didn't offer salvation along with my one pound fifty. I think I was being very silly. Jesus promised the disciples that *he* would make them fishers of men, and, of course, they went on to do very specific jobs. Let's trust that he will give us the job that is right for us, whether it's up-front evangelism or something less overt but no less essential.

Prayer

Lord Jesus, we all want to be part of your promise that we can be fishers of men, but we also want to make sure that we're doing the job that is right for us. Give us either the courage or the humility that we need to accept the role that you've planned for us. Amen.

Fishers of men (part two)

Matthew 4:18–20 (NIV) (again)

A fishing disaster I failed to mention in my previous note was the dramatic occasion when one of us hooked a seagull. It wasn't funny at the time. We were horrified. These birds had been wheeling around us since our arrival at the estuary. They wanted our bait, which consisted of little frozen fish from a local shop. At every cast, one or two birds would swoop down hoping to capture the tasty snack on a hook. We thought they'd never be quick enough—but one was. He flapped triumphantly up with his prize in his beak, only to catapult back to the water as he reached the full extent of the line. We were distraught.

Hurriedly I cut the whole thing free next to the reel, and we watched the puzzled bird fly up again with endless nylon cord trailing from its beak. Finally, to our enormous relief, bait, hook and all got dislodged and dropped into the water. I began to wonder if someone was trying to say something...

Later that year I took my youngest son to a trout farm. Here they provided set-up tackle, buckets to put your catch in, and, most importantly, a lake full of fish whose one apparent aim in life was to be caught by the general public. Those fish were almost jumping out of the water in their eagerness to take our bait. At first it was wonderful. We caught seven good-sized fish in an hour! Unheard of!

Was it the lorry arriving to dump vast quantities of replacement stock into the lake that put us off a bit after that? These fish had obviously been raised on the sweetcorn provided to us for use as bait. As far as the trusting incoming fish were concerned it was simply lunchtime in a different place. We took our seven fish home and grilled and ate them, but we couldn't think of ourselves as proper anglers. Those fish were not wild fish—those fish were in captivity before we caught them...

The trout farm reminds me of an awful lot of evangelism that I've encountered. All over this country converted Christians have the gospel preached to them every Sunday whether or not they need it or like it—placid fish volunteering to be caught yet again by those who want to feel like real fishermen.

Perhaps genuine evangelism is going to be rather more like the Plass family's experiences of angling. You might have a few disasters as you learn patience and technique, you might have to stand faithfully by strange waters that are 'known' to be a waste of time—you might even catch the odd seagull by mistake, but at least you'll know that you are fishing where the wild fish are, and that when you catch something it'll be worth it.

Prayer
Give us the courage to fish in strange waters. Amen.

When?

Jeremiah 29:13 (NIV)

'You will seek me and find me when you seek me with all your heart.'

This verse has dogged me for years. Why? Well, I suppose because it asks a question of me that I have never satisfactorily answered. I am always, like Goethe on his deathbed, crying, 'More light—more light!', but when opportunities come, am I prepared to seek God and the knowledge of God with my whole heart? Do I even really know what that means? The merest glance at my performance so far is not too encouraging.

Take me when it's late at night, for instance. Quite often I'll be the last one to bed, because I've sat up in my favourite armchair watching some obscure sporting contest. God is probably sitting in the other armchair getting very bored and sleepy. Round about midnight it suddenly occurs to me that there's a burning issue in my life, and I really need to discuss it with God. So vital is the issue that I *almost* turn the television off, but not quite. When the next commercial break comes, however, I finally get round to doing something dynamic—I turn the sound down. Hurriedly, I outline my problem or concern to God, still keeping one eye on the screen because I don't want to miss any of the Ukrainian formation chisel-balancing championship quarter-final if I can help it.

As the programme comes back on I say something along the lines of, 'Well, I'll leave it with you,' and then it's up with the volume and back to the chisels.

A bit of a caricature, perhaps, but not so far from the truth, I'm afraid. When I *am* disciplined and committed to prayer—and I mean disciplined, not chained—the burdens that constitute my particular cross become no less heavy, but are more neatly packed. It's rather like using one properly organized rucksack instead of fifteen overfull plastic carrier bags that are about to break.

So, why am I still wrestling with the carrier bags? Oh, I don't know!

Prayer

Father, I'm well aware that you aren't going to stop loving me because I don't spend enough time and concentration on my communication with you. I hope we're all beginning to understand that the place we occupy in your heart doesn't require any kind of religious rent from us. On the other hand, we miss out on so much when we don't get close to you. Forgive us for those times when we fail actively to seek you. Help us to be wholehearted in all our dealings with you—even when there's something good on the telly. Amen.

Dining with the King **Revelation 3:19–20 (NIV)**

'Those whom I love I rebuke and discipline. So be earnest, and repent. Here I am! I stand at the door and knock. If anyone hears my voice and opens the door, I will come in and eat with him, and he with me.'

Regular readers of my vapid outpourings will be well aware that certain ideas occur in everything I write, and that eating—or rather, the enjoying of meals—is definitely one of those.

Allow me a little indulgence as I describe one or two of my favourite scenarios.

There's a country pub about three miles from where I live that, on a weekday evening in particular, is a real joy to visit. Settling down at one of the bar tables with a good friend, two wine-glasses, a bottle of house red and a large bowl of chips comes as close to heaven on earth as most things I've experienced.

It was in exactly this situation that a close friend of mine and I decided that if we saved, scraped, borrowed and schemed it might actually be feasible jointly to buy some kind of small property in France. A big decision for us, but now we've done it. We have a dumpy little cottage in Normandy, and it's wonderful.

Here's another scenario.

I have a friend who regularly takes me to speaking engagements and the like. I can't eat much before speaking, but afterwards we quite often find a restaurant (usually Indian) on the way home, and enjoy a late meal. It may not be good for the digestion, but I can tell you that it's pretty good for the soul. I would say that we talk at more depth and with more mutual benefit at those times than on any other occasion. Unforced fellowship—that's what I'd call it.

I could continue the list.

Bridget and I, for instance, love to eat out in some quiet place where we can be 'us', instead of us defined by our responsibilities. We need that so much. It isn't just the food, or the place, or the company that makes these times so enjoyable and meaningful—it's a rich mix of everything, and it goes very deep, way down into the heart of habit and history and tradition and the real meaning of things.

And look—Jesus, the same Jesus who cooked fish and ate breakfast with his friends on that wonderful Galilee morning 2,000 years ago, says to us today that, if we will open the door, he will come in, not to pray with us, not to worship with us, not to read the scriptures with us, not to supervise our quiet times, but to *eat* with us.

How clearly we recognize the authentic voice of Jesus, and what a pleasure to eat with him.

Prayer

Come in, Lord. Please sit down. Let's eat and talk together.

Wanting to want to please him

Malachi 3:10 (NIV)

'Bring the whole tithe into the storehouse, that there may be food in my house. Test me in this,' says the Lord Almighty, 'and see if I will not throw open the floodgates of heaven and pour out so much blessing that you will not have room enough for it.'

I made a very silly joke once, but it wasn't so silly that I don't feel able to pass it on to you. I was talking to my friend Hilary McDowell, whose excellent book, *Some Day I'm Gonna Fly* (she paid me twenty pounds to write something nice about her book) was published at the beginning of 1995. We were at a breakfast laid on by her publishers, SPCK (another twenty quid) to celebrate the launch of Hilary's first solo work and it was a great occasion.

Afterwards I said to Hilary, 'You know, if this book really takes off you ought to think seriously about getting yourself an agent to deal with future contracts and that sort of thing.'

'Ah, yes,' said Hilary euphorically, 'but the Lord is my agent.'

'Well,' I replied, 'that's great, but even he takes ten per cent. You might as well get someone who'll throw in the contract work.' Gosh, how we laughed.

Malachi is full of God's outrage at the attitude of Israel in the areas of sacrifice and worship, most powerfully perhaps where he complains bitterly that the animals being offered are second-rate, damaged ones that are considered too inferior to present to earthly rulers, but *will do* for the creator of the universe.

We get very hung up in the modern Church about tithing—whether one should give a tenth of net or gross income seems, incredibly, to be an absorbing, ongoing debate. It seems to me that, through Malachi, God is saying that what he wants is a radical change of attitude, not a meticulous adjustment of percentages that will ensure he's getting his 'cut'.

God wants us to *want* to give extravagantly to him in terms of time and love and care for others, quite apart from purely financial giving. He longs for us to desire to offer him our very best, not the fag-ends of what we have and what we are, and it is this extravagant opening of the heart that will cause him to throw open the floodgates of heaven and pour out blessings. Beware, though—if your heart changes, so will your idea of what constitutes a decent reward...

A suggestion

Let's read the story of the rich young man again (Mark 10:17–23), and ask ourselves what Jesus would have told us to exchange for treasure in heaven. Would my face have fallen? Would I have gone away sorrowing?

Whose approval?

Matthew 6:3–4 (NIV)

'But when you give to the needy, do not let your left hand know what your right hand is doing, so that your giving may be in secret. Then your Father, who sees what is done in secret, will reward you.'

Giving secretly is not easy for mere mortals like me. I always like *someone* to know, don't you?

This very challenging (and annoying) passage roots around at the base of our faith like a very determined dog after a bone. Will that dog's snuffling activities uncover some foundations down there, or will it become clear that the structure of what we believe is far less stable than we thought? Because, dear reader, a very simple question is being asked here, and the answer to that question, whatever it happens to be for you and me as individuals, needs to be faced if we are to claim any reality for our faith. The question boils down to this: Is my belief in the presence of God real enough, close enough, and personal enough to motivate giving or prayer or acts of kindness without the need to receive 'applause' from anyone else?

This is really a question about relationship, isn't it? Do I need to tell someone else if I send some flowers to my wife when I'm away from home? No, I don't, because I can imagine her pleasure on receiving them, and I look forward to the moment when we are reunited because then I shall actually see, hear and touch her response. That will be my reward and it will be enough. Whilst I'm away and going about my work I hug to myself the secret knowledge of what I've done, and—the crucial point this—I enjoy it as much as she does. (At this point my wife looks over my shoulder and comments that she could do with it happening a bit more often).

The points that Jesus makes here are fearsomely clear and uncompromising. Whatever I do to attract the applause and approval of the world has no validity in the Father's eyes. Those things mean nothing. The things that I do in secret and that spring from a genuine desire to please him will be rewarded. But don't lose heart if your answer to that essential question left you feeling a bit depressed. I didn't come out of it too well either. Let's talk to God about it—he really is very nice...

Prayer

Father, some of us fall very short of the mark when it comes to the reality of our relationship with you. We want to value you and love you so much that our only concern is your approval, but we're not there yet. Teach us and hold us for as long as it takes. Amen.

My friend

Luke 23:34 (NIV)

Jesus said, 'Father, forgive them, for they do not know what they are doing.' And they divided up his clothes by casting lots.

Some people reckon that when Jesus said these words he was asking God to forgive all of us for our corporate sin in putting him on the cross as we did then, and as we have continued to do again and again and again ever since. Well, that makes sense, of course, but it's wrong. God told me it was wrong last night. He didn't really, but I wish he had, because it would support what I think.

You see, I think Jesus was a very immediate sort of character, and when you're having nails driven into your hands and you're an immediate sort of character, you tend not to produce carefully formulated prayers concerning the corporate sin of mankind. The interesting thing is that if the response is localized, it actually has a more powerful implication for all of us.

It almost sounds as though Jesus had a sudden, awe-inspiring awareness of the vengeful fury his Father was feeling towards the men who were wielding those murderous hammers on his beloved Son's hands and feet. Hurriedly he throws up a preventative prayer to make sure that they don't get thunderbolted before they have a chance to be saved by the very event that they were preparing Jesus for.

Those men must have approached the gates of heaven with a certain trepidation, to say the least. Perhaps the duty angel recognized them and frowned as he mentally replayed the scene in which they had played such a brutal part. Perhaps he whistled up a few of his mates and they all stood with folded arms, ranging themselves in a solid, accusing phalanx in front of the gates, silently conveying the message that if these killers of the Son of God thought they were coming in they could think again. And perhaps, just as those men turned away guiltily, Jesus himself broke through the ranks of angels and cried out, 'What are you doing? These are my friends—let them in. I've been so looking forward to seeing them...'

I'm sure this is a foul slur on angels, but they'll be able to get me later. The point is that I have to approach the gates of heaven one day as well, and I don't think I'll be waving an insurance policy called The Salvation Plan. I think—I know—that I'll be craning my neck to catch a sight of Jesus, my friend, who has promised to forgive the particular sins that are *mine*, and who will, without doubt, keep his promise.

Prayer

Father, forgive us, we don't know how much we hurt you...

Getting clean

Luke 7:47–48 (NIV)

'Therefore, I tell you, her many sins have been forgiven—for she loved much. But he who has been forgiven little loves little.' Then Jesus said to her, 'Your sins are forgiven.'

Do read the whole of this story. It begins at verse 36, and it embodies one of the greatest promises of all, a promise so familiar, and yet so difficult to believe for oneself, that it is easily overlooked or avoided.

Jesus *will* forgive our sins.

I've always been vaguely grateful to the woman in this story for showing me so clearly that real repentance will involve two important things. First, having recognized the authoritative personality of Jesus and his claims on our lives, we are likely to feel deeply sad and sorry that we are not as he would like us to be. Secondly, though, and this is so important, we *will want* to express this to him. And please don't be put off by those who say that feelings are to be avoided at all cost. People who say that may have a bit of a point—sometimes—but just look at the state of this poor woman, for goodness' sake! She is absolutely devastated by the knowledge that God knows and is affected by what she does and what she is.

Mustn't it have been unutterably wonderful when, after supporting her in front of this stuffy old big-wig, Jesus turned to her and very simply told her that everything was going to be all right because her sins were forgiven? The only one in the world who had the power and the authority to make her clean had, with four life-changing words, done exactly that. No emotion? Who's kidding who?

Would you like to feel that clean?

Let us pray

Lord Jesus, there are things in our lives, past and present, that make us feel wretched and sad. You know what they are. You're the only one who knows about some of them.

(Tell him about the particular things in your life—go on, there's no one else listening. If you get all upset it's not the end of the world. Tell him now...)

Jesus, that woman in today's reading heard your voice clearly saying that she was forgiven and made clean. Some of us are not very good at hearing your voice, and some of us don't believe it's really possible, but would you please help us to achieve anything from a tiny gleam to a blinding flash of awareness that you do indeed forgive us in exactly the same way? Thank you, Lord Jesus. Amen.

The second death

Revelation 2:10–11 (NIV)

Do not be afraid of what you are about to suffer. I tell you, the devil will put some of you in prison to test you, and you will suffer persecution for ten days. Be faithful, even to the point of death, and I will give you the crown of life. He who has an ear, let him hear what the Spirit says to the churches. He who overcomes will not be hurt at all by the second death.

A friend of mine came round fairly late one night for a coffee and a chat. He leads quite a large church in the next town, and he was a bit low on this occasion. A member of his church, a forty-year-old married man with three children, had collapsed and died earlier in the week.

'The thing is,' said my friend, 'there was no warning of any kind, no preparation possible. One minute he seemed to be as fit as a fiddle, and the next minute—gone.' He shook his head. 'I just seemed to run out of things to say this time.' He sat back and stared at the ceiling for a moment. 'I wonder if any research has ever been done on whether Christians have lower incidence of accidental or sudden death than other groups. I must say, despite all the stuff about counting the hairs on our heads, it looks exactly the same to me.'

I felt a lot of sympathy for my friend, and for the family who are hurting so much, but I also felt that much of the teaching about suffering that we receive is blinkered and blinkering, if I can put it like that. Suffering has *always* been a part of Christian living, beginning with Jesus and continuing to the present day in the lives of ordinary people like this young widow and her children. It's horrible, but let's not pretend that it doesn't happen. Christians appear to be afflicted by exactly the same things as everyone else. The difference is that Jesus inhabits our suffering and pain as well as our joys. He is in it with us.

Sometimes, certainly, God will intervene to remove suffering, but perhaps we should focus on the fact that he also intervenes to *not* remove suffering, and if *he* doesn't know what he's doing we've had it! He holds the most valuable part of us in the palm of his hand, and no one can harm or steal that part.

He asked the Christians in Smyrna to be faithful even to the point of death. Like them, the man who died this week will not be hurt at all by the second death. At the moment that won't be much help to those who loved him, but by the time he is reunited with his family they will realize that this was always the most important thing of all.

Prayer

Father, Jesus never said it would be easy, but he promised to be with us always. Help us to trust you whatever happens.

Unconditional love

Romans 8:38–39 (NIV)

For I am convinced that neither death nor life, neither angels nor demons, neither the present nor the future, nor any powers, neither height nor depth, nor anything else in all creation, will be able to separate us from the love of God that is in Christ Jesus our Lord.

These are very grand, stirring words, aren't they? The promise they contain is exactly what most of us (me included) want to hear, but there was a time when I felt sick every time I heard them because they sounded so hollow and meaningless to my ears. Why was that? Well, I was going through a difficult time, and confidence in God was part of those difficulties. Someone would read out a verse like the one quoted above, speak about the unchanging, never-ending love of God, then, a little later quote some other verse that apparently indicated the ease and finality with which any one of us could separate ourselves from God. It used to drive me mad. Since then, I've met other Christians, especially those whose confidence is never very high anyway, who are puzzled by the way in which this paradox is trotted out so readily by people who haven't really thought it through. For all those people (and for myself) here are a few humble(ish) observations.

God loves us without any condition whatsoever. Whatever we are or aren't—whatever we do or don't do, he will go on loving us just the same. Consider the story of the prodigal son. Could anything be more transparently clear than the passion with which this father regards the son who has left home. Let me spell it out.

Even as the prodigal was in the act of sleeping with prostitutes and pursuing whatever other vile activities he was engaged in, his father, knowing full well the sort of thing he was doing, was loving him and watching out for his return and planning the kind of celebration that would accompany that return. Do we honestly think that this consistency and depth of love and affection is going to be changed or reduced by lapses and mistakes made by the prodigal *after* he has returned home? Don't misunderstand me, I don't mean that we have a licence to sin. What I'm trying to convey is that this whole thing—this whole salvation/Jesus/crucifixion/resurrection/repentance/heaven *thing* is God's idea and initiative. He so loved the world...

Prayer

Father, thank you for the passionate, eternal love you offer us. Perhaps some of us have drifted away from home again. Call us back—help us to remember what Jesus told us about you. Amen.

A burst of colour

Genesis 9:13–15 (NIV)

I have set my rainbow in the clouds, and it will be the sign of the covenant between me and the earth. Whenever I bring clouds over the earth and the rainbow appears in the clouds, I will remember my covenant between me and you and all living creatures of every kind. Never again will the waters become a flood to destroy all life.

The rainbow guarantees that our world will never again be covered in water. This is good news, of course (although it can't be much comfort to those whose small corner of the world is destroyed by local flooding), but I think the rainbow promises much more than that.

It might be seen as a declaration that God has permanently abandoned the idea of wiping out humanity—a commitment, if you like, to working with the problem rather than against it. This promise has been kept. The life and death of Jesus is powerful evidence of the depth of that commitment. Nothing could be more important.

A less obvious interpretation of the rainbow promise was suggested to me by the work my wife was doing with a junior class on the subject of 'Light'. It was rather fun looking through all the stuff about prisms and mirrors and experiments involving pieces of black card with holes cut in them. I remembered all sorts of things that I'd almost completely forgotten. Prominent among these was the fact, astonishing and frankly unconvincing to me when I was a small child at school, that light is not really white at all, but is actually a mixture of colours known as the spectrum.

*R*ichard *O*f *Y*ork *G*ave *B*attle *I*n *V*ain. Of course he did! Red, orange, yellow, green, blue, indigo and violet—the colours that, when spun rapidly together on a cardboard spinning top, became white, proving that our teacher's ridiculous claim was entirely justified.

The spectrum that we call the rainbow is a clue, a hint, a promise, a guarantee, that the love of God is not a single, unvaried beam of light shining impersonally on us all, but a veritable explosion of colours, one of which will be the exact wavelength of light needed to reach and illuminate the dark places in my heart and yours.

Next time rain and sunshine happen together, and you feel as if you're living in a washing-machine, look up, and see how God is offering you, individually, what we Anglicans would call the sign of peace—in glorious Technicolor.

Thought

Richard of York may have given battle in vain, but he did make a very solid contribution to junior science.

Something to look forward to

1 Corinthians 2:9 (NIV)

However, as it is written: 'No eye has seen, no ear has heard, no mind has conceived what God has prepared for those who love him.'

A group of us were talking about heaven. I was putting forward the view that the quality of eternal life will be much more closely linked to our lives on earth than we imagine. 'Surely,' I said, 'the essence of all those beautiful things in the world must be there because they're part of him and part of us. I reckon anything good and innocent and beautiful down here has a chance of surviving in some form up there. For instance, I fully expect to play cricket in heaven.'

'Well, I'm not going, then,' said one of the ladies spiritedly. 'If you think I'm going to watch cricket in heaven you've got another think coming. It already lasts forever down here.'

'No, no,' I protested, 'you won't have to. Each of us has got our own list of things that mean a lot to us. We won't have to get involved in anything we don't like.'

Most of us had contributed something to this enjoyable if highly speculative discussion, but there was one chap, called Jim, who had said nothing. Jim was a man who really loved Jesus, but his language and general conversation in this context tended to be abstract and rather unimaginatively Bible-based. He listened to our discussion with a little smile of gentle scepticism on his face.

'It's quite a thought, isn't it,' said someone else, 'that we might be allowed to do or have the very thing we've always wanted most and never been able to have?' I was just about to answer when I noticed the smile had gone from Jim's face. In its place was an expression of what appeared to be deep spiritual longing. Rarely have I seen anyone with as much of his heart in his eyes as I saw in Jim's at that very moment. Probably some Bible verse, I thought, that will neatly dismiss everything we've been saying. 'Penny for 'em, Jim,' I said.

'Oh!' He seemed to come to with a start. 'I was just thinking how much I've always wanted—' The far-away look came back into his eyes—'I was just thinking how absolutely wonderful it would be if he would let me have, well—a lathe of my own...' Somewhere in heaven a note was made.

Prayer

Father, we don't really know any of the details about heaven, but we do know that you love us and that you care for us as individuals. The verse we've read today seems to be full of your excitement about planning good things for us, and we would like to feel a little of that excitement ourselves. Help us to remember that you made heaven and earth. Amen.

Ever present

Matthew 28:19–20 (NIV)

'Therefore go and make disciples of all nations, baptising them in the name of the Father and of the Son and of the Holy Spirit, and teaching them to obey everything I have commanded you. And surely I am with you always, to the very end of the age.'

How do we react to the idea—the fact—that Jesus is with us always? Is it embarrassing, encouraging, alarming, or doesn't it mean very much at all because he's not actually visible?

I remember an occasion, recorded in fictional form elsewhere, but a very real part of my experience, when a member of our church who'd been asked to do the talk on this particular Sunday set an empty chair before the congregation and invited everybody to consider it carefully.

'Just suppose,' he said dramatically, 'that Jesus were to suddenly appear sitting in this chair. How would you feel? Wouldn't you be deeply worried? Wouldn't you want to run away and hide because you were ashamed of your sins? Wouldn't you decide to stay well out of the way until he'd gone?'

Well, how would that have made you feel? On this occasion I felt almost the exact opposite of what the speaker said I should. I don't mean that I would have welcomed the chance to see Jesus because I hadn't committed any sins—don't make me laugh! No, I just wanted to be with him. The thought almost made me weep. I wanted him to take charge and tell me what to do and make everything all right. And that's what I want now, even if I can't see him. I want him with me—always.

Thought

What if he had not been with us always? Have a look at Psalm 123.

I'll be back

John 14:1–3 (NIV)

'Do not let your hearts be troubled. Trust in God; trust also in me. In my Father's house are many rooms; if it were not so, I would have told you. I am going there to prepare a place for you. And if I go and prepare a place for you, I will come back and take you to be with me that you also may be where I am.'

Have you noticed how some rock stars like to dwell on the humbleness of their origins and the fact that underneath the glitz and glamour they're just ordinary folk like you and me? You sometimes see television programmes in which such folk visit their old haunts and pose with picturesque locals as if they'd never left. You almost get the feeling—and you're meant to, of course—that for two pins they'd move back into a little semi-detached house as near as possible to the one they grew up in. I suppose that might be true for one or two of them, but generally speaking—I don't think so! Most 'stars' also become very inaccessible, admittedly for the best of reasons. If your face is one that's known by everyone you'll guard your privacy at any cost—if you've got any sense.

But there never was a greater star than Jesus. He voluntarily left the place where he was seated beside his Father to begin a human life in the most humble fashion imaginable. When his ministry began at the age of thirty-three he chose ordinary people to accompany him and carry the message on after his death. He refused all offers to take personal advantage of the power which was his to command and direct, and in the end suffered an agonizing criminal's death, no doubt leaving those who even bothered to think about it with a clear conviction that whatever he'd intended to start was now well and truly finished.

The resurrection restored Jesus to the highest possible place, beside his Father again. Now was the time, if he had wanted to use his glory as most humans do, to forget his short life, his miserable death and the little people who for three years had followed him round that tiny corner of time and space that was Israel 2,000 years ago.

But he didn't. He doesn't. Jesus is the mega-star who doesn't stay separate, the top man who will never forget his friends, the multi-millionaire who wants to share. He busies himself preparing nice rooms for us. And one day, when everything's ready, he'll come and get us, and we shall live in his Father's house, and I suspect we shall have a bit of a party. You, who read this now—you'll be there.

Thought

He is coming back, you know...

A bit bland?

Revelation 21:3–4 (NIV)

And I heard a loud voice from the throne saying, 'Now the dwelling of God is with men... God himself will be with them and be their God. He will wipe every tear from their eyes. There will be no more death or mourning or crying or pain, for the old order of things has passed away.'

For those of us who suffer it's a wonderful thought that God will take out his divine hanky, dry our eyes and tell us to have a jolly good blow. A lovely concept, but it leaves me uneasy. I can't imagine life with no tears at all, can you? I'm not sure that existence without negative content is very appealing. I don't mean that I have a loony wish to be constantly miserable, and, let's face it, I live in a country with little lacking in physical comfort so I'm very spoilt anyway. I *like* being fed, clothed and generally happy.

No, my problem is that most of my inspiration for writing in general and poetry in particular has its roots in personal difficulty and pain. I enjoy the business of mining these seams of conflict, digging out the raw material of experience and extracting the truth that it invariably contains. What kind of life will it be where the spices of mood-change and confrontation and anger and forgiveness and debate and clash and Frank Bruno's attempts to regain the world championship are all missing? Won't it be rather bland?

Panic in heaven. God clutches his head, crying, 'Goodness me, yes, of course! It'll all be rather bland. Of course it will. Fancy Adrian Plass spotting a glaring error like that and me missing it completely. I've been *so* stupid! I'll have to start all over again...'

I reach out through the mist of my own foolishness for an answer, and it comes, as always, in the form of a question.

'On the rare occasions that you've enjoyed real shalom peace, the gift you've always wanted most, would you happily have exchanged it for a little more conflict and confrontation?'

'No, but—'

'Was there *anything* lacking in those moments?'

'No, but—'

'If I offered you that peace now and for ever would you take it?'

'Yes, but—'

'Well, I'm not going to.'

'Oh, but—'

'That's why you feel the need to transmute experience into poetry. It's unlikely that you'll achieve total peace this side of heaven.'

'What about the other side of heaven?'

'Precisely.'

Thought

Perhaps conflict is raw peace—much tastier when it's cooked and allowed to cool.

Inspiration

Matthew 25:34–40 (NIV)

'Then the King will say to those on his right, "Come... take your inheritance... For I was hungry and you gave me something to eat, I was thirsty and you gave me something to drink, I was a stranger and you invited me in, I needed clothes and you clothed me, I was sick and you looked after me, I was in prison and you came to visit me." Then the righteous will answer him, "Lord, when did we see you...?" The King will reply, "I tell you the truth, whatever you did for one of the least of these brothers of mine, you did for me."'

C.S. Lewis and G.K. Chesterton are my literary heroes. Both make words dance. Clarity, profundity and entertainment are hallmarks of their work. Recently, though, I found my old copy of *The Unutterable Beauty* by Studdert Kennedy, the Anglican clergyman nicknamed 'Woodbine Willie' because of his habit of handing out cigarettes in the trenches during the First World War. I bought this anthology of poems soon after conversion at the age of sixteen. The vulnerability and reality of some pieces impressed me no end. Here's an extract from 'It Is Not Finished':

I cannot read this writing of the years
My eyes are full of tears
It gets all blurred, and won't make sense
It's full of contradictions
Like the scribblings of a child,
Such wild, wild
Hopes, and longings as intense
As pain, which trivial deeds
Make folly of—or worse.
I can but hand it in, and hope
That Thy great mind, which reads
The writings of so many lives,
Will understand this scrawl
And what it strives to say—but leaves unsaid...

I met an elderly lady once who recalled how her father became too sick to earn money to feed his family for some weeks. 'Studdert Kennedy came round every day,' she said, 'with a pint of milk and a loaf of bread, and I sat on his knee while he chatted to mother and father. Mind you, I don't know how he managed it, because he gave away everything he'd got. My mother would see him going out in the morning in jacket and waistcoat, and come back later with just a shirt.'

Kennedy thought nothing of his own good deeds, and, for the sake of others, he was vulnerable to the point of rawness in his art—a good and faithful servant who long ago entered his Master's peace. I thank God for his example and inspiration.

Thought

Loving humility really is a beautiful rose.

A man in a passion rides a wild horse.
Benjamin Franklin

PASSIONATE PARENTING ON THE PATH TO PARADISE

Some reactions to Hosea

Dear Father,

I am addressing this letter to you at the beginning of my notes on Hosea, because writing them was such a strange, emotional experience, and because there is one thing about the content of this book that I simply cannot understand, however hard I try. Of course, the fact that there is something I can't understand is hardly an earth-shattering surprise—why on earth should I expect to grasp more than anyone else? But, you see, it's not that I'm craving theological insight, or spiritual vision, or exegetical illumination (that's what they have in Blackpool during Bible weeks, isn't it?—sorry), or anything like that. It's just that everything I've thought and felt as I've read about Hosea's unending struggle to make people comprehend the depth of your love, and the intensity of your hurt and anger, leads me towards one genuine and serious question:

HOW CAN YOU, THE CREATOR OF THE UNIVERSE, BE A PARENT *AND* A PERFECT BEING?

I hope you don't think this is an impertinent question, by the way. Some people find the way I speak to you quite unacceptable. They say I should be in awe of you, and that, if I was, I would never address you in such familiar tones. Well, I've got news for them. I *am* in awe of you. The last thing in the world that I would ever want to do is get on the wrong side of you, partly because it would frighten me, but also because I know that you love me, and I hate the idea that I might be responsible for hurting you. I treasure our relationship. The knowledge that it is this relationship between father and child that you have chosen to describe the way things should be between you and me, is something that I hold carefully in my hands like the most precious of jewels. And, to an extent, it helps me to understand you, because I have four children of my own (not quite as many as you've got, of course), and I've learned so much about you through having them. We have much more in common than I thought.

For instance, I have learned that when one of my children is really naughty the love I feel for them burns, if anything, more brightly than ever. Everything in me wants the rift to be healed as soon as peace with honour becomes possible. In the past I tended to think that you probably 'went off me' when I misbehaved, and that a good long period of perfect behaviour would be required before you unbent sufficiently to smile in my direction again. I'm sorry that I misjudged you so badly. I should have known, shouldn't I, just by reading the Bible, that you always were more than ready to forgive anyone who is truly sorry.

I've learned also about that razor-sharp knife that cuts into the very centre of a parent's heart when a child is hurt or unhappy or abandoned or disappointed, and there is no immediate means of solving their problems. I know now that you feel all those things, but far more intensely than I do, and the knowledge of that point of identification makes me want to put my arms around you to comfort and be comforted. Is that wrong? It doesn't feel wrong.

I've learned that all sorts of different things happen between a child and a parent. Sometimes I simply play with my daughter. We do ridiculous things together and laugh a lot and play silly tricks on one another. Sometimes I help her (or try to help her) with work she brings home from school. We sit at the kitchen table together, puzzling jointly over maths problems that seem to bear no relation at all to anything I ever tackled when I was being educated. From time to time I get cross with her, especially when she deliberately annoys her older brother and ignites one of those dreadful squealing, squabbling, bickering arguments that are based on nothing, but drive everyone else mad. Sometimes I go and look at her when she is fast asleep and think about how much I love her. And you do all these things with us, don't you, Father? You laugh with us, and teach us, and discipline us, and look on us with great love when we are at peace.

All these things I have learned about you through having my own children, and the knowledge that you and I feel the same things (albeit on such a different scale) is a source of warmth and reassurance.

But what about the differences between you and me, Father? In one of the poems that I've written for this section there's a line that says you are 'burdened with perfection and with passion'. How do you do it, Father? How do you do it? How do you deal with those storms of feeling, when you are not allowed (not able?) to sulk for a while, or to blow your top when it would have been better to go out of the room and come back in again, or to blame somebody else when it was your fault in the first place, or to seek solace in three fingers of whisky, or to blame your own parents and their parents before them for the problems that have actually been caused by your own poor parenting, or to make threats that you can't carry out and have to climb down from later on?

How can you, the creator of the universe, be a parent *and* a perfect being? In this book, the story of the prophet Hosea, I can feel great waves of love and anger pouring from you towards those infuriating Israelites who meant so much to you, and, as a parent myself, I, in my own feeble way, feel *so* sorry for you. And it's still going on with with us, isn't it?

Do you sometimes wish that you were not perfect?

Love,

Adrian

Vicious circle

Hosea 1:1 (NIV)

The word of the Lord that came to Hosea son of Beeri during the reigns of Uzziah, Jotham, Ahaz and Hezekiah, kings of Judah, and during the reign of Jeroboam son of Joash king of Israel.

Commentaries on Hosea speak of the difficulty involved in finding coherent meaning in the book as a whole, but it looks as if the prophet gave an ear-blasting to at least six different kings of Israel, so we're actually talking about a long and complex period in the nation's history. The repeated pattern of anger and forgiveness needs to be seen as happening over a period of many years.

What a pain in the neck this chap Hosea must have been. Every time those in authority—kings or priests—cobbled together some morally threadbare system designed to accommodate the sinful excesses of the people, a system that would necessarily exclude the one true God, along would come Hosea to 'spoil' everything by telling the truth.

Some marriages (not mine, of course) can be a bit like this. Paul Tournier speaks about some wives becoming 'policemen' in their husband's lives, continually wagging a metaphorical finger when their spouses stray from the straight and narrow. A relationship once full of tenderness and mutual idealism becomes cold and strained as love is transformed to disapproval on one side, and annoyed resentment on the other. The wife takes on a parental role in order to cope with her husband's regression to teenage-style awkwardness.

This is more or less what's happening here with God and Israel, at least, as far as Israel is concerned. The God who provided for their every need, passionately caring for them when they needed him most, has become an irritating interference, a nagging marital partner who is no longer wanted, or a preaching parent who wants to stop everybody from 'having a good time'. The vicious circle of disapproval and resentment, one that is very difficult to break out of, is expressed here in very human terms. Much of Hosea's message from God is filled with the desperate pain-filled fury that characterizes those who have been betrayed and neglected.

Frankly, I can't believe that Hosea was on many people's Passover-card list, and he'd be no more popular now than he was then, but, oh, how we could do with him in this age.

Pray

You loved us then, you love us now. Through Jesus you revealed that you are not a policeman, but a father. Forgive our neglect and draw us back to you, Father, so that we don't have to face your anger.

Family matters

Hosea 1:4–9 (NIV)

Then the Lord said to Hosea, 'Call him Jezreel, because I will soon punish the house of Jehu for the massacre at Jezreel, and I will put an end to the kingdom of Israel...' Gomer conceived again and gave birth to a daughter. Then the Lord said to Hosea, 'Call her Lo-Ruhamah, for I will no longer show love to the house of Israel...' Gomer had another son. Then the Lord said, 'Call him Lo-Ammi, for you are not my people, and I am not your God.'

Dear Miss Osborne,

Early contact with the family provides the following information:

Father is unemployed, but states, usually very loudly from the upstairs window of his house, that he is a mouthpiece for God. *Hosea the Prophet* claims that God instructed him to marry an adulterous woman and use their relationship as a sort of visual aid to illustrate people's religious shortcomings. This did not produce queues of eager applicants, but Hosea did—incredibly—find a willing candidate with the somewhat muppet-like name of *Gomer*, a member of the *Diblaim* family, who have been known to this office for a number of years.

Hosea then moved to the fathering of three offspring by Gomer, and it is their welfare that causes concern. Hosea's choice of names alone indicates that all three are at risk.

Jezreel, the oldest boy, is named after a bloody and brutally inhuman massacre, because he is the symbol of God's decision to destroy the whole community. This has not exactly endeared the boy to local residents.

The second child, a girl, is called *Lo-Ruhamah*, which means 'Not Loved', a further sign of God's refusal to forgive the world in general. Such a name is unlikely to enhance a developing child's self-confidence.

Lo-Ammi, the second son, completes the set, as it were. His title conveys a message from God to all and sundry that they are not his people and he is not their God. Lo-Ammi doesn't get many party invites.

I recommend a social worker be appointed immediately, as 'Hosea the Prophet' and Gomer seem incapable of understanding that the God Hosea claims to represent would never allow children to be subjected to the hardship that these three have endured.

Yours

Vic Stapley

Pray

Father, the Old Testament continually throws up things about you that I just won't—can't—don't want to accept, but lead us into all truth, whatever the truth turns out to be.

Practical forgiveness

Hosea 3:1–4 (NIV)

The Lord said to me, 'Go, show your love to your wife again, though she is... an adulteress. Love her as the Lord loves the Israelites, though they turn to other gods...' So I bought her for fifteen shekels of silver and about a homer and a lethek of barley. Then I told her, 'You are to live with me for many days; you must not be a prostitute or be intimate with any man...' For the Israelites will live for many days without king or prince...

Defining forgiveness and working out how you actually do it is an ongoing preoccupation of many Christians, as you will have noticed in my introduction to the section on James. Those of us who try to follow Jesus are all too aware that we are directly commanded to forgive those who hurt us. When Peter asked his master how many times he was supposed to forgive his brother he probably assumed the answer would be something like, 'Well, two or three's more than enough—four at the most...' In fact, of course, as we all know, Jesus said that Peter should forgive 'unto seventy times seven', and he didn't mean that, having put up with your brother annoying you four hundred and ninety times, you were then free to smack him in the mouth. Forgiveness is meant to be for ever.

But isn't it difficult?

The experience many of us have is that we really try hard to change the way we feel about someone who's wronged us, and perhaps feel that we've succeeded, only to discover that all the old bitterness and anger comes flowing back when we least expect it. I suspect the reason for this is that 'being a Christian' tends to be a rather cerebral business nowadays. God is very practical, and, contrary to the belief of many, practicality and spirituality are not mutually exclusive. Read the book of James.

Hosea was commanded, not just to forgive Gomer, but to buy her back and physically reinstate her as his wife, even though she had committed adultery. Forgiveness would occur within the framework of this practical act of reinstatement, an act that was dependent, not on Hosea's feelings about his wife, but on his obedience to the will of God. Perhaps, if we can, by an act of obedience, allow or actively draw those who have injured us into areas of our lives where we would really rather not have them, the business of forgiveness will have a chance to become real. I'm not for one moment claiming that it will be easy, but then, whoever started the ridiculous rumour that it would?

Questions not to be avoided

Who have I not forgiven? What can I do?

Hurting the land

Hosea 4:1–3 (NIV)

The Lord has a charge to bring against you who live in the land: 'There is no faithfulness, no love, no acknowledgment of God in the land. There is only cursing, lying and murder, stealing and adultery; they break all bounds, and bloodshed follows bloodshed. Because of this the land mourns, and all who live in it waste away; the beasts of the field and the birds of the air and the fish of the sea are dying.'

Nothing changes much, does it? The first two verses could easily be describing the moral decline that seems to be common to all so-called civilized nations at present, and the third reflects the concerns and warnings constantly expressed by those who feel that the natural environment is in real danger of being damaged and misused by us.

Sometimes, you know, a deep, dark pool of fear is stirred in me. It happens when I face the fact that our society does not, by and large, give any credence to the idea that an all-powerful God will eventually react to this general decline. 'There is no acknowledgment of God in the land', says Hosea in this passage, and if anyone is looking for a strong theme on which to pray, this may well be it. Pray that more and more people will discover the missing piece of the jigsaw that makes sense of the whole picture. Pray that the terrible distortion of God's image that we as Christians are responsible for will not obscure the truth. Pray for healing in this increasingly immoral society and in the natural world. Pray that, at last, God will be acknowledged in the land.

Don't you find it interesting that God links death and decay in nature with moral and spiritual decline? What can he possibly mean by saying that 'the land mourns'? The New Testament view is that the whole of creation groans as it waits for redemption. Apparently everything that exists is from God, is linked with God, and is indivisibly part of his total creation. Somehow—and I certainly don't understand this—the pain and sin or elation and virtue that enter into our lives are registered in the very rocks themselves, and in the seas that surround us. We don't begin to comprehend the nature and complexity of this masterpiece of God's, but perhaps that ignorance is quite a good place to start.

Consider

Jesus tells us that there is great rejoicing in heaven over one sinner who repents, and that rejoicing permeates the physical world as well. Likewise, when we perform some small selfish act, the vibrations, however small, will be felt everywhere. Let's work towards a wider acknowledgment of God, and give the land a break.

Prophets and priests

Hosea 4:7–9 (NIV)

The more the priests increased, the more they sinned against me; they exchanged their Glory for something disgraceful. They feed on the sins of my people and relish their wickedness. And it will be: Like people, like priests. I will punish both of them for their ways and repay them for their deeds.

One morning I received an extraordinary letter from a Christian hotel in an exotic part of the world. After reading the first couple of paragraphs I laughed loudly, and Bridget looked enquiringly at me over the top of her coffee mug.

'I've been invited to be "Prophet in Residence" at a holiday hotel,' I said.

Bridget laughed at the title, but when I told her where the hotel was located her eyes reflected the greedy gleam in mine. Miraculously, we both felt strongly guided to accept the offer of a free holiday on this tropical island, one that we'd always wanted to visit. Alas, as I read on, I discovered that (rather surprisingly) I was expected to pay all my own travel expenses, a condition which abruptly ended my dreams of enjoying sun-soaked relaxation in exchange for the occasional, gently benevolent prophecy to my fellow residents.

'Oh, well', said Bridget, looking disappointed, 'you're not a prophet, so you couldn't have done it anyway.'

I nodded resignedly and reached for the marmalade.

I forgot all about it until fairly recently when a friend asked me quite seriously if I thought I was a prophet or not. My immediate reaction was to snort sardonically, but he persisted, so I said that apart from one or two isolated occasions, I had never been aware of God literally speaking through me. Later I reviewed what I'd said, and was a little horrified when I thought about how much (considering my non-prophet status) I've talked and written *about* God. What a cheek! In any case, I reflected, all Christians are priests nowadays, according to scripture, so the responsibility for what we say to others, and the way we represent our faith, is enormous, whoever we are.

I went all hot and cold as I remembered some of my verbal excesses—and this passage from Hosea hasn't helped much. God seems to be saying that the priests of Israel had completely misused the power that they held—instead of representing the ways and the will of God, they were, for their own benefit, fitting in with what sinful people wanted.

It can happen in such a way...

Prayer

Father, whether we're prophets or priests, help us to make sure when we talk to others about you, that we are speaking for you, and not for us.

Turning round

Hosea 4:12 (NIV)

... They consult a wooden idol and are answered by a stick of wood. A spirit of prostitution leads them astray; they are unfaithful to their God.

Here is an extract from a conversation I had with an old friend whom I shall call 'Rita'. Rita is one of those people in whose world everyone appears to make one physical revolution before speaking. Rita made us a pot of tea, then she sat down and said (after turning round, of course), 'I was out with Plank an' Emma last night, an' she was saying—'

Me: Plank?

Rita: Plank an' Emma, yea, an' she was saying—

Me: Plank? How can anyone be called Plank?

Rita: He just is. That's his name. What?

Me: It just seems a bit of an odd name. He can't have been christened Plank, surely?

(We both turn round before continuing our conversation)

Rita: Oh, no, his actual name's Ricky, but we all call him Plank.

Me: Yes, but why?

Rita: 'Cos he's thick.

Me: Ah! As in two short... yes, I see. And he doesn't mind?

Rita: No, you call him Ricky and he won't even turn round, but if you call him Plank he says, 'Yea, what?' He knows he's thick, see?

Me: I see.

Rita: Anyway, Emma turned round an' she said to me...

Whatever these Israelites were called, God must have been tempted to call each one 'Plank'. People made in the image God—indeed, a *particular* people rescued, nurtured and protected by him—had put its faith in wooden idols. Planks seeking revelation from planks. How could they have been so thick?

Where there is sin and self-absorption and no genuine will for change, it is virtually impossible to meet the eye of one who will never dilute his response to evil. Later, God complains that people do not cry out to him from their hearts, but 'wail upon their beds'. This reminds me of when I have persisted in deliberate sin, and paused only for long enough to moan that God isn't interested in me any more—you know the sort of thing I mean. No hint of repentance, just the complaint that I'm not allowed to have my self-indulgent cake topped with the icing of spiritual comfort. It's a small step from there to 'Plank Allegiance', and then nothing will go right until, like Rita's friends, we turn round and say something (from the heart) to God.

Prayer

We take the risk of turning to you, Father, because we know that not doing so is a much greater risk.

Religion and relaxation **Hosea 6:6 (NIV)**

For I desire mercy, not sacrifice, and acknowledgment of God rather than burnt offerings.

Some years ago I wrote a book called *Broken Windows, Broken Lives*, a fictional account of my experiences as a residential worker in a boarding-school for maladjusted boys. That horrible word 'maladjusted' simply meant that these children were unable to cope with the situations they had found themselves in. My job as Housefather was to look after the daily physical and emotional needs of about twenty-five of these kids, half the school in fact. I was twenty-one, and the fact that I thought I could do the job shows how naïve I must have been.

At first it all looked terribly easy. I accompanied an experienced member of staff called Bob as he woke the children, supervised showers and dressing, joined them for breakfast, and checked the small domestic tasks that each one performed before school-time. It all looked so relaxed and effortless. The boys were fully cooperative at every stage, and Bob never needed to raise his voice, let alone get cross. They just—did it. I remember, on that first morning, hearing screamed orders and swearing coming from the other side of the house, and congratulating myself on being on the side where the pleasant children were. I did just wonder why they'd put all the nice children on one side and all the difficult ones on the other...

The next morning, the first one on my own, I thought they must have switched the groups of boys around. But they hadn't. It was the altered staffing that made the difference. Where there had been cooperation and friendliness there was resentment and argument, where there had been calm there was loud noise and chaos, and where there had been willingness and industry there was laziness and grumbling. I hated it. To make matters worse, those on the other side, now looked after by Bob, had been transfigured, and were behaving like little angels.

I went through a long, painful period of instituting procedures, rules, fixed penalties and other aids to gaining control. The reaction of my charges was negative and grudging, and it was a very long time before I came anywhere near acquiring Bob's deceptively relaxed style of supervision, but I was so relieved when, eventually, temporary structures could be replaced by genuine relationship. Why, oh, why, did it take them so long to understand that I cared for them?

Prayer

Why, oh, why does it take us so long to understand that you care for us? Roll on the day when religion rolls away.

Pooh-sticks

Hosea 10:7 (NIV)

Samaria and its king will float away like a twig on the surface of the waters.

Have you ever played Pooh-sticks? A.A. Milne invented it, and it's very simple. You stand with someone else on a bridge over a river or a stream, and you each throw a stick into the water. Then you hurry to the other side of the bridge, and the person whose stick comes floating through first is the winner. It doesn't call for any great skill, but our family has always enjoyed it, particularly when the children were small. The bridge we especially like is on the outskirts of Alfriston, a beautiful old village set among the Downs, a few miles from where we live. You must go and see it if you haven't already.

In this passage God is saying through Hosea that he is capable of causing the most powerful nations, people and institutions to simply float away and disappear like one of those Pooh-stick twigs. You and I might find this fact very depressing or extremely encouraging, depending on what our 'twig' happens to be.

We might think it depressing, for instance, that money, or looks, or power, or human achievement, or life itself, or any of the other things that the world offers can be removed and discounted with such casual despatch. Many of us have invested everything we have and are and hope for in such trifles. The image of God leaning over a parapet and dropping our precious bundle of things into a slow-moving inexorable current that will take them away for ever is not an attractive one.

On the other hand, if our priorities have been rightly adjusted, we might be mightily heartened by the fact that he is just as capable of taking our blackest sins and sorrows—nasty charred old bits of wood, if you like—and dropping them with equal abandonment into the moving stream. If we then hurry across the bridge we shall be in time to see them come out on the other side, and we can watch as they become smaller and smaller before disappearing altogether in the far distance.

An exercise

Play Pooh-sticks with God. Stand beside him on the bridge and, with due consideration, hand him the things that you want to get rid of, one by one. When they've all gone, rush across with him and watch them float away. Then, I suggest that you walk off the bridge, across the green, and into Alfriston to celebrate, possibly with one of their very good cream teas...

Looking back

Hosea 11:1–4 (NIV)

'When Israel was a child, I loved him, and out of Egypt I called my son. But the more I called Israel, the further they went from me. They sacrificed to the Baals... It was I who taught Ephraim to walk... but they did not realise it was I who healed them. I led them with cords of human kindness, with ties of love; I lifted the yoke from their neck and bent down to feed them.

The person who wrote this passage must have been chosen by God because he knew what it was like to have difficult or rebellious teenage children (sorry—that's a tautology, isn't it?).

It may be foolish fancy, but I picture God sitting at home in an armchair flicking through old photograph albums in which his rescue of the children of Israel from Egypt is recorded. I've done the same sort of thing myself, sighed and wiped away the beginnings of a tear as those carefully preserved snapshots remind me of when my children were so dependent on Bridget and me for their most basic physical needs, that there was no question of division or serious conflict between us. We looked after them and they cuddled us—that was more or less the deal. As they get older, the loss (temporary though it usually is) of that simple arrangement can come close to breaking a parent's heart. This change in relationship is actually the door to a different but equally profound closeness, as long as we mothers and fathers will walk willingly through the door and close it firmly behind us, but the pain of the process can be unbearable sometimes.

Here is God the Father, then, cooing over the first tottering steps of his little ones, recalling the pleasure with which he healed them, fed them and removed obstacles from their path, but, at the same time, shaking his head in anguished disbelief over the fact that those same cherished children have now put their trust in other, man-made gods, and forgotten the one who loves them with genuine power and passion.

I don't want to appear disrespectful, but, as far as the pain is concerned, he sounds just like me, and I find that rather helpful. If God really does regard me with anything like the same torrential love as I regard my own children (and, of course, that's an understatement) then I probably hurt him far more than I have realized when I ignore him and turn to the alien gods who inhabit this little corner of the twentieth century. We are used to the idea of God being angry, but how will we react to the knowledge that he is hurt?

Prayer

Father, we have hurt you. Forgive us, and let us be close again.

Just for now

Hosea 11:8–11 (NIV)

'How can I give you up, Ephraim? How can I hand you over, Israel? How can I treat you like Admah? How can I make you like Zeboiim? My heart is changed within me; all my compassion is aroused. I will not carry out my fierce anger, nor will I turn and devastate Ephraim. For I am God, and not man—the Holy One among you. I will not come in wrath. They will follow the Lord; he will roar like a lion. When he roars, his children will come trembling from the west. They will come trembling like birds from Egypt, like doves from Assyria. I will settle them in their homes,' declares the Lord.

Forgive us if we say
We want to take you in our arms
Sad Father, weeping God
Breathless with the storms
Of anger—of compassion
Fists clenched hard around your grief
Around the marks
The cost
The proof
How can you give us up?
How can you hand us over?
Of course you never can
Never could
Never will
Burdened with perfection and with passion
Lay your head down
Let us hold you for a while
We will try to be to you
What you have been to us so many times
Peace, Lord, be a child once again
Do you remember Mary's arms?
So warm
So different
Rest quietly and soon you will be strong enough
To be a lion thundering from way beyond the east
We will come trembling from the west
We promise you
Like birds
Like doves
Like children who have suddenly remembered
Who taught them how to laugh

But just for now
Forgive us if we say
We want to take you in our arms
Sad Father, weeping God.

Free love

Hosea 13:4–7 (NIV)

But I am the Lord your God, who brought you out of Egypt. You shall acknowledge no God but me, no Saviour except me. I cared for you in the desert, in the land of burning heat. When I fed them, they were satisfied; when they were satisfied, they became proud; then they forgot me. So I will come upon them like a lion, like a leopard I will lurk by the path.

If I wanted I could take the light
One shining sheet of paper
Crush it in my fist
And so, it would be night
If I was so inclined
I could destroy the day with fire
Warm my hands at all your charred tomorrows
With the smallest movement of my arm
One flicker of my will
Sweep you and all your darkness from the land
But I cannot make you love me
I cannot make you love me
I cannot make you, will not make you, cannot make you
love me
If I wanted I could lift the sea
As if it was a turquoise table-cloth
Uncover lost forgotten things
Unwritten history
It would be easy to revive the bones
Of men who never thought to see their homes again
I have revived one shipwrecked man in such a way
The tale of that rescuing
That coming home
Might prove I care for you
But though I can inscribe I LOVE YOU
on the sea and in the sky
I cannot make you love me
I cannot make you love me
I cannot make you, will not make you, cannot make you
love me.

Hosea-fied?

Hosea 13:16; 14:4–6 (NIV)

'The people of Samaria must bear their guilt, because they have rebelled against their God. They will fall by the sword; their little ones will be dashed to the ground, their pregnant women ripped open... I will heal their waywardness and love them freely, for my anger has turned away from them. I will be like the dew to Israel; he will blossom like a lily.

The vivid contrast between these two passages is a recurring feature of much of the Old Testament. God appears to swing wildly from crashing, vengeful fury to warm, compassionate forgiveness with bewildering swiftness. I asked someone else to tell me honestly what they thought about the personality that seems to be revealed here. I needed to because I couldn't quite focus on what I thought myself. It's difficult to face one's own response to some of these passages because each response passes through the sieve of religious conditioning. I have to give myself *permission* to look at what I really think.

'Well,' said my friend, wrestling inwardly, but, unlike me, determinedly pinning half-truth to the floor, 'he comes over as rather immature, doesn't he? I mean, he's doing all the things that teachers and parents are told they should never do—making huge threats and then not carrying them out, getting murderously angry and then going all sort of sentimental. That's how I see it. Bound to be wrong, of course.'

'Mmm...' I felt the same. This God didn't seem much like Jesus.

Well, here's a thought. It's only a thought. Don't unofficially excommunicate me. Discuss it—consider it.

Hosea marries a woman who turns out unfaithful and unstable. Hosea is a maritally loyal but emotionally immature fellow of extreme passions, who loves this wife of his, and her waywardness drives him into bouts of irrational fury, followed by tearful expressions of love and forgiveness. God, who is casting around for someone to convey to Israel his anger, his pain and his willingness to start again, decides to use this inadequate but (crucially) available vehicle, even if the message gets grossly Hosea-fied on the way through. Hosea decides that a little licence is allowable in the area of his reasons for marrying Gomer in the first place, and there we are. God filtered through man. Not the first time—and, I can assure you, certainly not the last.

Prayer

Forgive me if I'm up the creek here, Lord, but this is a real problem for a lot of us. What we do know is that Jesus is the living expression of you, and for that we are deeply thankful.

All sin is a kind of lying.

St Augustine

UNAUTHORIZED EXCURSIONS

The story of David and Bathsheba

Yes, that's right, we're talking about David; the same David who killed Goliath, the Philistine giant; the same David who slew lions and bears when he was just a shepherd boy looking after his father's sheep; the same David who played soothing harp music to the manic-depressive King Saul, and was later driven into exile by that insanely jealous king when he could no longer stand the chant of the Israeli people:

'Saul has killed his thousands and David his ten thousands!'

We are talking about David, who mourned for his closest friend, Jonathan, the son of Saul, when he died next to his father on the field of battle, and then came back to Jerusalem and was made king, years after the great prophet Samuel had anointed the young shepherd boy with oil and declared that, against all the odds, it would be so.

This is David, who brought the ark of God back to the holy city at last and danced with joy in front of it, and, when his first wife, Michal, mocked him, said:

'I was dancing before the Lord who chose me and appointed me as leader of Israel, the people of God. So I don't mind acting like a

fool in order to show my joy in the Lord. Yes, and I don't mind looking even more stupid than this.'

This is David, who was promised by God through the prophet Nathan that he would become one of the most famous people in the world.

David.

You know, David really loved God. He *really* loved him. He loved his generosity, couldn't understand why he showered blessings on someone who had started out as nothing, with nothing. He said:

'You know what I'm like. Why do you do it? Because you want to. Because you said you would. Well, go ahead, and—thank you.'

David was so well set up! Wives, concubines, children, property—he had everything. Fair to everyone, justice to all, that was David's style. A good king. God's man. Every battle, every campaign began with the same questions to God: 'Should I go? Is it right? What do *you* want?' And always, the questions were answered, and the battles, the campaigns—hugely successful.

All was well. Life was rich and fulfilling. Israel was in good hands. How could a man like David possibly go wrong?

Where is the battle? **2 Samuel 11:1–3 (NRSV)**

In the spring of the year, the time when kings go out to battle, David sent Joab with his officers and all Israel with him; they ravaged the Ammonites, and besieged Rabbah. But David remained at Jerusalem. It happened, late one afternoon, when David rose from his couch and was walking about on the roof of the king's house, that he saw from the roof a woman bathing; the woman was very beautiful. David sent someone to inquire about the woman. It was reported, 'This is Bathsheba... the wife of Uriah the Hittite.'

It is so easy to go wrong.

One night David took a walk on the palace roof. It was springtime, the battle season, the season when kings usually went to war. It was a beautiful night. The air was vibrant, electric. He had tried to sleep, but he was just unable to relax. Not surprising. The army was away under the leadership of the great Israeli general, Joab. Joab's brief was a simple one—destroy the Ammonites, and he had already begun by laying siege to the city of Rabbah.

Of course the king couldn't sleep! David, the soldier, the ex-guerilla leader, the commander, the man of action, must have been regretting his decision to stay home. He must have been itching to abandon the luxury of his palace, to be where he knew he belonged, out in the field with his fighting men. It would take something very powerful, very stimulating, to push these thoughts of blood and battle from his mind.

He strolled slowly along the edge of the palace roof, gazing out over the city lying quietly in the moonlight before him. Suddenly he stopped, his gaze fixed on the courtyard of a dwelling house not far from the royal residence. A woman was bathing. She was naked—beautiful, more beautiful than any woman he had ever seen. He wanted her. He sent a servant to find out who she was.

He wanted her.

Never mind that he had wives and concubines of his own. Never mind that this woman turned out to be the wife of Uriah, a loyal warrior, who, at this very moment was fighting under David's banner in the struggle to capture Rabbah.

He wanted her.

Her name was Bathsheba.

He burned for her, and he wanted her—now.

Prayer

Father, sometimes when we should be at the battle we stay home. Forgive us and protect us.

Self-delusion

2 Samuel 11:4 (NRSV)

So David sent messengers to fetch her, and she came to him, and he lay with her. (Now she was purifying herself after her period.) Then she returned to her house.

David didn't burn for long. He sent for Bathsheba that night. He slept with her that night. And in the morning he sent her home.

Now, this is where we part company with all those who have never done anything wrong, because they just won't understand. You see, David knew he had done wrong. Oh, yes! No doubt about that. He knew God's law as well as anyone else:

Thou shalt not commit adultery.

For commoners and kings alike the law was just the same, and he knew it. Probably for the first time in his life, David had deliberately left God out of the reckoning. Now that the deed had been done it occurred to him that it might be better to avoid Nathan the prophet for a time. The old man could have heard something on his hotline from God, and David had never been told off by God before.

Anyway, perhaps the whole thing would blow over soon. Was it such a terrible sin? He had wanted her so *much*. The very power of his feelings had somehow seemed to make it right at the time. And Uriah, the husband, need never know. Bathsheba and her servants were silenced by royal command. No problem there. Yes, perhaps it would just blow over, and later on he'd make his peace with God too—when the dust had settled, as it were. And when Uriah came back from the war, he'd give him a fine present—in appreciation of his soldierly feats, of course. Uriah would feel very honoured. Well, anybody would, wouldn't they? Bathsheba would like that too.

David could continue to be the great and good king, loved and respected by all. It had just been a silly slip, quite out of character. Surely he was allowed to make one mistake. He'd got so many things right, for goodness' sake! Granted, Nathan might not see it that way, but he needn't see him for a while. Yes, surely the whole thing would blow over soon.

Thus, David talked himself into an uneasy peace, but deep in his heart he knew with dark and lonely certainty that, for the time being at least, he had lost God and was on his own.

Prayer

Father, protect us from the dangerous self-delusion that sin doesn't really matter.

Webs

2 Samuel 11:5 (and read 6–11) (NRSV)

The woman conceived; and she sent and told David, 'I am pregnant.'

It didn't blow over. It got worse—much worse. One of Bathsheba's servants arrived at the palace. She had a message. She would speak only to the king. No, she would *not* speak to David's servant. Yes, she *must* speak to the king himself, with no others present. When she was finally ushered into his presence she could hardly bring herself to speak. David was kind to her—coaxed her. At last, she told him. Her mistress, Bathsheba, was pregnant. What did the king suggest?

What indeed?

White-lipped and tense with shock, David dismissed the girl and considered alternatives.

Tell all? Confess to Uriah when he returned? Call Nathan? Confess to God? Confess that good king David had stolen a fighting soldier's wife and used her casually for a night?

No! He was David! He could never bear to be less than the sum of rich qualities that his name had come to mean throughout the land of Judah and far beyond. Self-preservation, that was all that mattered right now. There was another way, and it could work. If Uriah were to sleep with his wife in the very near future, then everyone would assume that the baby, when it came, was his. But Uriah was at the war. Uriah was at Rabbah.

David summoned him, and, when he arrived a few days later, greeted him personally, asked how the battle was going, talked as one old soldier to another, shook him by the hand, sent him home for the night, sent a present to his house.

That night David slept. The nightmare was over—or so he thought.

Uriah, an honest captain of fighting men, and a stickler for the rules, had refused to stay in the comfort of his own home while his troops suffered hardship at the front. He slept by the palace door.

How his eyes must have shone as he explained to the king why he hadn't gone home. David would understand. He knew what it was like. He too was a leader of men. Of course he would understand.

Thought

Oh, what tangled webs we weave...

Into the darkness

2 Samuel 11:12–13 (NRSV)

Then David said to Uriah, 'Remain here today also, and tomorrow I will send you back.' So Uriah remained in Jerusalem that day. On the next day, David invited him to eat and drink in his presence and made him drunk; and in the evening he went out to lie on his couch with the servants of his lord, but he did not go down to his house.

How did you feel when you learned that your clever ploy with Uriah had failed to work, David? Did you feel ashamed, or did you just feel wild panic driving your mind to work, to plan, to find a way—any way—to remove the problem?

Did Uriah guess that all was not well? That night, when you entertained him again at the palace, feasted him well, made sure that he drank far too much, talked about war and wives, did he suspect that something else was going on—something that he couldn't quite understand? Because he didn't go home that night either, did he? He slept in the servants' room again.

I wonder, David, do you think Uriah slept easy that night, or did he suffer strange nightmares of pointless, bloody fighting and dying, of a woman running naked through a storm, of another battle fought with something other than swords—a battle that he had already lost without ever being given the chance to fight?

And what about you, David? Did you sleep on that second night of Uriah's stay? I bet you didn't. I bet you lay awake thinking and thinking and thinking—what do I do if he doesn't go home *again*? And in the morning, when you knew that Uriah was still there, still in the palace, when you knew that plan A was not going to work, was that when you finally faced the fact that, other than the confession you would not contemplate, there was only plan B left?

Uriah had to die, didn't he? You had reached the point where you couldn't care less what you had to do as long as your crime was concealed, even if it meant committing another, even worse crime to do it.

Prayer

Father, give those who are about to step into utter darkness the courage to turn back.

Dangerous safety

2 Samuel 11:14–16 (NRSV)

In the morning David wrote a letter to Joab, and sent it by the hand of Uriah. In the letter he wrote, 'Set Uriah in the forefront of the hardest fighting, and then draw back from him, so that he may be struck down and die.' As Joab was besieging the city, he assigned Uriah to the place where he knew there were valiant warriors.

The morning after Uriah's second night at the palace, you wrote a letter to Joab, field commander of the armed forces. Joab would do whatever he was told. He knew which side his bread was buttered on. Was any part of you sickened by the words you wrote in that letter, David? You remember the words, don't you? It was quite a short message really.

'Joab, place Uriah in the front line where the fighting is at its hottest, then draw back and leave him. I want him dead.'

And who delivered this instruction to Joab? No prizes for guessing. Good old trusting Uriah, wasn't it? Reported smartly back at camp to deliver his own death sentence. Went out to face the fiercest of the Rabbah defenders without question, and died at the foot of the city walls, puzzled by the sudden, unaccountable lack of support, but proud to give his life in the service of the king who had so generously wined and dined and talked intimately with him only a few short days ago.

Plan B worked like a dream, didn't it, David? And all you felt was relief. In the space of a few short weeks you had trained yourself to stay deaf to the once-familiar voice that said:

'Thou shalt not lie.
Thou shalt not covet.
Thou shalt not commit adultery.
Thou shalt not murder.'

Like so many people before and since, David discovered that after only a few steps into the swamp of deceit and cruelty, he almost forgot what it meant to be clean. He was safe—safe from the judgment of men, that is. Uriah was well and truly fixed. Time to relax? Maybe.

Thought

Being safe according to the world's terms can be very dangerous indeed.

Nails

2 Samuel 11:25 (NRSV)

David said to the messenger, 'Thus you shall say to Joab, "Do not let this matter trouble you, for the sword devours now one and now another; press your attack on the city, and overthrow it." And encourage him.'

Surely, in some remote corner of David's heart, as he pronounced these hollow words, the shepherd boy, the honourable soldier, the servant of the Lord, was in anguish—furious with himself and everyone else.

Was David looking for someone to blame? If so, I wonder if God was his first choice.

Didn't you mean what you said when you called me?
Didn't you mean it at all?
When I was young and you knew you enthralled me,
Did you know then I would fall?
I was so sure, I was sure I would never,
Never be parted from you,
I'm just a king who has taken his pleasure,
What did you think I would do?

Was it a lie? Did you deceive?
Do you not love me at all?
Better to die if I believe,
That you don't love me at all.
I get the picture, you're talking of murder,
Let's put a name to the crime!
But I never wanted to go any further,
And you weren't around at the time.

Let's not pretend I'm the only offender,
I'm only joining the queue,
No, don't try to tell me your love is so tender,
I am just spoiling your view.
Will you forgive? I need to know,
Can it all be like before?
How can I live if you say no,
If it can't be like before?

You won't forgive, You will say no,
No, it can't be like before,
Somehow I'll live when you say no,
No, it can't be like before.

Didn't you mean what you said when you called me?
Didn't you mean it at all?
When I was young and you knew you enthralled me,
Did you know then I would fall?
I wish I could know and be sure in the morning,
That you will be there when I call.

Thought

Before and after Calvary, the nails are constantly hammered in.

A sock in the jaw

2 Samuel 11:26–27 (and read 12:1–7) (NRSV)

When the wife of Uriah heard that her husband was dead, she made lamentation for him. When the mourning was over, David sent and brought her to his house, and she became his wife, and bore him a son. But the thing that David had done displeased the Lord.

Bathsheba mourned.

Yes, that's right. Bathsheba mourned for her dead husband. When the king of Israel sends for you to sleep with him, you don't send a note back saying, 'I'm not that sort of girl.' You have no choice. Bathsheba didn't give away anything. Her husband was dead. She mourned for him.

As for God being displeased—yes, you could put it like that. God must have been, at the very least, displeased. But, however angry he might have been, it was more than nine months since David's stroll on the palace roof, and so far, not a word from God—no sign of Nathan. Everything had settled down. Perhaps it *had* blown over.

As David warmed himself by the fire in a corner of the royal palace one night his mood matched the winter season—cold but settled. The fear had almost gone, but so had the joy. The baby was a great pleasure, but real happiness was rare, to say the least. Still, the panic had passed. It was possible to relax nowadays. Sometimes he almost managed to forget the nightmare events of last year. It really began to look as if there was to be no comeback—no punishment.

He hardly heard the servant announce a visitor, and when he did turn towards the door he was not particularly interested—until he saw who it was. Then, his stomach seemed to turn to ice, and the old fear gripped him tight, so that, for a moment, he could only stare dumbly at the figure standing in the doorway. It was Nathan.

How relieved David must have felt on discovering that Nathan had only come round to tell a little story, but what a sock in the jaw that punchline must have been!

Prayer

Sock it to us, if necessary, Lord.

Facing up

Psalm 51:1–12 (and read 13–19) (NRSV)

Have mercy on me, O God, according to your steadfast love; according to your abundant mercy blot out my transgressions. Wash me thoroughly from my iniquity, and cleanse me from my sin. For I know my transgressions, and my sin is ever before me. Against you, you alone, have I sinned, and done what is evil in your sight, so that you are justified in your sentence and blameless when you pass judgment. Indeed, I was born guilty, a sinner when my mother conceived me. You desire truth in the inward being; therefore teach me wisdom in my secret heart. Purge me with hyssop, and I shall be clean; wash me, and I shall be whiter than snow. Let me hear joy and gladness; let the bones that you have crushed rejoice. Hide your face from my sins, and blot out all my iniquities. Create in me a clean heart, O God, and put a new and right spirit within me. Do not cast me away from your presence, and do not take your holy spirit from me. Restore to me the joy of your salvation, and sustain in me a willing spirit.

Oh, David, what a shock that little story was! What a heart-stopping, dumbfounding shock! Nathan played you like a fish, and now you were well and truly caught. He knew everything, and that meant that God knew everything as well. The whole thing was out in the open, and for the first time in your life you were face to face with a very upset God. The prophet went on to spell out every detail of your crimes, didn't he? And he left you in no doubt about the way God felt about what you'd done. Sadness, disappointment, anger.

Now, I have to tell you, David, I was very impressed with the way you handled the situation at this point. Nathan's accusation must have broken through all that brittle hardness that had built up over the last nine months, and reached the heart of the old David, the man who feared and loved his God. No excuses, no bluster, no attempt to blame anyone but yourself. You really *spoke* to God. And the amazing thing is that, all these thousands of years later, we know exactly what you said, because here are your very words in the fifty-first psalm, in God's book, the Bible.

Prayer

Thank you for the example of David's wholehearted repentance.

Another?

John 3:16 (NRSV)

For God so loved the world that he gave his only Son, so that everyone who believes in him may not perish but may have eternal life.

Nothing changes much, does it, David? Burnt offerings, church services, prayer meetings, Bible reading; all useless as long as they're being used as smart gear to cover up the grubby underwear. You really came clean when you talked to God about what you'd done, and I admire you for that. It took some courage.

But it didn't change the facts.

Charges: Adultery and murder.

Verdict: Guilty.

Statutory sentence on both counts: Death.

Jewish law, you see. Absolutely clear, and you can read it for yourself if you want. Leviticus, chapter twenty, verse ten:

If a man commits adultery with another man's wife, both the man and the woman shall be put to death.

Leviticus, chapter twenty-four, verse seventeen:

All murderers must be executed.

You should have died, David. You knew that, Nathan knew that, God knew that. You should have died, but you didn't. God listened to that prayer of yours, and it must have touched him in the same way that Nathan's words touched you. He forgave you—he let you live. He preferred to have you back as a loving friend rather than let the law take its course and lose you altogether, and it says in one translation of the story that God 'laid your sin upon another'.

Laid your sin upon another? Who?

Might it have been someone who was born thousands of years later in a small Judean town called Bethlehem (you knew Bethlehem well, didn't you, David?), someone who came specially to take the blame for people like you, and to make it possible for all of us to get back into friendship with God? He's even more famous than you, David. You didn't know him then, but you must have met him by now. His name is—well, you know his name, don't you?

I would imagine you and he have a lot in common. You were a man after God's own heart, despite your sins, and he is God's beloved Son who never put a foot wrong. I would love to be a fly on the wall when you two get together.

Thought

God so loved you...

Dominoes

2 Samuel 12:14–17 (NRSV)

'Nevertheless, because by this deed you have utterly scorned the Lord, the child that is born to you shall die.' Then Nathan went to his house. The Lord struck the child that Uriah's wife bore to David, and it became very ill. David therefore pleaded with God for the child; David fasted, and went in and lay all night on the ground. The elders of his house stood beside him, urging him to rise from the ground; but he would not, nor did he eat food with them.

David didn't die, but there was an immediate and chilling penalty to pay. The child, Bathsheba's child, David's child, a living testimony to the king's crime, was going to die.

Only a little baby, but he too had David's sin laid upon him. He became deathly sick. David lay on the bare earth day and night for seven days without eating, weeping, and begging God to let the child live. Meanwhile, Bathsheba watched daily as the little body lost strength, and the eyes that should have sparkled with interest and curiosity became dulled and lifeless, as though the baby knew somehow that this world was not for him.

Perhaps she sang softly as she sat and rocked him.

Peace now, baby,
Your daddy's praying outside
And your mummy's already cried,
For you,
Now your eyes are asking me why
She needed to cry,
Oh, baby, if only you knew.

Special baby,
You won't be staying for long,
But can you tell from the love in my song,
For you,
And the tears in your daddy's prayers,
That somebody cares?
Oh, baby, if only you knew.

Sorry, baby,
You won't see much of the sky,
But you have to learn how to fly,
Yes, you do.

Remember you after you die,
We won't have to try.
Oh, baby, if only you knew.

Listen, baby,
I'm all wrapped up in my pain,
And my tears are falling like rain,
For you,
But I know that we'll meet again,
And I will explain,
Oh, baby, if only you knew.

Thought

People get hurt like toppling dominoes after certain kinds of deliberate sin.

What matters?

2 Samuel 12:18–20 (and read 21–23) (NRSV)

On the seventh day the child died. And the servants of David were afraid to tell him that the child was dead; for they said, 'While the child was still alive, we spoke to him, and he did not listen to us; how then can we tell him the child is dead? He may do himself some harm.' But when David saw that his servants were whispering together, he perceived that the child was dead; and David said to his servants, 'Is the child dead?' They said, 'He is dead.' Then David rose from the ground, washed, anointed himself, and changed his clothes. He went into the house of the Lord, and worshipped; he then went to his own house; and when he asked, they set food before him and he ate.

On the seventh day the baby died. The king's aids were afraid to tell him the bad news. All that week he had been broken up by his son's worsening condition. Exhausted by lack of sleep and food, emotionally drained by hour after hour of tearful prayer, how on earth would David react to the news that the child was dead? Breakdown? Total collapse? Nobody could summon up the courage to tell him. In the end he couldn't help but see for himself that something was being kept from him.

Now, here are some things that David did not do at this point when he realized that, despite his pleadings, the baby had died.

He didn't collapse.

He didn't shout and rave at God because his prayers hadn't been answered.

He didn't lose himself in wild living in order to forget.

He didn't descend into the sludge of self-pity.

This is what he actually did, to the amazement of his aids, and every detail of it is recorded in this passage. He got up, brushed his hair, changed his clothes, went into the tabernacle to *worship* God, then returned to the palace and ate an extremely good meal.

Heartless? No. You really cared about that baby, David. Mind you, I can see why the people around you were puzzled. I suppose the fact was that they hadn't really understood how close you were to God before all this business started, and how intensely relieved you were to be back on speaking terms, as it were. He had become your first priority again, and that was what really mattered to you.

Question

What really matters to me?

Why?

Matthew 7:8 (NRSV)

For everyone who asks receives, and everyone who searches finds, and for everyone who knocks, the door will be opened.

David, I genuinely did want to understand how your relationship with God made it possible for you to cope with the death of your baby, but it took me a long time. You see, it was different for you. You were more or less brought up by God. You were never that important to your own father, and Saul swung from rage to affection and back again with bewildering speed and frequency. You loved them both, but it was God who really looked after you. It was God who gave you the love and guidance that you needed so much. You seemed to have *known* something about him that most of us don't, something that made it possible for you to accept the death of your baby without bitterness or anger. For your sake I am glad of that, but when I read that part of the story for the first time, I was left with one overwhelming question that I had to ask, because I'm me, and not you.

Why did God kill the baby? I mean—why did he?

I don't mean that I hadn't followed the logic of what happened. I understood the mechanics—cause and effect and all that. I could see that, but—why did God kill the baby?

The idea of him doing that hurt me, opened up a dark place inside me. It frightened me. Why did he do it? How could he do it?

Of course, there *were* answers. I'd heard them—used them even, when people had asked me the same sort of question.

It was a different age and culture.

Life was cheaper.

The baby might have died anyway.

God has his own reasons that we don't understand.

It's wrong to question God, in any case.

Take your pick. They all make a bit of sense, and they may be absolutely right. I nearly gave up, but, fortunately, God cares about the things that trouble us deeply.

Prayer

Father, thank you for listening to us when we are lost or confused. Help us to trust that you will not condemn us for genuinely needing to be at peace about issues like this one. We know that there are no final answers in this life, but we are grateful for the temporary ones.

An answer

Isaiah 53:5–6 (NRSV)

But he was wounded for our transgressions, crushed for our iniquities; upon him was the punishment that made us whole, and by his bruises we are healed. All we like sheep have gone astray; we have all turned to our own way, and the Lord has laid on him the iniquity of us all.

Why did God kill the baby?

I hadn't stopped hoping for an answer to that question, but in the meantime I had started to leave things like that out when I was talking to people about what I believed. It was a bit like when a friend asks you to write a reference for her and you don't exactly tell lies, but you avoid much mention of the weaknesses that might lose her the job. Well, that's just plain silly, isn't it? God doesn't need that kind of nonsense, surely. I know that the apostle Paul said the clay has no right to question the potter, but I couldn't help it. I really wanted to know—about the baby, I mean, David—your baby.

Why?

If there were prophets like Nathan around today (and if there are any, I haven't met them—not like Nathan, anyway) I would have asked one of them, but I couldn't, so I went on asking God directly, and, in the end, he gave me, not *the* answer, but *an* answer. His answer was about his own Son. It was about how he allowed Jesus to be put on trial and beaten and jeered at and kicked. He let his own dearly loved child be hurt and abused by the very people he came to save. He allowed us to crush him under the weight of the cross as he dragged it towards the site of his own death, refusing to release him from his burden for our sakes.

He let his 'baby' be nailed to a piece of wood without lifting a hand to save him, because if he had done, we would have been abandoned to judgment.

He endured the unspeakable pain of hearing his Son cry out that he felt forsaken, and let the situation be, because he loves us.

I began to understand, David, that, though there are many questions still to be asked, when it comes to the death of babies, he does know exactly what he is doing.

Prayer

Thank you for placing your child into our arms.

Full circle?

2 Samuel 12:24–25 (NRSV)

Then David consoled his wife Bathsheba, and went to her, and lay with her; and she bore a son, and he named him Solomon. The Lord loved him, and sent a message by the prophet Nathan; so he named him Jedidiah, because of the Lord.

It all sounds pretty good, doesn't it? David is not only back with God, he also gets to keep Bathsheba as well. The first baby's death was a great sorrow, but there are plenty more sons—Solomon, Absalom, Amnon, Adonijah—and David is back on track with God.

It looks like a full circle.

It looks like the end of a nightmare.

It looks as if the only way to end the story is to say that they all lived happily ever after. Unfortunately that is not the case. It is true that David stayed on good terms with God for the rest of his life, except for the foolish affair of the census, years later, and there is little doubt that this relationship continued to be a priority for the king, but the rest of it, well, the rest of it was a bit of a mess.

Nathan had warned David that another penalty of his crimes would be trouble in his family, and the prophet was absolutely right. Terrible trouble. Terrible times. Terrible hurts from Absalom, the son he probably loved most. Absalom was—well, you can read about Absalom and David in the second book of Samuel, one of the most heart-wrenching stories in the Bible. You can read about the death of Amnon, the treachery of Adonijah, and the end of David's life.

David never quite recovered the purity of intention and motivation that had so distinguished him before the Bathsheba incident, but then, in David's life, as in the lives of believers before and since, there can only be one hero, and that is God, the God of whom David himself said:

He has rescued me from my troubles.

Prayer

Thank you, Father, for allowing us access to this detailed and exciting account of David's life. It helps us to understand that everyone, no matter how close to you, is liable to fall. We pray that followers of David's type will be raised up to work for you in this age of respectable moderation in the Church—people capable of great virtues and great sins, who, in the end, choose to follow you. May you be the only hero in the lives of us all.

There is nothing new save
that which has been forgotten.
Mme Bertin

NEW BEGINNINGS

Chances to get up and go—again

The fact that Bridget and I have made three trips to Australia during the last few years is, in itself, evidence of a fairly dramatic new beginning. There was a time when financial pressures and the demands of seemingly eternal shift-work in childcare establishments were such that we felt very little hope of ever going much further than the corner shop. Once you've done it, of course, you know that you *can* do it, and therefore it's more likely that you'll do it again. We really are grateful to God for allowing us the opportunity to do things and to go to places that we would never have thought possible, and, of course, for inspiring people to believe that it's actually worth paying for us to come and speak to them. I still find that idea extremely difficult to accept, as do my close friends, who have stubbornly refused to pay me a heavily discounted sum per sentence for speaking to them when we meet at the pub.

Bridget has found the whole business of travelling and speaking just as exciting as I have, but, as she has recorded elsewhere, there has always been a gnawing worry in her mind that people are only tolerating her contribution to our presentations because she happens to be married to me, the one who writes the books. This deep insecurity tends to persist in the face of overwhelming evidence to the contrary. She won't thank me for saying this, but wherever we have appeared together she has received fulsome praise and expressions of appreciation. But then, that's the way it is with deep insecurities, isn't it? As a young teenager I was quite convinced that no normal girl would ever want to go out with me, and this conviction persisted even though I found myself going out with an extremely attractive one. Any girls who did like me, I reasoned, must have faulty powers of perception, and therefore, in this area at least, their views didn't count. Bridget's just the same. If an entire audience of five hundred people were to pin her to the ground and scream loudly and in unison in her ear that they appreciated her in her own right, there would be a short pause, and then you would hear a small voice from the bottom of the human pile saying, 'You don't really mean that.'

During our third trip to Australia this problem came to a head because of one particular comment during a radio interview, and seemed to be getting worse until a story told by a friend, and inspired by God, I'm sure, produced a new beginning in Bridget's ability to keep things in perspective.

The radio interview, live and conducted over the telephone, was set up as a promotional aid to our forthcoming appearance in Sydney, and included the following question, delivered in a flat, Australian drawl:

'What exactly does Bridget do? Does she hold up cue-cards, or come on stage wearing a leotard, or what?'

Bridget later said that, on hearing those words, she felt as if she had received a vicious punch in the solar plexus, a sense of reeling back, doubled up and breathless with pain and humiliation. Only pride enabled her to laugh and smile as though nothing had happened instead of bursting into childlike tears of hurt and anger.

All evening and all of that night Bridget fought to subdue the sense of rage and upset that was determinedly welling up in her. She said that it felt like emotional bruising. The same questions and fears ran through her mind over and over again as she lay awake.

'How could that *man* say such a thing? What a sexist, chauvinistic idiot! But supposing he was right! Am I being ridiculous? Even if I'm not, what's wrong with me that I've taken it so much to heart? Why am I still so vulnerable to the idea that I'm worth nothing in my own right?'

By morning the waves of pain had receded, but, just as is the case with acute homesickness for many people, when reason appeared to have achieved some level of healing, the memory of how threatened she had felt sent her reeling again. Bridget's peace had been stolen, and it was difficult for her to see how it was going to be recovered or replaced.

The day after that interviewer had unknowingly caused such a problem found Bridget and me, together with other people involved in our concerts, scrunched together in a van on our way to the next venue. It was during this trip that Karen Beckett, a marvellous singer and ideal travelling companion who accompanied us throughout the tour, suddenly announced, 'It was just around here that my husband and I nearly ruined a small turtle's life.'

It sounded too good a story to miss.

'What happened,' said Karen, 'was that we were travelling along the main road, when I spotted this little turtle right over on the other side of the dual-carriageway. He was just climbing up from the road to get on to the grass verge, so he must have spent ages crawling from one side to the other. I don't know how he'd avoided getting flattened by cars and trucks, but he'd done it somehow. Anyway, my kids had never seen a turtle before, so we stopped, and my husband, Trev, dodged the traffic to get across the road, and brought the turtle back across to where we were waiting in the car. The kids were knocked out by the little fellow, and they wanted to take him home, but then he did an amazing amount of wee all over us—frightened I suppose—and that sort of brought out the conservationist in all of us. It encouraged us to think it would be better to leave him in his natural habitat. So I put him down on the grass verge beside the car and we drove on.

'Well, we hadn't got much further down the road when I suddenly realized what we'd done. We'd left him on our side! The poor little creature was going to have to dice with death all over again, and the odds against him getting across unsquashed a second time were pretty heavy, to say the least.'

Bridget told me later that, on hearing the story up to this point, she said to herself, 'That's just how I feel. After years of trying to get to the other side of this dreadful self-image of mine, and just about managing to dodge the stuff life throws at me, one stupid remark has taken me all the way back to the place where I started.'

I wondered at the time why Bridget asked her next question with such a degree of intensity.

'What did you do?'

'Well,' said Karen, 'we turned around as soon as we got to a junction and went back. We felt pretty stupid, actually, but we couldn't face the idea of that little thing having to take such an awful risk all over again. He'd just started the repeat trip when we got back, so Trev picked him up, wee and all, and carried him over to the place where we'd found him. He must have had a great story to tell his mum! Eh?'

We all enjoyed the story, but Bridget not only laughed, she also felt the lingering remains of that recent bruising fade quietly away. She thought of all the times when family and friends had helped her to pick herself up in the past, leading her across roads that seemed too difficult to navigate on her own—phone calls she couldn't bring herself to begin; encounters she dreaded; apologies that were difficult to make; reconciliation that depended on her being more forgiving than she felt able to be. She thought also about the times when she and God had been on their own in situations where she felt totally inadequate, and she had been able to lean on him.

And it isn't only Bridget, of course. It's all of us. We all depend on each other and on God. Jesus promised that we would be left with a peace that can't be taken away, whatever the world throws at us. He will not leave us stranded on a roadside verge, so paralysed by our overwhelming sense of failure that we are incapable of moving forward.

No matter how deep the old wounds may go, and I know that they threaten to cut some of us in two, by God's grace it will always be possible to have a new beginning.

Prayer

Father, some of us are in desperate need of a new beginning. As we read your words and think about what they mean, give us fresh hope that we can move safely to the other side of difficulty and disaster. Be with us as we watch closely for opportunities to help others who need to make a fresh start, and clear our heads so that we may hear your voice offering wisdom and guidance. We trust that you will never forsake us, Lord—help our lack of trust. Amen.

A new song **Psalm 40:1–3 (NRSV)**

I waited patiently for the Lord; he inclined to me and heard my cry. He drew me up from the desolate pit, out of the miry bog, and set my feet upon a rock, making my steps secure. He put a new song in my mouth, a song of praise to our God. Many will see and fear, and put their trust in the Lord.

I identify with all of this section except for the first six words. I never have been a very patient person, with God or anyone else. As someone who is constantly required to put words on paper, however, I have special reasons for willingly testifying to the truth contained in the other fifty-nine words.

This process of crawling out of the bog (don't laugh, please) and having a new song put into my mouth is one that I experience every single time I begin a new piece of writing. And it doesn't matter how successful the last project might have been, because I still end up slumped gloomily in front of my computer, filled with the certainty that I will never write anything else ever again. As I sit there, I might pick up my last book and glance through it.

'How on *earth*,' I ask myself, 'did I manage to write all this? How could someone with a mind as empty and unproductive as mine feels now produce an entire book that other people might want to read?'

I really do get very depressed.

Convinced that my professional life is over, I dejectedly push a key or two, just for old times' sake, before putting my coat on and setting out for the Job Centre. A couple of words appear on the screen; they grow into a bad sentence; I put the sentence right; I have to write a second sentence in order to explain the first one; suddenly my interest is caught by some aspect of what I have written; I sit up in my chair and wriggle into a comfortable position; my fingers do a sort of piano-playing mime as they hover over the keyboard; I plunge headlong into composition; I am writing again.

Now, I am not talking about God giving me the words to write. What I am talking about is this eternally present divine principle of movement from despair to a new beginning. Don't give up. Whether your inspiration is lost in the area of looking after a dependent relative or composing a concerto, put yourself in the place where the work is to be done and listen hard. The music may begin with a few faint notes in the far distance, but there is always a new song to be sung.

Prayer

Father, may others hear you in the music of our lives.

A new start

Isaiah 62:2–4 (NRSV)

The nations shall see your vindication... and you shall be called by a new name... You shall be a crown of beauty in the hand of the Lord, and a royal diadem in the hand of your God. You shall no more be termed Forsaken, and your land shall no more be termed Desolate; but you shall be called My Delight Is in Her, and your land Married; for the Lord delights in you, and your land shall be married.

Since my mother died. I cannot tell you how sad Bridget and I feel that we can no longer jump in the car and drive up to Tunbridge Wells to see her. She was such a very significant part of our lives, and the pain of loss has not diminished much. She was a tough, generous, sometimes cantankerous, enjoyer of life, who allowed people to be exactly what they were. Bridget described her as 'my best friend'.

For the four years prior to her death, mum was confined to a wheelchair as the result of a stroke, and though she remained very much the person that we loved, there was an inevitable deterioration in the optimism and outgoingness that had characterized her before she became ill. Sometimes she was downright crabby.

Interestingly, most of our memories of mum go back automatically to the days before her stroke, when she was vigorously active in the village where she lived, and a warm, involved grandma in the lives of her grandchildren. That person was the real Marjorie Plass, but we had almost lost sight of that fact in the period before her death.

In our kitchen stands a framed enlargement of a photograph of mum when she was ten years old, the same age that Katy is now. The picture, taken in 1928, shows a tall, skinny little girl holding her skirts up as she paddles in the sea. She is gazing up inquiringly towards the shore, as if trying to hear what someone is calling to her. Young Marjorie's face, captured for ever in this long-ago moment is strong and confident, full of an optimism that needs no expression because it is a part of her. That child lived on in the adult that Mum became, sustaining her through some very difficult years. Strangely, in that sixty-two-year-old portrayal, I see more of the person I knew than in any other memory or photograph, which is just as well, because it will be the clear-eyed face of a child that Bridget and I shall recognize when we join her in heaven.

Thought

In heaven the child in us will be able to start again.

A new world

Isaiah 65:17–19, 25 (NRSV)

For I am about to create new heavens and a new earth; the former things shall not be remembered or come to mind. But be glad and rejoice for ever in what I am creating... I will rejoice in Jerusalem, and delight in my people; no more shall the sound of weeping be heard in it, or the cry of distress... The wolf and the lamb shall feed together, the lion shall eat straw like the ox; but the serpent—its food shall be dust! They shall not hurt or destroy on all my holy mountain, says the Lord.

Are you engaged in an eternal struggle to develop a living situation that you wouldn't cope with if you ever succeeded in creating it? Let me explain what I mean.

Take our family—please do. In my pathetic vision of the future there is total cooperation between all the members of the household. My second son, for instance, would spend a long time cleaning and preparing the bathroom for its next occupant after using it himself, my darling daughter would insist on doing her violin practice at least twice every day (without being reminded) at times convenient to the rest of the family, my third son would regularly wrest the carpet cleaner from my wife's hand, refusing to allow her to wear herself out when he could just as easily do it, and my oldest son would pop over every weekend to take his brothers and sister out for the whole of Saturday, leaving Bridget and I to potter about in the sort of happily pointless way we used to before we foolishly started begatting.

There are a couple of problems with this scenario. First, I contribute to the general air of chaos as much as anyone else. I am either fanatically, cataclysmically, intolerantly tidy in very short explosive bursts, or utterly slob-like for much longer periods. I'd have a job changing that very much now.

Secondly, despite the fact that we always seem to be fighting our way towards this domestic utopia, I'm not sure that I'd actually enjoy it if it came. Our family life has always been as rich as a Christmas cake, and I think I'd miss it if it became *that* civilized.

No, I think I'll leave the new earth to God. Something tells me that he will be able to pick out the very best of what was, and reproduce it in a new and excitingly shining form that will lose nothing of the granular richness of family life, and gain a great deal in addition because he'll be in charge instead of me!

A reminder

I've said it before and I'll say it again—heaven will be wonderful.

A new kind of law **Jeremiah 31:31–34 (NRSV)**

The days are surely coming, says the Lord, when I will make a new covenant with the house of Israel and the house of Judah. It will not be like the covenant that I made with their ancestors when I took them by the hand to bring them out of the land of Egypt... But this is the covenant that I will make... I will put my law within them, and I will write it on their hearts; and I will be their God, and they shall be my people. No longer shall they teach one another, or say to each other, 'Know the Lord', for they shall all know me, from the least of them to the greatest, says the Lord; for I will forgive their iniquity, and remember their sin no more.

For some people this particular new beginning may be the only real hope left in their lives.

I remember watching news of the apparently pointless roadside murder of Bill Cosby's only son, a socially concerned young man, often referred to by his famous American father as 'my hero'. As I watched pictures of the grief-stricken comic leaving home with his wife to collect the body of his son, I reflected on the fact, hackneyed but true, that wealth and position become meaningless in the face of such loss. I am quite sure that Bill Cosby would give his very last dollar and every shred of his international fame for the chance to be with his son once more. I have no idea what the religious beliefs of these two men were or are. I really hope that God's law has been written on their hearts, because if it has, there will be new and wonderful beginnings for both of them in the future, despite the agony that Mr Cosby was sure to be experiencing at that moment.

I really cannot imagine how anyone survives such a loss without the hope of reunion that Jesus promises. It's bad enough to lose someone close when you do believe, isn't it? What must it be like to face the solid wall of blackness that confronts those who see death as a complete full-stop?

People sometimes suggest that the readers of these notes are bound to be believing Christians, and most of them are, but I know that a minority are not. Please, if you have never known God, speak to him, and speak to those who do know him. Perhaps, if you do that, you, and eventually those you love, will experience your own new beginnings and be ready for anything that life throws at you.

Prayer

Father, hear the voices of those who need you. Write your law on their hearts and forgive their sins.

A new morning

Lamentations 3:15–23 (NRSV)

He has filled me with bitterness... my soul is bereft of peace; I have forgotten what happiness is; so I say, 'Gone is my glory, and all that I had hoped for from the Lord.' The thought of my affliction and my homelessness is wormwood and gall!... But this I call to mind, and therefore I have hope: The steadfast love of the Lord never ceases, his mercies never come to an end; they are new every morning; great is your faithfulness.

This sort of testimony infuriates some Christian groups. They dislike it so much because it's ragged and untidy and failing and just about impossible to contain within a neat religious package. For those who like their Christianity to proceed along man-made straight lines, these wild and hopeless cries from the heart are disturbing and threatening. And yet, for two very good reasons, it is absolutely essential that we hear and appreciate the meaning of such loud and painful shouts to God.

First, they reflect the way things actually are for many people, and you can argue until your face is bright purple with little pink spots all over it about how life ought to be for Christians, because all I shall say to you is that 'oughts' rarely work with clockwork precision. People get bashed and hurt and bewildered by events, and if we are honest we must admit that troubles seem to fall with equal weight on believers and unbelievers alike. Being Jesus to our neighbour, the highest calling known to men and women, involves hearing and embracing pain in each other without feeling obliged to trot out religious platitudes that make us feel better but bring the sufferer nearer to despair than ever. Jesus pleaded that we should love one another. Isn't it difficult?

Secondly, this kind of cry is immensely encouraging, because it concludes with a sudden surfacing of the knowledge, presumably based on past events, that the love of God will never end, and is new every single morning. When a man as unhappy and bowed down as this is rescued by that particular awareness, then his testimony is valuable indeed. This is no airy-fairy, pseudo-religious thing. In my life, and in the lives of many who are reading these words at this moment, it has sometimes only been possible to go on because, when you dwell in the kingdom of God, nightmares may come, but there is always the miraculous possibility of a new morning.

Prayer

Help us to be honest and faithful, Lord.

A new heart **Ezekiel 36:25–28 (NRSV)**

I will sprinkle clean water upon you, and you shall be clean... and from all your idols I will cleanse you. A new heart I will give you, and a new spirit I will put within you; and I will remove from your body the heart of stone and give you a heart of flesh. I will put my spirit within you, and make you follow my statutes and be careful to observe my ordinances. Then you shall live in the land that I gave to your ancestors; and you shall be my people, and I will be your God.

I have experienced no more powerful drive than the desire to make everything 'all right' for my children. Sometimes this leads to mistakes. Children should not always be protected from the consequences of their actions, and certainly there have been times when Bridget or I have jumped in far too quickly to rescue one of them from disaster. It's just that we love them so much, and we can't bear the thought of them being less than content. No doubt, in my case, this has more to do with my past than their present, but—well, you know what I mean.

Occasionally I've been really glad that we have this knee-jerk reaction to their problems. Once, for instance, the phone rang at five o'clock in the morning. When the phone goes at that time of morning it can only be bad news or an Australian. It was actually my oldest son, living in Kent at the time, and all he said was, 'Can you come down straightaway? I'm all right, but something bad has happened and I need you to come as soon as you can.'

I think Bridget and I were dressed and in the car within five minutes. Arriving thirty-five minutes later we found a police car parked outside the building, and learned that someone in the next-door flat had been attacked in the early hours of the morning. Hearing a banging noise, my son opened the door to find this unfortunate individual bound and gagged and covered in blood on the landing outside the door. He was still in a very shocked state by the time we got him home. We weren't able to make everything all right exactly, but, thank God, we were able to be there for him when he needed us.

Read this passage, and you will hear the passionate cry of a Father's heart for his children simply to be all right. This is a list of the things that he will do to make sure it happens. Until that work is completed God is there for us whenever we need him, and we don't even have to use a telephone.

Prayer

Put your Spirit within us, Lord.

A new commandment

John 13:34–35 (NRSV)

'I give you a new commandment, that you love one another. Just as I have loved you, you also should love one another. By this everyone will know that you are my disciples, if you have love for one another.'

How would the Church change if this commandment were to be generally obeyed? Would such a new beginning be welcomed? I have my doubts.

The problem, you see, is that Jesus doesn't say, 'Love one another as you have always loved one another in the past.' He says, 'Love one another just as I have loved you.' This is a very tall order indeed, not least because the love that Jesus showed to his disciples was a (to them) bewilderingly mixed bag of uncompromisingly tough straight-talking, overwhelming compassion, and a quite extraordinary willingness to trust them with powers and tasks that they can't possibly have understood. In other words, the principle of only doing what he saw his Father doing was applied as rigorously by Jesus to individual relationships as to his broader ministry.

How many of us would be ready to abandon items of our personal agenda because the love of God for the person before us demanded it? Would I? Would you? My heart sinks whenever another major issue arises in the life of the Church, not because I don't think we should confront issues, but because there will always be a little bunch of single-issue fanatics at both ends of the argument whose voices are louder and more strident than the saner arguments of those who have put Jesus first in their lives, and are prepared to be wrong if necessary.

The acid test will never change.

Jesus himself appears in the flesh, right in front of me, and says, 'Look, I see what you're getting at, Adrian, but, as it happens, you're wrong.'

My two possible responses are:

'Nevertheless, I think I have to pursue this point—I've thought it through very carefully.'

Or: 'Okay, Lord, you know best, I'll follow you.'

If I find that the first answer is the one I would give, then I have no business commenting on matters of faith and life at all. The business of loving as Jesus loved demands identification with the spirit of personal sacrifice that, in the end, sent him to the cross.

Tough, isn't it?

Prayer

Lord, teach us how to love you and each other. Heal your Church.

Communion

Luke 21:19–20 (NRSV)

Then he took a loaf of bread, and when he had given thanks, he broke it and gave it to them, saying, 'This is my body, which is given for you. Do this in remembrance of me.' And he did the same with the cup after supper, saying, 'This cup that is poured out for you is the new covenant in my blood.'

The church that we attend in Hailsham is small, and, being a sort of hall, has none of the grandeur or dignity of your average parish church. And yet, on those Sundays when we celebrate communion, I experience a sense of mystery and fathomless significance that could not be more profound if I was worshipping in the most extravagantly impressive cathedral in the country.

There is a danger in pulling to pieces the things that you love, but I have been trying to work out why this simple ritual has such an effect on me. One Sunday I sat at the back, watching the congregation make their way, row by row, to the front of the church, where they waited in a rough semi-circle to receive bread and wine from the priest and his helper. I know quite a lot of the people in our church, some very well indeed. As I looked at my brothers and sisters waiting like children to be given their share of the body and blood of Jesus, I felt like crying. I know the struggles that some of them have been through, as they know of mine. I know that quite a lot of people in our church feel far from worthy to be receiving such precious, jewel-like gifts from God. And yet, there we are, each time communion happens, going out like junior-school kids from their desks, tentatively putting out our hands in the eternally renewed hope that Jesus will place a share of himself into our humble safekeeping just as God placed his baby son into the world all those years ago.

We are a communion of uncertainty and hope, human beings of all shapes and sizes, but with exactly equal rights as children adopted into the family of God. In taking those few short steps from our seats to the front of the church we are, however nervously, expressing our faith in that proposition. Once we get there—he does the rest. It's beautiful.

Prayer

Thank you for your smiling presence at communion.

A new creation

2 Corinthians 5:17–21 (NRSV)

So if anyone is in Christ, there is a new creation... All this is from God, who reconciled us to himself through Christ, and has given us the ministry of reconciliation; that is, in Christ God was reconciling the world to himself, not counting their trespasses against them, and entrusting the message of reconciliation to us. So we are ambassadors for Christ, since God is making his appeal through us; we entreat you on behalf of Christ, be reconciled to God.

I was terrified when we first went to America. My books hadn't done very well there, except in a few individual churches and small pockets of the Christian community. I had been told some grizzly tales about widespread puritan attitudes that would find the sort of material I use offensive and unfunny. I suppose I'd been a bit spoilt really. Most audiences come to my meetings because they've already read something I've written and are therefore unlikely to be hostile. Many of those who bought tickets for our first meetings in the USA had no idea what they were coming to.

In the end it was a nerve-racking experience, but only for as long as it took to discover that Americans reacted in very much the same way as people in other parts of the world. One of the three venues Bridget and I spoke at was a huge church on the outskirts of Los Angeles. That evening there must have been more than a thousand people attending, and we had a wonderful time, the highlight of which was meeting and spending some time with the leader of the church. This man, an Australian as it happened, was precisely the kind of ambassador for Christ that American Christianity seems to need. Relaxed and vulnerable in public about his faults and shortcomings, Barry was totally committed to the task of presenting Jesus to those who are desperately in need of him, without allowing personal biases and attitudes to stand in the way. In the words of this passage, God was making his appeal through the minister, and, as far as we could tell, that appeal was emerging in a relatively pure form. The result was a very lively and unusually relaxed congregation in which individuals were free to pursue the business of conforming to Christ rather than to the man or woman at the front.

America is not the only place that could do with more leaders like this.

Prayer

Father, may people meet you in us, instead of us in us.

A new humanity **Ephesians 2:13–16 (NRSV)**

But now in Christ Jesus you who once were far off have been brought near by the blood of Christ. For he is our peace; in his flesh he has made both groups into one and has broken down the dividing wall, that is, the hostility between us. He has abolished the law... that he might create in himself one new humanity in place of the two, thus making peace, and might reconcile both groups to God in one body through the cross, thus putting to death that hostility through it.

The bitterness with which some Christians talk about their brothers and sisters takes my breath away.

I spoke at a weekend somewhere in England once for a church more or less divided down the middle over one issue. The issue was the vicar. One faction seemed sure their minister was, at best, useless, and at worst, some kind of devil's agent. The other faction felt—surprise, surprise—that he was the most saintly figure in the history of the Christian Church.

The leader of the anti-brigade picked me up from the station. All the way to the conference centre he filled me in on the vicar's failure as a preacher, his insensitivity to parishioners, his lack of hospitality in a home which had been supplied to him 'for that very purpose!', his inept chairmanship of the PCC, and his stubborn tendency towards sacramentalism. I asked him to tell me something good about the vicar. He grudgingly admitted that the vicarage garden was looking better nowadays. If only, he added, spoiling it, the vicar spent as much time with his parishioners as his flowers they would all be a lot better off. Later, at the Centre, I was cornered by members of the pro-vicar faction, anxious to put forward their point of view in case I had already been nobbled.

The vicar turned out to be a charming man close to cracking under the strain of a conflict that he clearly found quite inexplicable. It was a terrible weekend. When I openly challenged people there was temporary agreement that things were not as they should be, but nothing changed. I very rarely talk about such things, but it was as if something maliciously evil had crept into the very centre of that community.

Let's pray that the power of the cross will bring a new beginning for Christians locked in conflict.

Prayer

Lord Jesus, you are our peace. God forbid that your death should be in vain. Where there is bitterness and anger speak into the minds of those who need to change, and cast out evil from communities that have been deceived into losing sight of you.

A new self

Ephesians 4:17–24 (NRSV)

You must no longer live as the Gentiles live, in the futility of their minds. They are darkened in their understanding, alienated from the life of God because of their ignorance and hardness of heart. They have lost all sensitivity and have abandoned themselves to licentiousness, greedy to practise every kind of impurity. That is not the way you learned Christ! For surely you have heard about him and were taught in him, as truth is in Jesus. You were taught to put away your former way of life, your old self, corrupt and deluded by its lusts, and to be renewed in the spirit of your minds, and to clothe yourselves with the new self, created according to the likeness of God in true righteousness and holiness.

I sometimes think that I've been a Christian for too long. Let me explain.

I began toddling after Jesus at sixteen, so it's thirty-two years since I had any kind of perspective on life from the non-believer's point of view. Because of this I tend, like many Christians, to give myself a hard time over passages like this one. The guilt trap opens before me and I step meekly in, assuming that when I measure myself against such expectations I shall be revealed as a total failure. Now, there is some truth in that assumption, but it is not the whole story. Let's be positive for once. I'll tell you what I'm thinking, and you see if you agree with me.

First, I read this passage with the eyes of one who really does want to follow Jesus. Thank God for that! Good start, eh? Next, I may not measure up to what is demanded of me here, but I am at least conscious of that deficiency, and the gap between what I am and what I should be matters to me very much. I *want* to put away my former way of life. I *want* to be renewed in the spirit of my mind. I *want* to clothe myself with the new self.

Thirdly, I have made some steps in the direction that God wants me to go. They might have been small ones, and they might have been interspersed with the odd backward one from time to time, but I know that they have happened and I thank God for that as well.

It would be very sad if the effects of that guilt trap were to obscure the good work of God in our lives. We may not be much, but what we are and what we shall be is made possible by him, so let's thank him for it.

Prayer

Thank you Father for helping us to grow, however slowly, into the likeness of yourself.

A new covenant

Hebrews 9:11–15 (NRSV)

But when Christ came as a high priest of the good things that have come, then through the greater and perfect tent (not made with hands, that is, not of this creation), he entered once for all into the Holy Place, not with the blood of goats and calves, but with his own blood, thus obtaining eternal redemption. For if the blood of goats and bulls... sanctifies those who have been defiled so that their flesh is purified, how much more will the blood of Christ... purify our conscience from dead works to worship the living God! For this reason he is the mediator of a new covenant, so that those who are called may receive the promised eternal inheritance, because a death has occurred that redeems them from the transgressions under the first covenant.

What a strange gap there is between the grandeur and cosmic significance of this passage, and the things that actually happen to people when they receive forgiveness through Jesus from God. I'm glad we are given glimpses in the Gospels of the ordinariness of much of Jesus' life on earth.

I can't help wondering how Jesus would have replied to questions about forgiveness and eternity and heaven from someone like—well, like Mary or her sister Martha. He obviously spent a lot of time with these two. Their place was probably a sort of second home. Surely there must have been times—after a good meal, say—when one of the sisters would have said something like, 'Tell us what it's really all about, Master. Why have you really come? Tell us what heaven's really like! What are we going to do there? Don't tell us a parable or preach us a sermon—come on, the disciples won't be back for half an hour, tell us what it's all about.'

Do you think Jesus might have chuckled on hearing this, and given the kind of quiet, intimate answers that we would die to hear from his lips? Do you think his eyes might have misted over a little as he spoke about heaven, the place where he had been with his Father before time began, and to which he would return much sooner than the two women realized? Do you think he gave away any secrets? I'd love to have been there, wouldn't you?

Don't worry, the new covenant isn't just a few well-chosen words in a big black book. It's something that Jesus has done for you, because he loves you, and when you meet him it will all seem, in the very best sense, so ordinary.

Prayer

Thank you, Jesus, for giving yourself.

A new name **Revelation 2:17; 3:12 (NRSV)**

'To everyone who conquers I will give... a white stone, and on the white stone is written a new name that no one knows except the one who receives it'... 'If you conquer, I will make you a pillar in the temple of my God; you will never go out of it. I will write on you the name of my God, and the name of the city of my God, the new Jerusalem that comes down from my God out of heaven, and my own new name.'

One of the most interesting pieces of graffiti I ever saw was on a bridge that crossed a stream in a very upmarket area to the east of Harpenden. The first interesting thing was that these three words were the only defacement of the stonework. The houses on either side of the little stream and in the whole of that part of the world were very, very large and expensive, not at all the sort of places that are generally supposed to produce wall-scribblers. One young rebel, however, had obviously decided to break the mould by leaving his mark in bright yellow chalk. In large capital letters he had written:

NIGEL IS OBDURATE

Somewhat obscure and tentative perhaps, in comparison with the daubs that one sees on the walls of public toilets nowadays, but no doubt the writer felt better for it, and I expect Nigel was mortified, don't you?

Psychiatrists tell us that the act of writing on walls and doors has a lot to do with identity. Once you have written your name or made your mark on a surface that is bound to be seen by others, you make that place your own and feel a greater confidence in being who you are. Or something like that.

Now, before the Thought Police saddle up and ride out to get me, I am not about to say that God goes around scribbling nasty things in public places, but I am interested to note from this passage that Jesus declares his intention of writing the name of God, the name of the city of God and (intriguingly) his own new name, not on a wall or a door, but on us. Don't you find it encouraging that Jesus might believe in us enough to write his name on you and me so that we are publicly and eternally connected to him? The deal is that if we are obedient to him he will demonstrate his total confidence in us by intertwining his identity with ours.

Should we go for that? I think the writing's on the wall, don't you?

Prayer

We would be proud to bear your name, Lord Jesus. Be patient with us.

A new heaven

Revelation 21:1–5 (NRSV)

Then I saw a new heaven and a new earth... And I heard a loud voice from the throne saying, 'See, the home of God is among mortals. He will dwell with them; they will be his peoples, and God himself will be with them; he will wipe every tear from their eyes. Death will be no more; mourning and crying and pain will be no more, for the first things have passed away.' And the one who was seated on the throne said, 'See, I am making all things new.'

I enjoy most of my life, but sometimes I feel weary and sad. As a child I knew some unhappy nights, but the morning had miraculous powers of regeneration. I particularly liked going out in the summer just after the sun came up so that I could watch the light streaming like a river of gold over the red brick footpath that ran along the front of our house. That wonderful daily display of brand-new-ness suggested that any change for the better might be possible.

Years went by and the magic of the morning became diluted. Waking up no longer had the automatic effect of dispelling inner darkness, and the dull ache of lost innocence was perpetually present. I still loved the early morning sun, but the feeling that it heralded change was a memory instead of a reality.

Becoming a Christian helped a lot once I understood that instant and total joy was not handed out with each copy of 'Journey Into Life'. The concept of a fallen world explained a lot about the way in which life seemed to offer so very much, but to deliver in such a variable way. The world may be imperfect, but all around us, and particularly in the natural world, are clues and indications to the way God originally intended that things should be.

Things have gone well for me in so many ways. I know that. I have a family that loves me and a job that brings an enormous amount of satisfaction. I have travelled to places that I never thought I would see and met people who have become very important to me, and yet there is a part of me that is sick of this fallen planet. I look forward to nothing more than the wonderful, brand new morning that is promised in this passage. All things will be made new and we shall no longer feel weary or sad, because heaven and earth will be exactly as they were always supposed to be.

Prayer

Can't wait to see it, Father.

Can it be true, what is so constantly affirmed, that there is no sex in souls? I doubt it, I doubt it exceedingly.
S.T.Coleridge

TRAVELLING TWO BY TWO

The sexy Song Of Songs

Reactions to this particular set of notes have been most interesting and varied.

A few Christians clearly identify and agree with Mr Cholmondley-Warner, one of Harry Enfield's comic creations, who describes sex as 'conjugal unpleasantness'. I received a distinct impression from some of the people who talked to me that they felt God must have had some kind of brainstorm on the day when he allowed this particular book to be included in the Bible.

I remember, on a different occasion, one of those same people expressing the view that, although Jesus was a normal man in every other way, it was highly unlikely that he ever experienced sexual temptation. I can understand this person's reluctance to attribute such a basic and intrusively unruly human experience to someone who, for her, epitomizes purity, but, as I have said elsewhere, if he was not tempted in that way, then he was definitely not 'tempted as we are'.

Those who do react to the content of the poem with extreme distaste might like gently to ask themselves why they have such a personal aversion to this aspect of God's creation. They might also reflect on the fact that, as far as Orientals are concerned, the Song of Solomon is considered to be eminently chaste, honouring marriage and the joys of married life. Far from being an unfortunate and inexplicably accidental addition to God's otherwise admirable book, it is actually a vigorously positive endorsement of the kind of committed marital relationship that is under such constant attack in these days.

If anyone suggests to you that God is coldly legalistic and negative about this side of life—show 'em the Song of Songs!

By contrast, others, and especially women, have reported a sense of liberation as they enjoyed the celebration of simply being a woman that lights up these stanzas. One quite elderly lady talked with bright innocence about being 'thrilled' by the extravagantly appreciative way in which parts of the female body are described. For two pins I would pass her exact comments on to you, but unfortunately the Bible Reading Fellowship has only supplied me with one.

A second and more general objection has been that, while one might choose to read and interpret the book as an allegory of Christ's love for the Church, there is little substance in the text itself to support the view that it is intended to be understood in this way. As a non-theologian I have little to say in reply to this comment, except that, in a sense, I don't really think it matters either way. I consider it perfectly legitimate to enjoy the whole thing as poetry and nothing else (I hope all who use these notes will read right through it from that perspective in any case before looking at the different sections I've commented on). The trouble is that getting on to the old allegory trail is a bit like those times when, as kids, we used to ride down steep, bumpy hills on our rickety go-karts that never had any brakes. Once you've started it really is very difficult to stop—so I didn't.

Whatever the legitimacy or otherwise of this approach, I feel quite safe in assuming that the passion of God for his Church is at least as extreme and all-embracing as the love that is declared in these verses. It is, after all, Jesus who casts himself in (among many others) the figurative role of bridegroom to the Church that makes up his body on earth, that Church being composed, as you know, of you and me. Perhaps it is a measure of how far humanity has fallen, that some of us trip so heavily over the physical aspects of this relationship when it is used as a metaphor, that we forget to look up and see the value and significance of parallels with the fierce love, the passionate loyalty, the deep commitment and the rich fulfilment of married life at its best.

In any case, physical passion is not fornication, any more than a sunset-soaked poppy is a life-destroying drug. Both were created to be beautiful, and God has not changed his mind about either.

Prayer

Father, help us to read and enjoy this beautiful poem on any and every level that will provide nourishment for our spirits. We thank you for the gift of love between those men and women who dedicate their relationships to you, and we ask your forgiveness for those times when we have tended, in our minds, to turn something beautiful into something smutty. Thank you particularly for the relationship of Jesus to his Church. Help us to understand the depth and richness of that relationship, and to receive the passion of your love for us. Amen.

The power and the perfume

Song of Solomon 1:1–4 (NIV)

Solomon's Song of Songs. Let him kiss me with the kisses of his mouth—for your love is more delightful than wine. Pleasing is the fragrance of your perfumes; your name is like perfume poured out. No wonder the maidens love you! Take me away with you—let us hurry! Let the king bring me into his chambers. We rejoice and delight in you; we will praise your love more than wine. How right they are to adore you!

It's refreshing to plunge into an atmosphere as rich with the ecstasy of lovers as the Song of Solomon. I pray you will feel closer to the heart of God, and more safely held by the divine intelligence than ever, as you read this passionate allegory of spiritual desire and union. There is something reassuring about God electing to use such a human scenario in which to reveal his feelings for us.

One line in this early passage, though, the one about the lover's name being like perfume poured out, makes me rather sad. Don't misunderstand me, I love the idea. It reminds me of visits to our home by special friends and family members. When one of my children calls out that one of these favourite people is at the door, the very mention of the name seems to add a new and sweeter scent to the day. I felt the same thing even more pungently as a child. One of my brothers would yell, 'Mum's back!', and suddenly everything was—well—all right again. The house was warm and normal and scented with safety.

My sadness is about the name of Jesus. Since becoming a Christian in the mid-1960s that name has had the power to strengthen me, warm me, support me, make me cry, remind me who I belong to and what I should be doing, or a combination of those things. For some, however, the word 'Jesus' triggers feelings of something very close to disgust and repulsion, largely because the man who bore that name has been relentlessly presented by far too many of those who claim to follow him, as a passionless and really rather pathetic personality, who bleats thinly and unattractively about the need for people to stop doing bad things. How sad.

The Song of Solomon tips the balance way over in the other direction, without one jot of moral or spiritual compromise, and the sweet scent of the name of Jesus is on every page.

Prayer

Restore the power and perfume of your name, Lord.

The place where we are

Song of Solomon 1:5–6 (NIV)

Dark am I, yet lovely, O daughters of Jerusalem, dark like the tents of Kedar, like the tent curtains of Solomon. Do not stare at me because I am dark, because I am darkened by the sun. My mother's sons were angry with me and made me take care of the vineyards; my own vineyard I have neglected.

Some aspects of this poem are very difficult to understand, but it appears that the girl in this passage has been sent by her brothers to work in their vineyard under the hot sun. As a result she is bronzed and beautiful, and in this state she is later encountered by Solomon (disguised as a shepherd?), who falls in love with her and eventually makes her his bride.

The theme isn't an uncommon one—I suppose Cinderella is more or less the same story in a different form—but, as a picture of Christian experience it has a particular significance, namely, that the Holy Spirit will find us and demonstrate the power of love to us in the place where we are, rather than in the place where we perhaps thought we ought to be. Often, in addition, the face of God appears to us at first in the guise of a person or set of events that are without specifically Christian labels of any kind.

Today, as I look back to the days before I became a Christian, I can see, as I was unable to see then (or for some years after my conversion, to be honest), the ways in which God fathered me in times of desolation. I recall, for instance, a café in Tunbridge Wells where, as a lost, bored, broke and singularly unattractive teenager I spent much of my time. The manageress, an Italian lady named Inez, was one of the very few rays of light in an otherwise bleak world. She fed me occasionally, smiled at me, talked to me, made me feel I was not entirely a waste of time. I hope she reads this. I'd love her to know how grateful I was and am. Today, I also thank God for being there for me, in her, at a time when I didn't even know he existed.

If you want to meet Jesus you are not in the wrong place, because that is the place where he will find you, and then you *will* go to the ball.

Prayer

Father, some of us feel that we have been badly treated and have ended up in the wrong place. Visit us with your love, Lord, in the place where we are.

For ever in love

Song of Solomon 1:12–17 (NIV)

While the king was at his table, my perfume spread its fragrance. My lover is to me a sachet of myrrh resting between my breasts. My lover is to me a cluster of henna blossoms from the vineyards of En Gedi. How beautiful you are, my darling! Oh, how beautiful! Your eyes are doves. How handsome you are, my lover! Oh, how charming! And our bed is verdant. The beams of our house are cedars; our rafters are firs.

Being in love is such a total thing, isn't it? This passage has that dreamy, all-absorbed, repetitive quality that one associates with the whole business of falling head over heels in love.

Two friends of ours fell in love when we were living in the Midlands. We knew them both very well, but separately, if you know what I mean. In fact, they probably first met at our house. Philip and Jane were both halfway through their fifties, and we were surprised and a little alarmed on first hearing that a relationship had not only begun, but was rocketing down the road towards marriage! How would these two very distinct and independent personalities cope with sharing personal space at this stage in their lives? I went out for a drink with Philip and asked him how things were going. He was in a state of terminal gooiness. Apparently he and Jane felt exactly the same about absolutely everything.

'Isn't that a remarkable coincidence?' said Philip.

'Yes, Philip,' I confirmed superfluously, 'that's a remarkable coincidence.'

'Do you know,' went on Philip dreamily, 'I was sitting in this very same pub with Jane the other evening, and she accidentally spilt some of her drink on my trousers.'

'Oh, dear,' I said, 'how annoying that must have—'

'I said to her, "Jane, don't worry, I count it a privilege to have your drink spilt on me—I really do..."'

I didn't listen to any more after that. Philip and Jane are happily not counting it a privilege to spill drinks all over each other nowadays, and I hope they'll have a very pleasant life together.

Why have I been rambling on about my friends? Well, it interests me to reflect on the fact that the idyllic 'in love-ness' expressed in these verses from Solomon's poem will never actually fade when it comes to our relationship with God. Read it again and reflect on the fact that this dream is for ever.

Prayer

Help us to never fall out of love with you, Lord.

A lily among thorns **Song of Solomon 2:1–3 (NIV)**

I am a rose of Sharon, a lily of the valleys. Like a lily among thorns is my darling among the maidens. Like an apple tree among the trees of the forest is my lover among the young men. I delight to sit in his shade, and his fruit is sweet to my taste.

This is a beautiful piece of writing, isn't it? No comment of mine can add very much. There is one little thing that strikes me, though. (Yes, yes, you're right—there's always some little thing that strikes me). It's the line where the man compares his love among maidens to a lily among brambles. What does this mean?

Here are two possible interpretations, both of which have interesting implications.

First, there's a suggestion of vulnerability. Brambles are notoriously apt to choke or impede the growth of more tender plants. Perhaps there's a hint here of the risk taken by God in allowing Jesus to be exposed as a real man to the tangles and thorns of unsaved humanity. Certainly, the sight of that baby, fragile and dependent, in the stable in Bethlehem, is one which God and all his angels must have gazed on with great pride and great fear. How would we look after him? What would happen to him in the end? The answer, of course, is that Mary and Joseph seem to have done very well, but, between us all, we crucified him. The lily was crushed but not destroyed.

This principle of the vulnerability of Jesus is, I believe, an important part of our understanding of how the body of Christ on earth should function today. A later note mentioning Mother Teresa might explain more of what I mean by that.

The second interpretation is simply that something very beautiful and special is growing in the midst of us, however wild and cheap life on News at Ten (and in our living-rooms) may seem sometimes. In each one of us, in the centre of every situation, at the heart of every storm, plague and tragedy, the flowering, or the first shoots, or, at the very least, the seeds of the growth of love can never be destroyed. And, just in case anyone thinks that's soppy talk, let me say, on behalf of myself and many others, that it is the lily among the brambles that has made it possible to survive on many, many occasions.

Prayer

Jesus, so vulnerable, so beautiful, so strong, help us to stand.

Ordinary heroes **Song of Solomon 2: 4–7 (NIV)**

He has taken me to the banquet hall, and his banner over me is love. Strengthen me with raisins, refresh me with apples, for I am faint with love. His left arm is under my head, and his right arm embraces me. Daughters of Jerusalem, I charge you by the gazelles and by the does of the field: Do not arouse or awaken love until it so desires.

'Mum! I'm home, Mum, guess what—Robert Wilson's asked me to go round his tonight, an' I'm faint with love. Get the raisins out an' bung us an apple—I need a bit of sustaining...'

Initially it seems difficult to relate the stylized romance of such a distant culture and time to contemporary experience, but, in fact, human beings have been more or less the same throughout history, and especially when it comes to affairs of the heart. Only the context and the details change (although even raisins and apples reappear nowadays as muesli, don't they? Presumably Solomon's lover's mum made sure she had a good nourishing breakfast before going out romancing every morning).

Understanding the relative 'ordinariness' of biblical characters can help to develop a constructive relationship with scripture. For years, presumably influenced by grimly dramatic lithographs in our big family Bible, and feature films in which Charlton Heston or Victor Mature gazed at the horizon accompanied by a full orchestra, my vague notion was that people like Moses and Samuel were (a) American (b) fifteen feet tall, and (c) incapable of speaking any sentence that didn't drip with cosmic significance. What rubbish!

God has always dealt with frail human beings because there isn't any other sort about. Some of the great characters of the Old Testament had particular talents and qualities, but, on reading accounts of their lives we discover that they also had pronounced faults and weaknesses. A barrier to personal involvement in passages like today's, and in much of the rest of the Bible, is this illusory feeling that our emotions, experiences, relationships and spiritual battles are somehow puny and unimportant by comparison with the 'heroes' of scripture.

Rest assured; if you've ever been in love, you will understand the Song of Solomon, and if you're serving God in the twentieth century, you are already starring in an epic all of your own.

Thought

If the Bible had been written today, in our society, would we have the Book of George, and the Book of Irene, and the Book of Stan, and the Book of...?

A season for all men

Song of Solomon 2:10–13, 16–17 (NIV)

My lover spoke and said to me, 'Arise, my darling, my beautiful one, and come with me. See! The winter is past; the rains are over and gone. Flowers appear on the earth; the season of singing has come, the cooing of doves is heard in our land. The fig-tree forms its early fruit; the blossoming vines spread their fragrance. Arise, come, my darling; my beautiful one, come with me.'... My lover is mine and I am his; he browses among the lilies. Until the day breaks and the shadows flee, turn, my lover, and be like a gazelle or like a young stag on the rugged hills.

This must be one of the most famous springtime rhapsodies of all time, sung by one, not only enraptured by the new season, but also in love, a pretty unbeatable combination.

One of the clichés of Christianity is the spiritual symbolism of the seasons, isn't it? We're born, we live, we pass through the evening of our lives, we die, we are born again. These parallels have only become clichés, of course, because they really do resonate, not just with specifically Christian cycles, but with the very rhythm of living itself. As the years go by my gratitude for seasonal change intensifies. Living through a year in this country is like travelling in majestic slow motion on the most magnificent theme park ride that could ever be devised.

The symbols? Well, for me there are symbols within symbols. Here's an example.

In front of our house stands a large Japanese flowering cherry. The tree has obviously been there for years. For forty-nine weeks of the year, this sturdy growth is undistinguished, but when the spring comes it explodes into a triumph of pink blossom. For three weeks a huge orb of colour shines over the street like the most precious of precious jewels, glowing with particular magnificence under blue skies. After this brief but spectacularly successful run the performance ends, and our neighbours start getting annoyed about soggy blossom all over their front gardens.

When I was ill over a decade ago, the blooming of that tree was like a sign from heaven, suggesting to me that God employs a special magic to bring beauty out of dullness. Every year I look forward to a repeat of that little exercise in optimism, a sort of arboreal rainbow, a symbol within a symbol.

I love springtime.

Prayer

Thank you for the seasons and the possibility of change.

Lost lovers

Song of Solomon 3:1–4 (NIV)

'All night long on my bed I looked for the one my heart loves; I looked for him but did not find him. I will get up now and go about the city, through its streets and squares; I will search for the one my heart loves. So I looked for him but did not find him. The watchmen found me as they made their rounds in the city. "Have you seen the one my heart loves?" Scarcely had I passed them when I found the one my heart loves. I held him and would not let him go till I had brought him to my mother's house, to the room of the one who conceived me.'

Of all the heart-rending letters that people send me from time to time, the ones that upset me most (perhaps because I can identify with them) are those in which a desperate but unfulfilled desire for God is expressed. Like the speaker in this passage these unhappy souls cry out in the dark night of their desolation for some sign or indication that they are not alone—that God really does hear them and love them, that they will eventually be united with him and that—well, you know—that everything will be warm and fuzzy and wonderful.

Often, these folk have already sought and received most of the statutory varieties of advice, and are hoping I might offer some new, super-effective idea that will transform their lives. Oh, dear!

I suppose if God was a system, or a mechanism, or even a sheet of MFI instructions, I might be able to help in that way, but he isn't—he is a creative, dynamic personality who cannot be adjusted or programmed to produce a particular effect.

When you set against that the complexity of each of the human beings who has dealings with him, the problem appears to become even more insoluble. What I can say, from personal experience, is that if you are one of these lost lovers, a right time will come to rise from your bed and go about the city, in the streets and in the squares, looking for your God, and then you will meet him. But it must be the right time, the moment that he has chosen for you.

When you do find him—and you will—don't take him for granted. Don't let him go.

Prayer

Father, hear the cries from the dark and stretch out your arms towards us. We want to be with you so much.

Too good to be true

Song of Solomon 4:1, 5–7 (NIV)

How beautiful you are, my darling! Oh, how beautiful! Your eyes behind your veil are doves. Your hair is like a flock of goats descending from Mount Gilead... Your two breasts are like two fawns, like twin fawns of a gazelle that browse among the lilies. Until the day breaks and the shadows flee, I will go to the mountain of myrrh and to the hill of incense. All beautiful you are, my darling; there is no flaw in you.

When I was a teenager an advert appeared in *The Times*. The small panel on the back page simply offered a free car—a mini—to the first person who replied. There were no strings attached, nothing to be paid, in fact, no catch at all. Someone could have had a car for nothing, but not a single person responded. Presumably readers thought they'd be 'done' in some way. Of course, that was exactly the reaction the advertisers had expected; nevertheless, the car really was there for the taking.

Do you think people were silly to be wary? Well, look at this passage, which offers something rather more valuable than a mini, and ask yourself whether you think it's for real. Let me explain.

The Song of Solomon is many things, including, as I mentioned in the introduction, a picture of God's love for his bride, the Church. That, in case you didn't realize it, means you—and me. Now, I'd like us to ask ourselves the following question. Leaving aside items such as having breasts like two fawns, do we honestly believe that this is what God sees when he looks at us?

Are we—not just beautiful—but very beautiful to him? Does he really think us lovely? Could we possibly be without flaw in his sight? Is it conceivable that we stir such excited pleasure in his breast?

He says this is all true. Perhaps there's a catch. I don't think so. Even less than when the Plass family go fishing. We are so much in the groove of self-criticism that we forget we are caught up with Christ. We are as beautiful as he is, not because of what we are or do, but because he is in us and we are in him. Can we accept that? Come on—we missed out on the mini—let's have a go.

Prayer

Some of us don't feel very beautiful, Lord. Help us to get lost in your love.

Sweet nothings **Song of Solomon 4:9–11 (NIV)**

You have stolen my heart, my sister, my bride; you have stolen my heart with one glance of your eyes, with one jewel of your necklace. How delightful is your love, my sister, my bride! How much more pleasing is your love than wine, and the fragrance of your perfume than any spice! Your lips drop sweetness as the honeycomb, my bride; milk and honey are under your tongue. The fragrance of your garments is like that of Lebanon.

I wish I was a little better at the old sweet nothings. Mind you, my wife would be deeply suspicious if I suddenly nestled up and told her that honey and milk are under her tongue, and the scent of her garments is like the scent of Lebanon. As for claiming that I regard her love as much better than wine—I'm not at all sure she'd believe me.

Seriously, it does seem a pity that many marriages deteriorate, not just into lack of romance, but actual conflict. A dismally common view of marriage is exemplified by a scene I once witnessed in a laundrette. As I entered a loud argument was going on between a man and woman in their early sixties.

'You don't understand listenin', do you?' shouted the lady. 'All you can do is make a noise!'

'Go on, get out of it!' returned the man furiously. 'You're nothin' but a stupid, mouthy old ratbag!'

'Don't worry!' she snapped. 'I don't want to be anywhere you might be!'

And with that, she swept through the door and disappeared.

A pear-shaped lady who'd observed hostilities from beside the drying machines shifted slightly on her seat and addressed the man in dispassionate tones. 'She your wife, then?'

The man stopped muttering and stared at her.

'Married to 'er!' he said incredulously, 'I wouldn't marry 'er if she was the last woman on earth!'

'Oh,' said the pear-shaped lady, dispassionate as ever, 'I thought she must be your wife the way you was talkin' to 'er.'

An extreme example of how marriage is seen, perhaps, but it does seem such a shame that so many marriages begin as romances, only to decline to the point where your marriage partner is the only person you're ever really nasty to.

Prayer

Lord, we can't reach Solomon's standard, but we'd like to bring some romance back into our marriages. Help those of us who are married to see our partners with fresh eyes, and begin to appreciate them all over again.

Unlocking

Song of Solomon 4:12–16 (NIV)

You are a garden locked up, my sister, my bride; you are a spring enclosed, a sealed fountain. Your plants are an orchard of pomegranates with choice fruits, with henna and nard, nard and saffron, calamus and cinnamon, with every kind of incense tree, with myrrh and aloes and all the finest spices. You are a garden fountain, a well of flowing water streaming down from Lebanon. Awake, north wind, and come, south wind! Blow on my garden, that its fragrance may spread abroad. Let my lover come into his garden and taste its choice fruits.

I mentioned earlier that I occasionally look back with horror to the time when, as a teenage truant of fifteen or sixteen, I wandered aimlessly around Tunbridge Wells with no money and no prospects. It isn't the idea of the aimless wandering that causes my horror—that has remained one of my favourite hobbies—it's the memory of how I dealt with feelings of gross inadequacy about most of my relationships. I developed a habit of scathing sarcasm that probably alienated more people than I ever imagined at the time. Lowest form of wit it may have been, but for a pain-filled loser like me, it was the most effective way of ensuring that I made some impact on someone, sometimes.

I'm sure people were infuriated by my sardonic attitude. I don't blame them. But I think if they'd known what a yearning there was within me to give and receive warmth and emotion at exactly the same time as I was attempting to cut every other ego in sight down to size, they would have been amazed.

With a few friends, predictably those who demonstrated unequivocally that they valued me, I dropped my act, but those people were few and far between.

A significant effect of encounters with God over the last few years has, thank goodness, been a release of the natural, childlike desire in me to love and be loved for what I am, however unimpressive that turns out to be. I believe and hope that my sarcasm has been transfigured into satire nowadays. As I read today's passage I see and sense in the heart of it God's promise that all the locked, beautiful gardens within us will be thrown open one day, and all the sealed fountains allowed to overflow with feelings and thoughts and words that have hardly seen the light of day before. I know that some of you who are reading these words today need that more than anything else in the world.

Prayer

Unlock us and release us, Lord. Walk in this garden. Drink from this fountain.

What do you think about God?

Song of Solomon 5:8–11, 16 (NIV)

O daughters of Jerusalem, I charge you—if you find my lover, what will you tell him? Tell him I am faint with love. How is your beloved better than others, most beautiful of women? How is your beloved better than others, that you charge us so? My lover is radiant and ruddy, outstanding among ten thousand. His head is purest gold; his hair is wavy and black as a raven... His mouth is sweetness itself; he is altogether lovely. This is my lover, this my friend, O daughters of Jerusalem.

Because of travelling so much as a speaker I see an enormous number of churches in the course of a year, and I meet hundreds of Christians doing work of various kinds, from full-time ministry to the making of coffee on a Sunday morning. I never tire of hearing what's happening, especially from people who are really caught up in their activities. James Herriot wrote that enthusiasts are attractive, but fanatics are irresistible. I agree. Quite often, though, when I have been listening for some time to a description of recent youth-group activities or progress with the new church extension, I throw in a question that I've asked more times than I've had cold dinners that were supposed to be hot at missionary fundraising meetings.

'What do you think about God?'

The usual reply, after a moment's puzzled silence, is, 'What do you mean?'

'Well, what do you personally think and feel about God—about Jesus?'

Some people wouldn't be able to answer this question if I stood and waited all day, because, at this stage in their lives, they have not met him in any conscious sense. Others speak with varying degrees of eagerness or devotion, but the ones I really enjoy are those whose eyes and manner soften, as they attempt, incoherently or lucidly, to tell me how much they love him, and, perhaps, how proud they are to be working for him.

That's more or less what is happening in this passage.

'What's so special about this man of yours?' the women ask.

The reply is lyrical and overwhelming, containing words that, for 2,000 years, have summed up the feelings of true believers about Jesus.

'This is my beloved and this is my friend.'

Prayer

Help us to put you at the centre of our work for you, Lord, and to give a good, warm account of you when we are asked.

Open our eyes **Song of Solomon 6:1–5 (NIV)**

Where has your lover gone, most beautiful of women? Which way did your lover turn, that we may look for him with you? My lover has gone down to his garden, to the beds of spices, to browse in the gardens and to gather lilies. I am my lover's and my lover is mine; he browses among the lilies. You are beautiful, my darling, as Tirzah, lovely as Jerusalem, majestic as troops with banners. Turn your eyes from me; they overwhelm me. Your hair is like a flock of goats descending from Gilead.

Have you ever wondered why God has allowed Mother Teresa to become known to such a wide public? Wouldn't it have made more sense to leave her to quietly get on with her work among the poor in India, while the blow-wave evangelists do all the up-front stuff. Clearly, God wanted to make some sort of point, and this passage may offer a clue as to what it was.

'Where has your beloved gone?'

When that question is asked of Christians you can expect a wide variety of responses. Some are quite sure he is contained within a specific liturgical framework, others just know that the only venue at which he can be reliably expected to put in an appearance is their very own church between ten-thirty and twelve o'clock on a Sunday morning. Yet others have him stuck down solidly to the pages of the Bible, a number are certain he lives at Butlin's, and there are even a few who would locate him somewhere inside a television set, firmly under the control of a steely-eyed American evangelist.

What would Mother Teresa say? I suspect that she might reply in a rather similar way to the maiden in these verses, that he has gone to pasture his flocks in the gardens. But for Mother Teresa the flocks are sick, filth-ingrained, homeless people, and the gardens are the teeming streets of India. I believe that God raised this remarkable woman to prominence to remind us that our beloved is still to be found among those who need him, and to help us understand that if our spiritual sight is corrected we might be able, like Mother Teresa, to see Jesus in the eyes of beggars, and lilies on the streets of Calcutta.

Prayer

Open the eyes of our understanding, Lord, to see where you are to be found. May we see hope where there was only despair, and beauty where there was only ugliness.

On the contrary **Song of Solomon 7:1–2, 6–9 (NIV)**

How beautiful your sandalled feet, O prince's daughter! Your graceful legs are like jewels, the work of a craftsman's hands. Your navel is a rounded goblet that never lacks blended wine. Your waist is a mound of wheat encircled by lilies... How beautiful you are and how pleasing, O love, with your delights! Your stature is like that of the palm, and your breasts like clusters of fruit. I said, 'I will climb the palm tree; I will take hold of its fruit.' May your breasts be like the clusters of the vine, the fragrance of your breath like apples, and your mouth like the best wine. May the wine go straight to my lover, flowing gently over lips and teeth.

Solomon must have been a wow at Old Testament parties, mustn't he? What a chat-up line! I wonder how he would have got on nowadays. I'm not sure how the average modern girl would react to being told that her navel is a rounded bowl that never lacks mixed wine. I'm a bit confused about the rounded thighs like jewels as well. Jewels? I expect those references had cultural significance. The rest of this passage, though—my goodness!

If those who condemn the Bible (without reading it) for being bland and passionless were to study passages like this, they might have to shift their attack to a different front altogether. Perhaps they would end up complaining that such blatantly sensual expressions of sexual desire are inappropriate to a book claiming to be the living word of God. After all, they might point out, he is uncompromisingly critical of sexual immorality in many other parts of the very same book. But, of course, that *is* precisely the point. Sadly, the Church has tended to emphasize the negative aspects of sex, so that for many it has become an area of dark repression and guilt. God is often perceived as being concerned only with preventing people from enjoying themselves.

Read the passage again. Allegorically or literally, its message is clear. This climber of palm trees, this holder of branches, this connoisseur of wines and kisses, is as far removed from being anti-sex as it is possible to be. God is not just mildly and benignly tolerant of physical love, he is extravagantly in favour of it when it is enjoyed within the context of a spiritually committed relationship. He designed it, and saw that it was good. And it is.

Prayer

Lord, help us not to be frightened about things that you have given us. We'll try to be positive when talking about these things to people who don't know you.

Nowhere in particular

Song of Solomon 7:10–13 (NIV)

I belong to my lover, and his desire is for me. Come, my lover, let us go to the countryside, let us spend the night in the villages. Let us go early to the vineyards to see if the vines have budded, if their blossoms have opened, and if the pomegranates are in bloom—there I will give you my love. The mandrakes send out their fragrance, and at our door is every delicacy, both new and old, that I have stored up for you, my lover.

A few weeks before this note was written, Bridget and I took David and Katy over to France to spend a few days at the small cottage in Normandy that we own jointly with some local friends. This dumpy little dwelling, blessedly lacking in everything beginning with the prefix 'tele', stands next to a tiny junior school in a sleepy village, and has only three rooms, one dining-sitting-doing-things sort of room, and two bedrooms. The optimistically named 'bathroom' is designed for people at the lower end of the not-very-tall range, but it allows you to do whatever you need to do, albeit in rather contorted postures.

Ours is not a smart cottage. It probably qualifies for a quarter-star rating, but it and the fascinatingly lit valley it overlooks are full of strong magic. Those who stay there invariably seem to relax, and that's exactly what we did on this occasion.

I'm potty about France anyway, but there was something extra special about this visit. Something inside me sat down and took it easy for the first time for a very long time. We went for little walks to nowhere in particular, we cycled through farms to a place where the river runs beneath an old crumbling bridge and talked to a little brown goat who seemed anxious to get to know us, we went up to the nearby forest and collected kindling for the open fire, we ate long lingering breakfasts at the table by the window that overlooks the valley and we played French cricket on the lawn (an area of rough grass at the side of the house).

Something about this passage is almost tearfully reminiscent of those all too few peaceful days when we laughed together and looked at things together and simply rejoiced in being people who loved each other in a place that was lovely. It doesn't happen very often, does it? When the Lord and his bride are truly united it will happen for ever and ever.

A prayer

Come soon, Lord Jesus.

Permission to feel   Song of Solomon 8:6–7 (NIV)

Place me like a seal over your heart, like a seal on your arm; for love is as strong as death, its jealousy unyielding as the grave. It burns like blazing fire, like a mighty flame. Many waters cannot quench love; rivers cannot wash it away. If one were to give all the wealth of his house for love, it would be utterly scorned.

What do you think about unreliable people? I'm infuriatingly erratic at times. Kind people who write to me might get a reply the very next day, or they might end up sending me one of those embarrassing little following notes that say: 'I enclose a copy of the letter I sent to you last year, as the original was clearly lost in the post...'

Unreliable people are maddening at times (I have a degree in Hypocrisy), but they can also be vivid and stimulating. When options are not obliged to arrange themselves in straight lines, anything can happen, with wonderful or terrible results.

The same is true of emotions. When I was a young Christian we were 'warned off' emotions, as though they were dangerous ogres, sitting on our shoulders, whispering deceitful distractions to lure us from the straight and narrow. Generally speaking, I accepted this caution, but I was a bit puzzled. Why, when my original encounter with Jesus had been such an emotional affair, and I was such an emotional person who felt everything so deeply, was I supposed to ignore feelings?

Nowadays, I see the defensiveness that probably crept into such teaching. At those times when God cannot be seen, heard, touched, smelled, tasted or otherwise sensed in any way, the only thing likely to rein in your average youth group is a previously implanted suggestion that the way you feel, however dismal, has no real relevance to the situation. And, yes, there is a real, crucially important point to be made about trusting what or who you know, at the times when you stop feeling. But one of the things that the Song of Songs in general, and this passage in particular, teaches us, is that because God's love affair with the Church is a passionate, emotional business, feelings are an essential part of our relationship with him.

Like those unreliable friends, our emotions have an alarming, but necessary and potentially very creative role in our spiritual lives. Be wary by all means, but not wooden.

A prayer

Open our eyes and our hearts, Lord, to your love, strong as death, your passion, fierce as the grave.

The great storm comes at harvest time.

French proverb

GATHERING AS WE GO

Harvest in the Bible

It's so easy to forget important things, isn't it?

I was in a group that was being asked to talk about the experience that had excited each of us more than any other. It was a Christian group, and therefore, for better or worse, most of the answers tended to be about conversion or baptism or healing or something similar. One or two people did mention things like hang-gliding and the birth of their children, but, in the main, specifically spiritual adventures dominated.

I didn't say anything for a long time, because I was trying as hard as I could to answer the question with strict accuracy. In the back of my mind I felt that I knew what that answer was, but, although a long list of candidates jostled for front position in my mind, it was very hard to pin down the truth.

What about the time in Africa in 1995, for instance, when we hired a small plane and flew out from Johannesburg to spend three days at a game lodge on the edge of the Kruger National Park? Now, that was exciting! Very early each morning we were taken out in an open-topped jeep to spot animals in the wild. We would then return for a huge breakfast at the lodge. In the evening, we would set out once more, equipped with powerful torches on the front of the vehicle, to explore the vast acres of African bush as darkness fell. Both of these daily trips lasted for at least two hours. I cannot begin to convey the thrill of seeing, in their natural habitat, creatures that I had only ever seen in zoos or circuses before. We tracked the path of a lion right into the undergrowth, and saw where her recent kill had been hidden. As we gazed at the remains we suddenly realized that the lioness herself was regarding us with ominous suspicion from the top of a very adjacent hillock. We caught a leopard in the beam of our torch and followed it through the long grass as it sought cover. We came across giraffes, elephants, wild dogs, and one very satisfying rhinoceros. This experience could easily have been the one that I was thinking of, but—no, that wasn't it.

Something to do with writing? Well, that could easily be what I was trying to remember—that amazing day when I signed copies of *The Sacred Diary* for two and a half hours at Spring Harvest, at a time in my life when everything else seemed to be going wrong. Surely that must have been the most exciting moment in my life? No—still not it.

Seeing my children born? Mindblowing, but—no.

First kiss? Definitely not (I was trying to eat fried chicken at the time).

Getting married? No, too frightening.

What about the day when we moved into the first house that we'd ever owned. That was *tremendously* exciting. But it still wasn't the thing tickling the back of my mind.

So what on earth was it? I strained to remember. It was frustrating. The finger-tips of my memory were just managing to touch the extreme edge of whatever this thing was. It was something much further back than those other experiences—something so vibrantly, electrifyingly exciting that the very aura of this unidentified recollection set my nerves tingling and jingling in anticipation of—*what*, for goodness' sake?

'Radishes!'

My sudden triumphant cry was received by the rest of the group as though I had uttered some sort of vegan swear word.

'Radishes,' I repeated, 'my most exciting experience of all time was seeing my radishes come up when I was about three.'

Of course it was. Nothing had come close to it since. I remembered it all now. I could see the small square of garden at the edge of my father's allotment, the one that was specially mine. I could see myself carefully making a groove in the earth with a stick, then sowing seeds from the packet that I'd bought at the shop in the village where they seemed to sell everything under the sun. On the back of that packet was a picture illustrating the Platonic ideal of radishness, a bunch of huge radishes, their luxuriant, emerald growth sprouting from crimson red tops that merged into creamy white at the base. That was how my radishes were going to look. After covering up the seeds with earth I impaled the empty packet in two places on a stick as I had seen my father do, and stuck the stick into the ground at the end of the row, just in case, by some miracle much greater than the miracle of plant reproduction, I should forget what I was growing there. I think, also, I had a vague and strictly private notion that the plants might appreciate some kind of reminder of what they were supposed to be as they emerged from the earth.

Kneeling by my newly planted row, I would study the length of raised earth intently, wondering if the mysterious underground process of turning into radishes had actually begun yet, and hoping that if I hung around for a few minutes more I might actually spot the very first tiny spot of green to appear as the pioneers of my crop struggled towards the light.

For part of every single day I squatted by that bed, checking my radishes, becoming very slightly agnostic about the promised metamorphosis as time went by. Then—oh, the indescribable joy of discovering one morning that miniscule green shoots had begun to appear in exactly the right places—the places where little me had ordained that they should appear by sowing the seeds in that very nearly straight line the other day. The promise had come true—things *did* grow!

As all ex-radish enthusiasts will clearly remember, in the early stages of growth a radish plant consists of two tiny oval leaves pushing out in opposite directions, for all the world, I used to think, like two little hands extended in such a manner that each plant seemed to be saying, 'Well, here I am!' I believe I only just stopped short of naming each radish individually.

All I dreamed of from that first day of visible growth was harvest. I was terribly impatient. Days went by. At the first sign of embryonic red globes emerging from the earth I wanted to pull my radishes up. I *so* wanted to pull my radishes up! I was restrained by higher authority, but only just.

'What if they grow too much?' I inquired worriedly. 'What if they grow right up out of the ground and fall over and get eaten by—by cats?'

'Cats don't eat radishes.'

'Oh.'

At last the shining day arrived. Higher authority decreed that some of my radishes might be ready for pulling up. There can be few more profound and innocently sensual experiences than harvesting your own crop from the rich earth. And, at three, or any other age really, can there be a greater thrill than to walk into your own kitchen, as casually as you can in view of the fact that you are positively shivering with delight, to present your own mother with the firstfruits of your own labour? Real, proper teatime on that first day of harvest always featured *my* radishes. I was so proud.

This section is all about harvest, the first and last notes concerning prayer, without which there can be no harvest. As we work our way through it, let's bear in mind that the planting, preparation, daily attention and eventual reaping of our personal harvest for God needs to be conducted in exactly the same spirit of wonder and innocent excitement that I experienced as a child with my garden. Our limited contribution to the needs of the kingdom of God may appear small to us, but I can assure you that, if we offer them in the right spirit, they will be taken from our hands with the same seriousness and gratitude that my mother showed when she took those radishes from me when I was three, and which Jesus himself must have shown when he took two loaves and five small fishes (and a couple of radishes?) from a little boy on a hillside 2,000 years ago.

Prayer

Father, our harvest for you will be small, but we offer it to you with the confidence that you love all gifts from your children. Thank you for the miracles you do with radishes and the like. Amen.

Honestly!

Isaiah 29:13 (NIV)

The Lord says: 'These people come near to me with their mouth and honour me with their lips, but their hearts are far from me. Their worship of me is made up only of rules taught by men.'

Prayer can be so many things, but I think I find a sort of respectful friendship at the centre of all my honest dealings with God. The honesty is a relatively recent addition to my prayer life. Until I reached my mid-thirties I was very similar to the people who God is addressing through Isaiah in this passage. My mouth produced some well-rounded, well-organized sounds in the theoretical direction of God, but my heart was occupied elsewhere. Things changed after my wife and I said a very honest prayer for once.

'God,' we said, 'we know that we haven't done very well with anything up to now, but we really want to go all the way with you. We realize that we don't understand what that means, but whatever it costs, and however much it hurts, please let it happen. Amen.'

For once our prayer didn't bounce off the ceiling and fall on our heads, and it was in that same year that, through illness and recovery, I discovered the reality of God's fatherly love in a completely new way. Part of that new way was a relaxation in prayer, an understanding that, as the friends of Jesus, we are warmly welcomed to the presence of God. There seemed to be only two requirements—be there, and be honest. God could handle anger, tears, boredom, badly phrased prayers and just about anything else as long as they were offered to him as a child offers its moods to a parent.

I am not a disciplined sort of person at all, but I found myself settling into a flexible routine which included some sort of apology, prayers for friends and enemies, and, most important of all, a period spent just *being* with God, enjoying his joy in being with me. I wish I could pretend that this idyllic-sounding scenario has continued without pause since then, but I am a perverse human being. I abandon regular prayer times for weeks on end and wonder why my life feels shapeless and unsupported. Then I begin again and wonder why I ever stopped.

But it's always okay—as long as I'm honest, we just start again.

Prayer

Let us pray.

Give as good as you get **Exodus 23:15–16 (NIV)**

No-one is to appear before me empty-handed. Celebrate the Feast of Harvest with the firstfruits of the crops you sow in your field.

God must be so tired of receiving our left-overs.

I remember sitting with friends in a local restaurant, discussing the need for new elders in their church, a quite large Brethren assembly along the coast from us.

'The problem is,' said Jean, 'that everyone's so busy. There are three or four people who'd be really good, but they just can't spare the time. It's not fair to ask.'

I nodded and sighed automatically as I usually do. There's probably far too much sympathetic nodding and sighing in the Church nowadays. Afterwards I realized what my response ought to have been. Why should God be offered leaders on the basis that they have time? Why shouldn't he be offered leaders on the basis that they are right for the job, or (forgive me for suggesting such a thing) that he is calling specific individuals to become whatever he wants them to become? Why shouldn't priorities be altered so that we *create* time for the most important purpose of all?

I don't think God wants the fag-ends of our time, or our effort, or our money, or our concentration, or our love. Whatever the harvest of our lives might be, he wants the firstfruits, not the scraps. If you want to encounter God at his most scathingly angry on this subject, read the book of Malachi. I tend to avoid it.

I am reminded of an ancient aunt of mine who lived in Wales. After breaking several bones in one leg she was confined to a wheelchair and unable to take part in the village activities that had meant so much to her. One of the local ladies organized a collection among Auntie Susan's contemporaries, and used the proceedings to purchase a rather straggly plant in a pot, which was duly presented to the invalid.

'The thing is,' the collector confided to my wife, 'I only asked them for ten pence each, so they hardly noticed they'd parted with anything.'

Sums it up, really, doesn't it?

Prayer

Father, help us to offer our best to you. We want to seek the kingdom of God above all things, but we get distracted. Show us what we should be giving from our harvest.

Urgent message **John 4:35 (NIV)**

Do you not say, 'Four months more and then the harvest'? I tell you, open your eyes and look at the fields! They are ripe for harvest.

I entirely agree with C.S. Lewis when he says that there are going to be a lot of surprises in heaven. I believe that God is just, and I suspect that a lot of people are going to receive rewards that they never knew they had earned. If that's not true, then the twenty-fifth chapter of Matthew doesn't mean anything. Conversely, there will be others, Jesus tells us, who will be unacknowledged by God despite their loud claims that they wrought miracles in the name of his Son. I would like to believe that everyone will be saved (no, I can't claim to know exactly what that means) but if I also want to follow the Jesus of the New Testament, I can't help but be infected with the passionate urgency revealed in passages such as this. Jesus came to save sinners from some kind of eternal separation. He was perfectly clear about that, whatever anyone else wants to think. We leave the surprises to him, and get on with the harvest, that seems to be the plan.

I joined a church for a street mission in London once. Before we left the church building we prayed, and one lady gave a very dramatic prophecy about the 'scythe descending, and a mighty harvest to be reaped'. When we reached the spot, on this very cold day, there were only two 'ears of corn' to listen to us, and neither of them seemed very interested. Our speaker, a man who has a real ear for God, said that the Lord was calling someone with a marriage problem, someone with a hearing disorder and someone with respiratory difficulties. None of these materialized and we all trudged dismally home. A year later, the speaker was stopped by a man who said, 'I was walking past when you did that street thing. I had trouble with my ears, bronchitis, and my marriage was falling apart. I was too embarrassed to stop, but I found a church and I became a Christian.'

God had mobilized that whole event to save one man. The harvest goes on.

Prayer

Father, show us what you're doing, and we'll join in.

Mean?! Me?!

Leviticus 19:9–10 (NIV)

When you reap the harvest of your land, do not reap to the very edges of your field or gather the gleanings of your harvest. Do not go over your vineyard a second time or pick up the grapes that have fallen. Leave them for the poor and the alien. I am the Lord your God.

One of the vices I hate most is meanness and penny-pinching. There's nothing worse than being on holiday for instance with the kind of person who waits outside the café for you because 'there's no point in paying for coffee when we can have it for nothing back at the cottage'. I don't mean that I approve of spending indiscriminately (although I'm pretty good at doing that on the rare occasions when I've got any money to do it with). It's just that I get depressed when any streams of availability dry up. I guess that goes back to my own childhood when we never knew for sure whether my father would part with the housekeeping money on a Friday, or take offence over some imagined misdeed of my mother, leaving us all to wonder how we would eat for the rest of the week. I've hated all wilful withholding of resources ever since.

Imagine, then, my horror at discovering that I have exactly the same vice developed to the point of miserliness in my own make-up. It only erupts occasionally, like some underground molten river, and it isn't only to do with money, but it's very real. A sort of panicking insecurity drives me to greedily clutch to myself every scrap of time, or ready money, or attention from others, or whatever is around at the time. I reap to the very edge of my field, and I gather the gleanings of my harvest. It is a far from attractive characteristic, and I'm always very relieved when the tension relaxes in me and I'm able to, as it were, release my grip.

I realize that it's a rather alarming prospect, and it's probably very cheap psychology as well, but try having a look at the thing you dislike most in others, then honestly assess the extent to which it's replicated in your own character. Maybe I'm the only one!

Prayer

Father, let the weakness we see in ourselves encourage generosity towards others in their weakness.

What's the catch? **Luke 5:4–11 (NIV)**

When he had finished speaking, he said to Simon, 'Put out into deep water, and let down the nets for a catch.' Simon answered, 'Master, we've worked hard all night and haven't caught anything. But because you say so, I will let down the nets.' When they had done so, they caught such a large number of fish that their nets began to break. So they signalled to their partners in the other boat to come and help them, and they came and filled both boats so full that they began to sink. When Simon Peter saw this, he fell at Jesus' knees and said, 'Go away from me, Lord; I am a sinful man!' For he and all his companions were astonished at the catch of fish they had taken, and so were James and John, the sons of Zebedee, Simon's partners. Then Jesus said to Simon, 'Don't be afraid; from now on you will catch men.' So they pulled their boats up on shore, left everything and followed him.

Saatchi and Saatchi would have found Jesus a very frustrating client to have. He refused just about every opportunity to exploit his natural advantages. Here's a good example. After a night remarkable only for its barren fish harvest, Peter and his mates, having heard some great stuff from the benevolent hijacker of their boat, go along with Jesus' suggestion that they should let their nets down one more time. Peter's reactions of fear and astonishment when the huge catch comes in are very understandable, but I wonder if the Saatchi and Saatchi side of him peeped through for just an instant, speculating perhaps on the possibility of this strange man joining the piscatorial team on a full-time basis. There would be two good reasons for not suggesting such a thing.

First, Peter must have sensed that this was far from being a commercial gesture. Jesus was saying—or rather showing—that material success was easily and abundantly available to him. It was a one-off, almost casual demonstration of power. And that leads directly into the second reason.

Peter must have been puzzled, fascinated and strangely thrilled by the fact that this Jesus, who seemed to have total control over the environment, was calling him, a simple fisherman, to join in some inexplicable task called 'fishing for men'. Thrilling for us as well to realize that he *needs* us to help bring in the only harvest that really counts.

Questions

Have we seen the power? Would we follow?

How much? Haggai 1:5–10 (NIV)

Now this is what the Lord Almighty says: 'Give careful thought to your ways. You have planted much, but have harvested little. You eat, but never have enough. You drink, but never have your fill. You put on clothes, but are not warm. You earn wages, only to put them in a purse with holes in it.' This is what the Lord Almighty says: 'Give careful thought to your ways. Go up into the mountains and bring down timber and build the house, so that I may take pleasure in it and be honoured,' says the Lord. 'You expected much, but see, it turned out to be little. What you brought home, I blew away. Why?' declares the Lord Almighty. 'Because of my house, which remains a ruin, while each of you is busy with his own house. Therefore, because of you the heavens have withheld their dew and the earth its crops.'

'There's a hole in my bucket...'

As I intimated in the section on Old Testament figures, the message of Haggai is timeless. The recipients of the prophet's message were lurching from disappointment to disappointment; from dismal failure to dismal failure. They were working hard, eating and drinking well, dressing in good clothes and earning plenty of money, but somehow they were never quite full or refreshed, never warm, and never in funds. Nothing satisfied them because the most important dimension of their lives was lacking. They had failed to build a house for God. The old temple lay in ruins while they lived in their smart panelled houses.

No wonder the so-called 'health and wealth' movement is dying a death. The notion is fundamentally ludicrous. Any Christian movement that fails to accommodate Jesus at the very heart of itself will go through that same cycle of trying and failing endlessly, until the ruins of humility and dependence are swept away and rebuilt at the centre.

The present-day Church is paying heavily for the Debenham's sale style of evangelism that says you can have the whole salvation package in return for one small down-payment of an assenting prayer. Jesus' teaching on repentance and cost is not popular. How could it be when its clear implication is that you give your harvest freely to him, and happily accept whatever he gives back to you?

We cannot have our divine cake—and eat it.

Prayer

Come and live in me, Jesus. Just give me a minute while I clear out all this stuff...

Heavy rock

Matthew 13:5–6 (NIV)

Some fell on rocky places, where it did not have much soil. It sprang up quickly, because the soil was shallow. But when the sun came up, the plants were scorched, and they withered because they had no root.

For a while my wife worked in what used to be called an approved school. The teenage girls who were resident in this grim establishment were mainly delinquent or out of control. Many of them were very disturbed and all were grossly inadequate. The lives of these kids were characterized by disruption, conflict, divorce and general emotional chaos. Some had been abused sexually, and others had been beaten regularly. The atmosphere of this boarding school was far from jolly.

Very occasionally the school would be visited by Christian outreach groups, who spent an evening describing the faith and calling girls to repentance. Hearing that everything would change once they invited Jesus into their lives, many of the girls would repent in floods of tears, desperate to embrace something that offered so much. The hit-and-run evangelists would depart rejoicing over their success, leaving the new 'converts' to wonder why nothing seemed to have changed when they woke up the next morning.

Quite apart from the fact that evangelism without follow-up is irresponsible, these poor girls had no root in themselves. The good earth that is formed by consistent experiences of trust and love and security was simply not present in their lives. They were rocky places, the hearts of those children.

But there will be a harvest there as well. God loves each of those desperate kids, and he is quite capable of breaking up rock to form new soil. It can be a long process, though, and it will probably require Christians who are not infected with quick-fix disease to commit themselves to long-term support and contact and caring for individuals whose lives were shattered before they even had a chance to get started.

If you really want to help someone like that, ask God to show you who needs a friend. But, be warned, he'll probably answer your prayer.

Thought

We are all responsible for our own actions, but some of us don't know how to take responsibility. We need to share the burden of learning with someone who won't give up too easily.

Enveloped by love

Luke 11:5–7 (NIV)

Then he said to them, 'Suppose one of you has a friend, and he goes to him at midnight and says, "Friend, lend me three loaves of bread, because a friend of mine on a journey has come to me, and I have nothing to set before him." Then the one inside answers, "Don't bother me. The door is already locked, and my children are with me in bed. I can't get up and give you anything." I tell you, though he will not get up and give him the bread because he is his friend, yet because of the man's boldness he will get up and give him as much as he needs.'

My children were fascinated to know why I started to spend a part of each morning sifting through a pile of brown envelopes that lay on my desk in the upstairs sitting-room a few years ago.

'Well,' I explained, 'each of these envelopes has got a letter inside it. All of the letters are written to God, and each one is about someone I know or someone I want to pray for.'

'Are you going to send them, then?' asked David.

'Well, I don't think there's much point in posting them,' I replied seriously, 'but every day I hold each one up to God and ask him to look after the person I've written about.'

The boys looked through the pile of sealed envelopes with great interest, noting the name written on the front of each. Joe became very animated when he discovered one marked 'ENEMIES'.

'Those are the difficult ones,' I said, 'but I'm supposed to pray specially for them, so I just grit my teeth and do it.'

'Tell us who your enemies are, Dad,' said David.

'No, that wouldn't be fair.'

'Does it work?'

'I'll tell you in a few months.'

And in a few months I was able to tell them that it really *did* seem to work! Persistent prayer seems to gradually massage events and circumstances and people and attitudes into a position nearer to God, or nearer to what he wants.

Thought

I hope I'm in someone else's envelope—even as an enemy...

People who are anxious to shine
can never tell a plain story.
George Borrow

STORY POWER —TALES TO TRAVEL BY

Parables

A good story is such a wonderful thing, isn't it? Ever since I was a small boy, books, mainly fiction, have been an essential item on the list of things-that-comfort-me. We tend to take such basic skills as reading for granted, but even when I didn't quite know who to thank, I was always immensely grateful for this simple path to distraction. I may have been uncertain and nervous as an infant, but I developed reading skills very early, and learned that, whatever storms might be brewing in the outside world, it was nearly always possible to slip quietly and quickly away into the warm safety of a book.

By the time I was ten or eleven I had become a sort of print monster, seeking out and indiscriminately devouring every scrap of reading matter that presented itself to me. Bizarre combinations of books would be scattered around the end of my bed—Pope's translation of Homer nestling up to *Little Grey Rabbit*, a couple of Famous Five books piled on top of Conrad's *Nigger of the Narcissus*—they were all grist to my fiction-consuming mill, whether or not I understood them (certainly, the deeper meanings of some passages in *Little Grey Rabbit* elude me to this day).

I once made the mistake of telling one of my own children how

I went about persuading my parents to buy me a particular book that I wanted.

I explained that I had read all of a certain series of books by Enid Blyton (that terrible writer whose books are mysteriously enjoyed by generation after generation of children who stubbornly refuse not to like them), and that I now desperately wanted the latest in the series, a book entitled *The River of Adventure*. Neither Christmas nor my birthday were in sight, and as my parents were not very well off, I was well aware that seven and sixpence was far more money than they would care to part with, especially as the book was bound to appear in the library eventually anyway. But I was merciless. I embarked on a callous, long-term campaign which simply involved saying the words 'River of Adventure' over and over again, the theory being that eventually my parents would crack under the pressure and I would get my book.

'River of Adventure—River of Adventure—River of Adventure—River of Adventure—River of Adventure...'

Those were the words that began to drive my mother and father mad over the weeks that followed. I was as stubborn at the age of ten as I sometimes can be now, and I WANTED THAT BOOK. I was determined to go on repeating the phrase until my mission was accomplished, and nothing was going to stop me. Looking back, I find it interesting to reflect on the stages that my poor parents went through in their response to this ploy. They were mildly amused at first, perhaps thinking my insistence rather touching, but that phase soon passed. Their amusement turned swiftly to irritation as they discovered that their every waking hour in my presence was filled with the same phrase, accompanying all else that happened, like the bass-line of a track being played on someone else's hi-fi in the next room.

Irritation was followed by downright anger and threats, all of which failed to stem or even briefly interrupt my flow, the content of which had, by now, resolved itself into a sort of condensed version of the original.

'Rivererervanture—Rivererervanture—Rivererervanture—Rivererervanture—Rivererervanture...'

They never really stood a chance, did they? But they did try everything. They ignored me.

I went on saying it.

They talked reasonably to me.

I went on saying it.

They made promises for the distant future.

I went on saying it.

They told me in serious, end-of-our-tether tones that enough was enough.

I went on saying it.

'Riverererventure—Riverererventure—Riverererventure—Riverererventure—Riverererventure....'

Finally, wild-eyed, haggard and defeated, they bought me the book. It was one of the few victories in a not very victorious childhood.

When, some years ago, I told one of my sons this story, he listened with enormous interest, then gazed speculatively at me for a moment.

'Nintendo,' he said, 'Nintendo—Nintendo—Nintendo—Nintendo...'

My love affair with books, and particularly my use of them as a distraction from the tricky business of living, grew so intense at one stage that it was almost life-threatening. I am somewhat embarrassed even to recall this fact, but I got into the habit of cycling to school with a book resting on my handlebars so that I could have a little read as I went along. Yes, yes, you are absolutely right—the results were utterly catastrophic. I can still recall the sensation of shock and horror when my world exploded because I had smashed into the back of a parked car or delivery van. And the unbelievable fact is that it happened several times. Nothing put me off!

As a pedestrian I was in no less danger. I gave up smoking many years ago now, but at the time it was just about the only other thing I did apart from reading. A packet of cigarettes and a novel—that was my distraction kit. The trouble was that, when I grew older and was out of work, I took to walking the streets with a cigarette in one hand and a book in the other, with as little regard for what was in front of me as I'd had in the days when I rode my mobile reading desk to school. I even continued to read—oh, blush!—as I crossed the road. What a trail of disgruntled drivers and fellow-pedestrians I must have left behind me.

I can only imagine that God had a whole legion of angels on my case, working overtime to prevent me from being prematurely dispatched to a place where I would be judged on the absence of my name from the most important book of all.

By the time I got married my reading habits had become a little more sane, but I can still recall Bridget's puzzlement on witnessing the lengthy procedure that I usually went through before going to bed. I might spend as much as half an hour selecting three or four books to take to bed with me, and then, exhausted by the lengthy selection process, read one of them for two minutes before turning off the light and settling down to sleep. She was no less puzzled by the complex explanation that I offered for this strange behaviour.

'You see,' I explained, 'I have to have one very worthy, serious sort of book that I can tell myself I *might* read—although I know I almost certainly won't, and then I have to have one of my old thumb-sucking books in case I need to feel safe, and I do like to have at least one book that I haven't read yet but really want to some time but probably won't start tonight, and last of all I have to have the book I'm actually in the middle of reading at the moment—to actually read, you see....'

All right, I may be slightly crackers, but I think it is this lifelong love of stories that enables me to go on finding so much satisfaction in being a writer myself. People sometimes ask me where ideas come from when you have to write all the time, but a very large part of the answer is that I am probably more interested in finding out what happens at the end of my stories than anybody else. When I was in the middle of writing *An Alien at St Wilfred's* I had no idea what the outcome of the story would be, but I *so* relished the fact that I was there with those five characters in the dimly lit interior of the church on those four Thursday evenings, waiting to find out how the arrival of 'Nunc', the alien, would change the lives of those who encountered him. In *Stress Family Robinson* I wasn't sure until near the end of the book whether Dip, family-friend of the Robinsons, would move in to live with the family or not. I didn't want to know until then. I was enjoying the story too much.

I have also very much enjoyed narrating stories to live audiences over the last ten years. It is in this situation that one learns how stories grow and change and improve with the telling.

Here, in this section, which describes the beginning of Jesus' ministry and the way in which he taught through parables, we focus on the work of one of the greatest natural storytellers of all time. It is such a joy for me to know that Jesus used the medium of fiction to communicate cosmic facts, and I do not think I am imagining the sense of satisfaction with which one feels these stories were developed and honed over the course of his ministry. Here is a performer who knew his audience intimately through years of gritty, day-to-day contact with them, and who worked hard at recycling events and experiences from real life until they became the multi-layered, verbally economical masterpieces that we know, and perhaps undervalue, today.

As those who have been bored by countless sermons will be aware, a good point cannot be made by a bad story. The parables of Jesus are not just arid, minimum requirements for passing on dry old chunks of teaching. They are in the very best tradition of 'Once upon a time' and I love them.

Prayer

You are a God of stories. Thank you for teaching your Son all the best ones. Amen.

Butterflies

Matthew 4:12–17 (NIV)

When Jesus heard that John had been put in prison, he returned to Galilee... to fulfil that which was said through the prophet Isaiah: '...Galilee of the Gentiles—the people living in darkness have seen a great light; on those living in the land of the shadow of death a light has dawned.' From that time on Jesus began to preach, 'Repent, for the kingdom of heaven is near.'

The butterflies must have fluttered in Jesus' stomach when he heard the news about John's imprisonment. Clearly, this was, to use an appropriately theatrical term, the 'cue' he'd been waiting for. Three years of ministry lay before him, to end, not with applause but with very unpleasant death. It was a long way from the wings to the stage—from Nazareth down to Capernaum; long enough, no doubt, to wonder whether his recent victory over temptation in the desert was really going to carry him through the teeth-grindingly difficult events and encounters that were about to begin. So very lonely.

Did he carefully control the panic in his breathing as he approached the place and time when the words he said and the things he did would be remembered, recorded and subsequently studied by millions of people for thousands of years? If the thought of that didn't make him nervous he wasn't human—and he was, so it must have done.

My own experience is that it's much better when you've actually got started. The waiting is awful. I don't feel the gut-wrenching fear that used to accompany all my speaking engagements, but my sweat glands still get a bit of violent exercise at times. In 1993 the most difficult situations I faced were a prison service where disruptive inmates had already been removed before I started to speak, and a spot at the London Palladium in a Christmas show attended mainly by Christians. These vastly disparate settings caused equal terror in my frail psyche. The disgruntled prisoners had certainly never heard of me, and it was clear I'd have to earn every second of their attention. The Palladium audience probably knew who I was, but this was the Palladium, for goodness' sake! What on earth was I doing here?

These events turned out all right in the end, but on both occasions, when my cue came, I was terrified. The bad news is that we don't escape the fear, the challenge, or the need to use an act of will to step onto the centre-stage of God's plan for us. Jesus went through it, and so, in our own small way, shall we. The good news is that God is in charge of the epilogue.

A thought

No resurrection without crucifixion.

Fond fathers

Matthew 4:18–22 (NIV)

Jesus... saw two brothers, Simon called Peter and his brother Andrew. They were casting a net into the lake... 'Come, follow me,' Jesus said, 'and I will make you fishers of men.' At once they left their nets and followed him. Going on from there, he saw... James son of Zebedee and his brother John. They were in a boat with their father... Jesus called them, and immediately they left the boat and their father and followed him.

Do you remember *The Magic Roundabout*? It was a TV programme that always ended when a funny little character called Zebedee bounced in on a spring, and told everyone it was time for sleep. The biblical Zebedee came to my notice much later, so that, even now, I picture the father of James and John ricocheting around the boat, trying to persuade his piscatorial sons to go to bed. I need to dispel this image, because I suspect that, like the father of Simon and Andrew, he was actually quite an impressive fellow. What kind of parenting produced, in each case, two sons who were fit and ready to join the Son of God as he stepped out to save the world? We have no details, but it seems likely that years of care, teaching and prayer had been invested in those four boys.

We once met an elderly man named George who had spent over thirty years praying each day that his son, Frank, would one day love Jesus. George was a quiet, devout Christian, more concerned with deeds than words, and his devotion was rewarded when, aged thirty-six, Frank was well and truly converted.

We met Frank. Not only was he converted, but he had become an air-punching, spirit-intoxicated, promise-claiming, chorus-singing servant of the living God. When we bowed our heads for grace, Frank spoke in tongues, interpreted his own tongue, sang a solo chorus and praised God for the fellowship and the food. We felt quite exhausted by the time he'd finished.

Frank chided his father for not entering more vigorously into things of the Spirit. I watched George's face as he listened. In the quiet, loving smile with which he regarded his son, I read a deep and serene trust that the same God who had answered his prayers after so many years would temper and focus the zeal of this exuberant new disciple.

George was proud of his son, and so, I suspect, were Zebedee and the father of Simon and Andrew. They might not have quite understood what was going on, but perhaps, in their spirits, they sensed that losing a son is not really a loss if he has gone to be with Jesus.

A prayer

Help us not to grow weary in prayer.

Why not?

Matthew 4:23–25 (NIV)

Jesus went throughout Galilee, teaching in their synagogues, preaching the good news of the kingdom, and healing every disease and sickness among the people. News about him spread all over Syria, and people brought to him all who were ill with various diseases, those suffering severe pain, the demon-possessed, those having seizures and the paralysed, and he healed them. Large crowds... followed him.

I am tempted, as I have been on other occasions, to bypass my first reaction to this passage, because it seems too ragged and personal. People who write Bible notes are not expected to be anything but shiningly positive—surely? It was just three words that affected me so strongly: '... he healed them'.

Jesus seemed to heal everyone who came to him, whatever their sicknesses, and many say that he does the same now. There's no doubt that he heals *some* people. My friend Jenny Larcombe was healed quite dramatically after years of suffering, and most of us know, or have heard of, at least one person who has had a similar experience. But, for every one of those who get better, there are countless others who do not. There are plenty of books by self-styled experts on this subject, some telling us off for not having enough faith, some explaining that we are using the wrong techniques when we pray, and others pointing out that God answers prayers in a variety of ways that might not correspond to what we actually want.

I expect each one of those books contains a bit of truth, but I get fed up with all this rationalization sometimes, don't you? When I read those three words this time, all I could think about was my friend Ian, who has been suffering terrible back pain for some years. Sitting at my word processor, I closed my eyes and, as I have done many times before, implored God to touch him, just as Jesus touched those hurting people two thousand years ago. I pleaded, I prayed in tongues. I even wept a little. That was yesterday. This morning I phoned Ian's wife to ask how he is. He's just the same really. I wanted to be able to tell you, through this note, that God had healed him—but, so far, he hasn't.

A prayer

Father, I've known you for many years now, and one thing I'm sure of is that I can be honest with you. I love you, and I believe that you love me, but I don't understand why you don't heal Ian, and I wish that you would. Thank you for accepting my puzzlement and my trust. Amen.

Roots

Matthew 13:3–9 (NIV)

He told them many things in parables, saying: 'A farmer went out to sow his seed. As he was scattering the seed, some fell along the path, and the birds came and ate it up. Some fell on rocky places, where it did not have much soil. It sprang up quickly, because the soil was shallow. But when the sun came up, the plants were scorched, and they withered because they had no root. Other seed fell among thorns, which grew up and choked the plants. Still other seed fell on good soil, where it produced a crop—a hundred, sixty or thirty times what was sown. He who has ears to hear, let him hear.'

In the section on Harvest I mentioned the girls my wife used to work with, in connection with this passage, but it also reminds me of some of the children I encountered in residential establishments. I remember Steve, for instance, who despite being the most inefficient thief in the universe, seemed quite incapable of curtailing the activities that constantly got him into trouble. Steve *always* got caught.

'I don't understand it,' said his mother to me one day. 'I've always been a good mother—given him stuff for his birthdays and all that. Last year I gave him this big construction set. Twenty-five quid that cost—at least, it would have done if I'd paid for it...'

Then there was Tony, who lived on a notorious local estate, and had been placed in the secure unit after being arrested and charged with arson. Tony's explanation of the motivation behind his crime went as follows: 'What happened was, my mate asked me to burn his flat down for the insurance, so I said, "Look, I'll burn your flat down for you, but I don't want to get involved."' As I pondered this elusive piece of logic, Tony, who was actually a very warm-hearted lad, offered graphic descriptions of everyday life in his large, tumultuous family.

'When people come to the door,' he said cheerfully, 'we might beat 'em up, or we might not. It depends on how we're feeling at the time.'

The seeds of these children's lives had been planted in such rocky ground. The soil of consistent love, good example and self-control was very shallow. I've described elsewhere how readily such children will reach for the gospel, only to despair when it seems to take no root. But it is worth repeating that rocky places *can* be broken up. Soil can be deepened and enriched. Thorns can be cleared. It's hard, long-term, sweaty work that sometimes lasts a lifetime, but it can be done.

A prayer

Father, increase our willingness to support people who had a rotten start. Help us not to give up.

It's not *what* you know **Matthew 13:10–13 (NIV)**

The disciples... asked, 'Why do you speak to the people in parables?' He replied, 'The knowledge of the secrets of the kingdom of heaven has been given to you, but not to them. Whoever has will be given more, and he will have an abundance. Whoever does not have, even what he has will be taken from him. This is why I speak to them in parables: "Though seeing, they do not see, though hearing, they do not hear or understand."'

When I come up against passages like this I wish I was a theologian or a Greek scholar or an intellectual. Being none of these things, my normal inclination is to rush to the little row of William Barclay commentaries on my shelf.

'Oh, William,' I cry in panic, 'please tell me what this means, so that I can rearrange your explanation and pass it on to the readers as if it were my own.'

But I'm not going to do that this time. You can look up Barclay for yourself if you want to. I'm going to tell you what *I* think it means.

The odd thing about Jesus' reply to his disciples is that, in fact, they didn't understand the secrets of the kingdom of heaven any more than the people did, except in one very important sense. The disciples had, as we saw in chapter 4, responded immediately and spontaneously to the person or the personality of Jesus.

They followed him.

They were still vulnerable, flawed human beings, but their special knowledge—the thing that they *had*, and which would be added to, was a commitment to, and a relationship with, Jesus. The crowds who listened to Jesus did not yet have this, so that the truths expressed in the parables (and in this one particularly, perhaps) took away even the spiritual security that had been theirs. Whether or not they understood in detail is irrelevant if we define a parable as a story that keeps the listener occupied at the front door while the truth slips in through a side window. Now they had to deal with that truth.

What all this means, if you're getting as confused as I am, is that we shall never have a more precious possession than our relationship with the Son of God. The knowledge of our need for him is the core of all wisdom, and though we may well meet people who can argue our faith to pieces, no one can destroy our love for Jesus.

A thought

Wisdom is very much to be desired, but, when it comes to the crunch, knowledge of Jesus is all the knowledge we shall need.

Flying blind

Matthew 13:14–17 (NIV)

'In them is fulfilled the prophecy of Isaiah: "You will be ever hearing but never understanding; you will be ever seeing but never perceiving. For this people's heart has become calloused; they hardly hear with their ears, and they have closed their eyes. Otherwise they might see with their eyes, hear with their ears, understand with their hearts and turn, and I would heal them." But blessed are your eyes because they see, and your ears because they hear. For I tell you the truth, many prophets and righteous men longed to see what you see but did not see it, and to hear what you hear but did not hear it.'

When I first became a Christian I was terribly shocked by everyone else's short-sightedness. I read about the slave trade and knew without a doubt that if I'd been alive at the time I would have seen how evil it was. What idiots those bygone Christians must have been! I was also quite sure that I could never have been taken in by Hitler's ravings—it would have taken more than a bunch of crazed Nazi thugs to fool someone as spiritually aware as me. As far as the present day was concerned, I found it difficult to believe that most people were blinded to the truth about Jesus as I clearly saw it. In fact, by and large, I was probably the most clear-eyed and perceptive person in the universe.

Curiously, the realization that my spiritual vision was actually very limited, coincided with an abrupt deterioration in my physical sight. For the first time in my life I had to wear glasses, and, apart from the fact that I could now sing 'We will magnify' with real gusto, I didn't like it very much. The first time I put spectacles on I felt as if an insect was gripping my head from the front. The good thing was that suddenly I could see the words I was reading without having to screw my eyes up and develop a headache.

Spiritual vision works in a very similar way. Clear sight can only be achieved with outside (inside?) help from the Holy Spirit. Without this help, Christianity is about as exciting as eating a recipe, and it gives you a terrible headache. The thrilling thing about what Jesus is saying here is that it is possible to see clearly who he is, and what his message means, otherwise he wouldn't have bothered to come. Calloused hearts *can* be softened, and dimmed eyes *can* be filled with light.

A prayer

I thought I saw everything, but now I know that I see very little. I want to see, Lord. Please open my eyes.

Grappling with greed

Matthew 13:18–23 (NIV)

'Listen then to what the parable of the sower means: When anyone hears the message... and does not understand it, the evil one comes and snatches away what was sown... This is the seed sown along the path. The one who received the seed that fell on rocky places is the man who hears the word and at once receives it with joy. But since he has no root... when trouble or persecution comes... he quickly falls away. The one who received the seed that fell among the thorns is the man who hears the word, but the worries of this life and the deceitfulness of wealth choke it, making it unfruitful: But the one who received the seed that fell on good soil is the man who hears the word and understands it. He produces... a hundred, sixty or thirty times what was sown.

Is the sower in this parable wasteful, or generous, or just very enthusiastic?

That was the question that first came to my mind as I read this story, but it was very quickly eclipsed by another question provoked by the phrase 'deceitfulness of wealth'.

I recently travelled to the north-east of England to do an evening at a local theatre on behalf of a Christian retreat centre that was about to open. The basis on which I had agreed to go was that, after expenses had been deducted, profits from the evening would be split 60/40 in my favour, an arrangement that usually works very well. As far as I was concerned, it was one of those really enjoyable evenings. The theatre was packed to capacity with more than five hundred people, and the response was as positive as I could have wished.

Afterwards, as I ate an Indian meal with the organizers, I knew inwardly that I should ask only for my expenses and donate the rest of my 60 per cent to the project. Imagine my horror on discovering that, although I'm usually fairly generous on a personal level, a small but dominant part of me was too greedy to give up the cash. I wanted to scoop it in and make it mine. I didn't want to give it away. I felt very miserable about being me, so, as I sat there, filling my face with Tandoori chicken, I gave the whole problem to God. 'You sort it out,' I said, 'I can't.' I was very relieved a little later to find myself giving away the money with hardly a thought. I was very grateful to God—I really was.

So, my question on reading this passage was about this newly discovered tendency to grasp at money. Am I deceived by wealth? The answer is, I think I could be, but the generous sower has cleared a few thorns that were choking me, so I think I'll be all right.

A question
Does he *come first?*

Large field—small crop **Matthew 13:24–30 (NIV)**

Jesus [said]: 'The kingdom of God is like a man who sowed good seed in his field. But... his enemy came and sowed weeds among the wheat... When the wheat sprouted... the weeds also appeared. The owner's servants... said, "Sir, didn't you sow good seed in your field? Where then did the weeds come from?" "An enemy did this," he replied. The servants asked him, "Do you want us to go and pull them up?" "No," he answered, "because... you may root up the wheat with them. Let both grow together until the harvest. At that time I will tell the harvesters: First, collect the weeds and tie them in bundles to be burned, then gather the wheat and bring it into my barn."'

This parable is an aerial photograph of the entire history of the Christian Church. For centuries critics have tended to see the weeds rather than the wheat, and have judged Jesus accordingly. The Inquisition, the endless sectarian conflict, the cruelty that has been inflicted in the name of Christ by those who don't know him, the agonizing boredom of many church services—these are just some of the ugly growths that have done the devil's work for him over the years. God has allowed the mess that men and women make of the Church for the sake of saving those who truly follow him, and it happens on all sorts of levels.

At one time Bridget and I were heavily involved in the running of a church youth club which, at its busiest, attracted anything from forty to sixty young people to the rather small house we shared with the curate. From those large numbers a much smaller group of five or six was, as it were, distilled. Out of this little band which met on a different evening for discussion and Bible study (because they wanted to), three have become ministers of the Church. Not for one moment am I suggesting that all the other club members were disposable weeds, but it does seem that in many situations you need a large field to produce a small crop.

The principle operates on an individual level as well. Your life may be producing a 100 per cent crop, but mine certainly isn't. God is allowing a lot of weeds to flourish beside the worthwhile things that are growing in me. Fortunately, like the owner in the parable, he knows where they came from, and he will know how to get rid of them when the right time comes.

A prayer

Father, protect the part of us and the Church that is yours.

Grown by God

Matthew 13:31–32 (NIV)

He told them another parable: 'The kingdom of heaven is like a mustard seed, which a man took and planted in his field. Though it is the smallest of all your seeds, yet when it grows, it is the largest of garden plants and becomes a tree, so that the birds of the air come and perch in its branches.'

The idea that wonderful things grow out of something very small and simple is not an easy one for the world to grasp, but it has always been God's way. I can't imagine any earthly committee, however wise, agreeing that the birth of Jesus in a stable in Bethlehem would make the ideal start for a salvation plan.

God sees mustard seeds where others see none. Take my own case.

Imagine the scene: a decision-making meeting in heaven about twelve years ago. Around the table an angelic committee is studying files, each of which has the words ADRIAN PLASS embossed on its front cover.

'No,' says one angel, shaking his head as he leafs through the file, 'not much here, I'm afraid. He's cracked up and useless. Doesn't go to church any more, he's left his job—how someone can do that with three kids depending on him...'

'Look at this.' Another heavenly being takes up the dismal story. 'Getting drunk most nights and disappearing for hours on end. I don't know how his poor wife has put up with it. He seems to enjoy letting himself sink into a moral swamp.'

'Have you read what he's saying to people about the Church?' A third angel holds up his opened file and taps the page with his finger. 'So scathing and destructive. It's hard enough keeping that outfit going as it is, without this kind of negative talk.'

'So,' says yet another committee member, shutting his file with a bang, 'what we have here is a drunken, critical, irresponsible, spiritually bankrupt, morally deficient no-hoper. An ideal case for dumping. Am I right?'

A murmur of agreement passes round the table as, one by one, the angels close their files and sit back in their chairs. Only one member of the committee has not yet expressed an opinion. God, who has been listening silently at the head of the table, gazes thoughtfully into the distance, and speaks for the first time. 'I think,' he says quietly, 'we'll give him an international writing and speaking ministry...'

A prayer

Father, some of us have reached the bottom. You once planted a mustard seed of faith in us. May it begin to grow now. Thank you.

Real life

Matthew 13:33–35 (NIV)

He told them still another parable: 'The kingdom of heaven is like yeast that a woman took and mixed into a large amount of flour until it worked all through the dough.' Jesus spoke all these things to the crowd in parables; he did not say anything to them without using a parable. So was fulfilled what was spoken through the prophet: 'I will open my mouth in parables, I will utter things hidden since the creation of the world.'

Whether you regard the life, death and resurrection of Jesus as a mustard seed or as yeast, it is easy to forget how remarkably that small beginning has grown into a situation where, in this country alone, almost every city, town, village and hamlet contains at least one building that celebrates the coming of the Son of God. This is certainly evidence of the power of the gospel, but, more sadly, it is also evidence of the way in which the devil has been able to prevent the yeast of God's presence from working itself right into the dough of everyday living. A friend of mine took over a big city mission a couple of years ago, and raised more than a few religious eyebrows by immediately closing down the three mission churches that were operating at the time. His explanation for doing this was simple.

'They aren't doing any mission,' he said. 'Each church has got its own little congregation that turns up on Sundays, and that's all right as far as it goes. They don't do anyone any harm. But they're not there to be harmless. The mission churches are supposed to be bringing God to the community, and they're not, so we'll close them down until we've decided how to do what we're here for.'

Christianity cannot be stored in barns called churches.

Why should things hidden since the creation of the world be uttered in parables? Why? Because, when the world was created, man was able to walk with his God through a garden in the cool of the afternoon. He didn't have to wait until the verger had unlocked the church and the vicar had arrived. Parables are about real life. The yeast was part of the dough when Adam walked with God.

We need our churches—of course we do. But let's not forget that the end of all our work for God will be the removal of buildings and rituals and religion, because he will be in all things, and we will have him, and he will have us, and all will be one.

A thought

Those of us in ministry are working enthusiastically towards doing ourselves out of a job.

Unauthorized

Matthew 13:36–43 (NIV)

Then he left the crowd and went into the house. His disciples came to him and said, 'Explain to us the parable of the weeds in the field.' He answered, 'The one who sowed the good seed is the Son of Man. The field is the world, and the good seed stands for the sons of the kingdom. The weeds are the sons of the evil one, and the enemy who sows them is the devil. The harvest is the end of the age, and the harvesters are angels. As the weeds are pulled up and burned in the fire, so it will be at the end of the age. The Son of Man will send out his angels, and they will weed out of his kingdom everything that causes sin and all who do evil. They will throw them into the fiery furnace, where there will be weeping and gnashing of teeth. Then the righteous will shine like the sun in the kingdom of their Father. He who has ears, let him hear.

Now, you're in luck here, because I can throw an entirely new light on these verses. Recently, a distant relative called Bill Rae died leaving me everything. In his will Bill insisted I should investigate an ancient Eastern pot in his attic, because 'the contents would help communicate parts of the Bible more accurately than hitherto'. I found the pot and, inside, an ancient scroll, which I submitted to experts.

Their report estimates the scroll's age at 2,000 years (well, they say two years, but I'm sure that's a typing error) and describes the content as 'a copy of Matthew's Gospel, with significant differences from the familiar version'. It certainly looks authentic, right down to the chapter divisions and verse numbers. I'll quote you a little of what I believe to be the *original* version of the above scripture. We've been so naïve!

'The Son of Man will send out his angels, and they will gently remove from his kingdom everything that causes what we rather archaically refer to as sin, and all who, for reasons beyond their control, do evil. They will install them in a rather comfortable private hotel where there will be counselling and laughing and cleaning of teeth, and a general sense of relief that all the fiery furnace stuff was just for effect. And the righteous need not have bothered really, nor the Son of Man if it comes to that. Still, never mind, he said some good things...'

A warning

He who has ears, let him hear.

A question

What is the one-word anagram of Bill Rae?

The inspiration of joy

Matthew 13:44 (NIV)

The kingdom of heaven is like treasure hidden in a field. When a man found it, he hid it again, and then in his joy went and sold all he had and bought that field.

For all too many people this parable ends rather differently:

'The kingdom of heaven is like treasure hidden in a field. When a man found it he hid it again, and set off with great joy to sell all he had, but he dithered about so much that he missed that day's market, and by the time he'd asked a few close friends for advice and slept on it for a night his joy had faded, and it didn't seem such a good idea after all. He was able to think of a thousand good and responsible reasons why it would be better to leave buying the field for a while, and anyway, the treasure would probably still be there when he went back in a few years' time. By then he'd be able to afford the field without having to sell absolutely *everything*. Much more sensible...'

Opportunities to act on the inspiration of joy don't happen very often in most people's lives, and they can result in great blessing or great sadness depending on whether they're taken or not. Sadly, much treasure is lost, for the 'best possible' reasons.

It can happen to writers sometimes, when consciousness is suddenly illuminated by an idea burning with such brilliance that one *knows* (as far as it's possible to know with any creative activity) that it will work. After a night's sleep these inspirations can look very drab indeed, especially if you then share them with somebody else, and that person's unenthusiastic response dulls whatever shine might have remained. I'm beginning to learn to trust the memory of these shining moments, to believe that the excitement will return when I actually put them into practice, and *not* to spill them to anyone else before pursuing the original vision.

We live in a society where nostalgia has become an industry, and for many people the future functions as distraction from an unacceptable present. Jesus is suggesting here that when we do discover the secret treasure of joy—the eternal *now* of union with him, it is worth giving, losing, selling everything so that it becomes truly ours. The world is very deceptive, and we shall be a long time dead. Grasp the chance.

A prayer

Lord, we discovered you—our treasure—in a moment of joy, but some of us never came back to make sure of owning that joy. Give us new resolve now to give all that we are and have for you.

Selling up

Matthew 13:45–46

'The kingdom of heaven is like a merchant looking for fine pearls. When he found one of great value, he went away and sold everything he had and bought it.

I have a friend who is continually finding the only thing he ever really wanted. The problem is that it's something different each time. Neglected and abused in his childhood, Sam, a single person who works in one of those expensive West-End clothes shops, has a bottomless pit of emotional need, made worse by disastrous relationships in the past. He has more or less given up the idea of marriage, fearing that he will never be able to sustain that kind of lifelong closeness. Nowadays, Sam's 'pearls' tend to be things rather than people. I can't count the number of times the phone has rung and it's turned out to be Sam, full of excitement because, at last, he really does know what he needs to make him happy. There was the art-studio in the back garden: Sam was going to devote himself to developing a neglected talent for sketching, and he simply had to have a special place and special equipment with which to do it. He nearly bankrupted himself in the process of finding enough money for this project, but today the 'studio' has become a garden shed and Sam sketches nothing.

He arrived outside our house once, driving an almost brand-new Land Rover. 'It's been my dream for years,' he said, patting his new baby fondly. 'I'll probably be in debt for the rest of my life, but it doesn't matter, everything's going to be different now. I shall probably sell up and drive round the world.' He didn't do anything of the sort, of course, and it wasn't long before the new vehicle was replaced by a heap of rust, thus releasing credit potential for the incredibly versatile electronic keyboard that was going to give Sam what he *really* wanted.

Now and then Sam gives up for a while. During these periods he phones us a lot and comes close to despair. He is a Christian—has been for years, but, perhaps because he is such a damaged personality, his faith doesn't bring him much peace. He does encounter Jesus, though, in the caring and concern of many Christian friends, and I think he is aware of the reality of that encounter. We pray that one day he will stop sorting through the worldly pearls of buildings and cars and the countless other things he's tried, and settle for Jesus, who will certainly cost everything, but will at last give him what he always needed.

A thought

Sometimes our task is to be temporary guardians of someone else's fine pearl.

Bad fish

Matthew 13:47–50 (NIV)

'The kingdom of heaven is like a net that was let down into the lake and caught all kinds of fish. When it was full, the fishermen pulled it up on the shore. Then they sat down and collected the good fish in baskets, but threw the bad away. This is how it will be at the end of the age. The angels will come and separate the wicked from the righteous and throw them into the fiery furnace, where there will be weeping and gnashing of teeth.'

The people who heard this parable originally can have had no idea that, in two thousand years' time, fried fish, cooked in furnaces of a more compact and worldly nature, would be available on the streets of every town and village in this country. Jesus' account is about something very different. Can you imagine the smell when bad fish get slung into the eternal ovens of hell? Ugh!

Do you sometimes worry that you're a bad fish? I do. I'm in the net, but am I fresh? It's not easy to feel the kind of assurance that we would like to feel, and it's no use holding Bible verses under my nose to show that we *should* be absolutely sure, because lots of us aren't—so there!

Elsewhere Jesus points out, for instance, that people will say to him that they healed the sick and drove out devils in his name but he'll say that he never knew them. He'll call them doers of evil. I know churches where people do those sorts of things all the time. Do you honestly think that any of those engaged in such—apparently—crucial spiritual tasks believes that he or she is a bad fish? I don't think so.

In another place he says that calling out 'Lord, Lord!' is meaningless if you don't really do what you're told. Well, I hear lots of marvellous prayers—really impressive ones. Would some of the performers of these offerings recognize the scent of bad fish in the air around them, or is it so familiar that they can't even smell it any more?

Then there's the twenty-fifth chapter of this Gospel. Read it. Worrying, isn't it? Do I feed the hungry? Do I give water to the thirsty? Do I invite strangers in? Do I clothe the naked? Do I look after the sick or visit those who are in prison? If I don't give these things proper priority and consideration I need to take a long deep breath—there'll be a smell of bad fish around, and I'd better do something about it.

A commitment

I will read the Gospels as though I had never read them before, and find out what being a good fish really means.

Understandable **Matthew 13:51–52 (NIV)**

'Have you understood all these things?' Jesus asked. 'Yes,' they replied. He said to them, 'Therefore every teacher of the law who has been instructed about the kingdom of heaven is like the owner of a house who brings out of his storeroom new treasures as well as old.'

I love this bit, don't you? Can't you just picture the disciples sitting and listening with great enjoyment to the stories Jesus was telling, and then suddenly, to their horror, being confronted with an inquiry as to whether they had understood everything? I should imagine there was a brief, jaw-dropping pause, followed by general, quite spuriously confident nods of agreement.

'Understood all these things? Oh yes. Eh, lads?'

'No trouble at all...'

'Got it, yes—quite clear, thanks.'

'Yep! Yep! Bad fish—yep!'

'Seeds, yeast, weeds, treasure—'

'Don't forget the pearls.'

'Ah, yeah, that's right, yeah, pearls as well, yeah.'

'Nets.'

'Nets, yeah...'

'It's all about the kingdom of er—'

'God.'

'That's it, God, yeah.'

'Yeah...'

A little smile of amusement must have played around Jesus' lips as he listened to the 'yes' of his disciples. I think it's extremely unlikely that they had anything but the haziest idea of what their master was talking about at this stage. Later, of course, after Jesus had died and risen, and the Spirit had come, they would have pored over every recollected word, catching for the first time a vision of the great reality that is contained in these deceptively simple little stories.

We have the Spirit with us now, so don't worry if you feel you don't understand all that you read in the Bible. He will reveal anything that you need to know.

A prayer

Father, thank you for the new treasures—the teachings of Jesus. We want to understand what he is saying, and particularly what he is saying to us as individuals. Holy Spirit, be with us as we read—let us adventure together.

He preaches well that lives well.

Cervantes

GAINING FELLOW-TRAVELLERS

The woman at the well

Personal evangelism, or rather my failure to do it, was one of the things that caused me quite a lot of guilt when I was a young Christian. Mind you, I started off with enormous vigour. For a time, as I have already recorded in *The Unlocking*, I spread the word indiscriminately, and, I have no doubt, extremely annoyingly, all over Tunbridge Wells. On reflection, I was probably fortunate to escape public execution by a mob composed of all those who had, quite reasonably, decided they would rather spend an eternity in the hell I was trying to save them from, than ten minutes trapped in the corner of a café by me and my large Bible.

As time went by, a conspicuous lack of results caused my zeal to be abated (my tongue was writing cheques that my experience and scholarship couldn't cash, to borrow an expression I heard in a film), but the feeling that I should be telling everyone I met about Jesus never really went away, and has remained with me, although its outworking has been highly modified since those early days.

Interestingly, in one sense my attitude to evangelism has come full circle. The stark message of judgment and salvation with which I harangued people when I was sixteen is exactly the message that now seems to me the most crucial thing for people to hear. The difference is, quite simply, my awareness that the gospel is driven by the love of God, and not by the neurotic need of any organized branch of Christianity to fit each potential convert into its own unvarying pattern of behaviours and attitudes. The need for people to be saved is paramount, but, as Saint Paul would undoubtedly have said if he had been alive in this age, 'Verily, there existeth more than one way to skinneth an cat.' I certainly had not appreciated this when I was converting the world at sixteen.

The fact is that almost any form of evangelism can be effective, including the traditional ones.

Bridget and I were very struck, for instance, during a large Christian festival that we attended in Australia, by the work of one South American evangelist, unknown in this country, as far as I am aware, who spoke for a fairly short time in a not particularly impressive way, but was immediately besieged by hundreds of people wishing to make some kind of movement towards Jesus. It seemed to me, especially after we had met and spoken to this chap over one or two meals, that this was a man who was as near to being fully committed to his master as it is possible to be, and, much more importantly, that he was a man who had actually received the specific gift of evangelism that Paul mentions in the fourth chapter of Ephesians. There were other speakers at the same conference who produced talks that were longer, wittier and far more obviously seductive than those of the South American, but they simply did not achieve anything like the same results. God had tapped this fellow on the shoulder.

The provision of such useful services as mother and toddler groups to the secular community by individual churches can be a valuable means of evangelism, as long as the service is offered in a genuine spirit of charity, and God is allowed to direct the means and the pace of evangelism.

Keeping one's mouth shut can be an excellent form of evangelism.

Making *real* friends with someone can result in highly effective evangelism—the *most* effective as far as I can tell from what I hear as I travel around the world.

I'm sure this is only the beginning of a much longer list of ways in which the message of salvation can be given to those who need to hear it, but is there one thing that they all have in common? Well, I would venture to suggest that wherever people are drawn to Christ, you will find someone who really has tackled the business of sorting out priorities. This is what Jesus himself had to do before beginning his three-year ministry, and we learn about it in the following verses, which come from chapter four of Luke's Gospel:

Jesus, full of the Holy Spirit, returned from the Jordan, and was led by the Spirit in the desert, where for forty days he was tempted by the devil. He ate nothing during those days, and at the end of them he was hungry.

The devil said to him, 'If you are the Son of God, tell this stone to become bread.'

Jesus answered, 'It is written: "Man does not live on bread alone."'

The devil led him up to a high place and showed him in an instant all the kingdoms of the world. And he said to him, 'I will give you all their authority and splendour, for it has been given to me, and I can give it to anyone I want to. So if you worship me, it will all be yours.'

Jesus answered, 'It is written: "Worship the Lord your God and serve him only."'

The devil led him to Jerusalem, and had him stand on the highest point of the temple. 'If you are the Son of God,' he said, 'throw yourself down from here. For it is written: "He will command his angels concerning you to guard you carefully; they will lift you up in their hands, so that you will not strike your foot against a stone."'

Jesus answered, 'It says, "Do not put the Lord your God to the test."'

When the devil had finished all this tempting, he left him until an opportune time.

Luke 4:1–13 (NIV)

In Matthew's version of the same story angels appear at this point and minister to Jesus.

The trouble with passages like this is that, over the years, they become almost impossible to see clearly, just as a painting on the sitting room wall can become such a familiar part of the domestic scenery that the content and meaning of the picture, which meant so much once, no longer makes any impact on those who see it every day. An additional problem with this crucially important event in the life of Jesus, is that the common perception of those forty days in the wilderness, the one that is, as it were, fixed on the walls of our minds, is a religious picture, a tidy, formalized, cleaned-up, harmless version of one of the greatest and most gritty acts of heroism in the history of this world. Behind those silly images of a tall, blue-eyed, freshly showered and shampooed Son of God, dismissing Satan with a casual waft of the wrist, is something much deeper, much more ragged, much more meaningful and challenging to us, and, ultimately, much more beautiful because it is full of love.

During the sheer hell of forty hungry days and forty freezing nights in the desert Jesus had to learn, through facing these three temptations of the devil, to steer away from material prosperity, indulgent use and enjoyment of power and an illusory sense of personal safety, the very items that topped the priority list of most human beings then, and still do today. Only by doing this could he bring about the greatest miracle of all, the reunion of his Father with millions—billions of people who were and are profoundly loved, but profoundly lost. Grasping the logic of this divine principle is *so* difficult for limited human beings like us. It doesn't appear to make any sense.

We are not helped by the way in which that side of the Church which is vulnerable to temptation has, in recent years, tried to rationalize—forcibly to steer—these low spiritual priorities back on to the top of the list. Some churches have almost redefined material prosperity as a sort of spiritual gift; some misguided aspects of what is called Holy Spirit ministry offer power without loving responsibility to people who shouldn't be in charge of a sausage sizzle, and, perhaps most subtly of all, there is a form of 'Kingdom Now' teaching that manages to avoid, for the 'best possible theological reasons', the realities of death and heaven and especially hell. These movements are all the more dangerous because their mutant growths emerge from seeds of truth.

Prosperity, power and personal safety—these are the things that Jesus deprioritized, as the Americans put it, and the message is pretty clear for us as well. While we are, in the very heart of ourselves, depending more on these worldly assets than on the God who sent his Son to die for us, we are not free to offer him the best possible job of evangelism, or anything else for that matter.

I know it's not easy—even I'm not stupid enough to think that—but it wasn't easy for Jesus either. He didn't go through the desert experience on a bye, like some fortunate Wimbledon competitor. He could have failed. He could have decided that he wanted money and women and power more than he wanted to be obedient to his Father, in which case we wouldn't be sitting in our churches every Sunday morning because there wouldn't be any churches to sit in. Jesus had no idea whether he would overcome temptation or not. If that was not the case, then he wasn't really tempted and he wasn't really a man.

He came through in the end as we know, and he did it for us. He did it because he knew he was our only chance. He knew that disaster on a vast scale was just waiting to happen if he didn't overcome those temptations. I must say that I think the Church seems to have lost sight of this dramatically urgent reason for the coming of Jesus.

Earlier in the week that has just ended as I write, I was talking to someone in the street, and he was saying what a shame it is that Christianity doesn't have as many interesting activities and events attached to it as other religions. I was just embarking on the old familiar nodding and agreeing that we Christians are so good at, when I suddenly thought—what are we talking about? The central issue is not (or shouldn't be) reminiscent of some 'Blue Peter' versus 'Magpie' competition (remember 'Magpie' on ITV?). It's not about who can offer the best way to make working models of combine harvesters out of milk-bottle tops. If Christianity is true, and I think it is, we are talking about a looming cosmic disaster, and, as well as presenting things in the best possible way—of course we want to do that—we should primarily be saying to people, 'Look, you do what you like—believe what you like, but I tell you this, if you're going to reject Jesus, you'd better be pretty blinking sure you've got it right!'

Two thousand years ago the Son of God gritted his teeth, locked his priorities firmly in place, and set out, steering in a very straight line towards certain death. He did it for us.

Prosperity, power and personal safety—where do they come on my list, and what am I going to do about it? Once they have descended to their proper place, and commitment to God has become my priority, I shall be prepared to pass on the message of salvation as well as it can be done, in the way and the place that is appointed and right, just as Jesus did with this woman from Samaria 2,000 years ago.

Prayer

Father, we really would like to be involved in passing on the message of salvation, but some of us are unsure and nervous about what might be involved. Please help us make a serious attempt to place you at the top of our list of priorities, and to be so filled with the excitement of your love and the urgency of your desire to save, that, impossible though it may seem at the moment, our very lives are alight with the gospel. Amen.

All the thirsty people **John 4:6–10 (NJB)**

Jesus, tired by the journey, sat down by the well. It was about the sixth hour. When a Samaritan woman came to draw water, Jesus said to her, 'Give me something to drink.' His disciples had gone into the town to buy food. The Samaritan woman said to him, 'You are a Jew. How is it that you ask me, a Samaritan, for something to drink?'—Jews, of course, do not associate with Samaritans. Jesus replied to her: 'If you only knew what God is offering and who it is that is saying to you, "Give me something to drink," you would have been the one to ask, and he would have given you living water.'

Nowadays we hear quite a lot about groups of Christians marching around the edge of a town or part of a city 'claiming it for the Lord'. One hopes that they get involved with the centre of such areas as well. A friend of mine was asked to run a house for homeless men in the East End of London when he was still very young. Each night he set off in the dark to seek out places where these men (many of them alcoholics) settled for the night. Sometimes he was so frightened that he turned round and ran home again. He was only a part-time coward, though. He persisted, and the project thrived. He took Jesus to people who might not have met him otherwise.

Here we see Jesus taking himself into an area that Jews normally avoided like the plague. He did not walk round it; he walked into it.

Having despatched the disciples (why *did* it take twelve men to collect the groceries?), he then defied convention even further by not only speaking to a Samaritan woman, but actually asking her for a drink. Like the homeless men that my friend visited on their own ground, she was curious about the motivation for this unusual behaviour. The answer in both cases was the same—Jesus had come, bringing the water of life.

It is not easy to go into places that are unfamiliar or threatening in some way, but if we want to follow Jesus, that is what will happen. It may be the people next door, it may be the pub down the road, it may be deepest Borneo, but if he calls us, we either go—or disobey.

A prayer

Lord, am I avoiding anyone or anywhere that you want me to visit? I need courage. Please give it to me when I need it, so that I can take you to those who need living water.

Unpoisoned water John 4:11–18 (NJB)

'You have no bucket, sir,' she answered, 'and the well is deep: how do you get this living water? Are you a greater man than our father Jacob, who gave us this well and drank from it himself with his sons and his cattle?' Jesus replied, 'Whoever drinks this water will be thirsty again; but no one who drinks the water that I shall give him will ever be thirsty again: the water that I shall give him will become in him a spring of water, welling up for eternal life.' 'Sir,' said the woman, 'give me some of that water, so that I may never be thirsty or come here again to draw water.' 'Go and call your husband,' said Jesus to her, 'and come back here.' The woman answered, 'I have no husband.' Jesus said to her, 'You are right to say, "I have no husband"; for although you have had five, the one you now have is not your husband. You spoke the truth there.'

Sometimes self-indulgence and sin appear very much more attractive than the path of virtue, especially when it is the path of arid, bloodless duty. When a stress-related illness forced me out of work and my world was collapsing around me, I wrote these words:

Who made these poison pools in desert lands
So sweet and cool?
A welcome lie,
The chance to die with water on my lips.
I've seen how others try to die
Unpoisoned in the sun,
I do not think that I can do as they have done.

In this passage, Jesus is offering clean, healthy, running water to replace both the poisoned water of negative behaviour and the aridity of loveless virtue.

In the case of the Samaritan woman, it is her predilection for a broad choice of close gentlemen friends that constitutes the poisoned water that will kill her in the end. What a mind-numbing shock it must have been when this rather impressive stranger's innocent-sounding suggestion was followed by such an accurate stab of insight.

God understands our failings. He knows the weaknesses that are responsible for bad decisions and developments in our lives. But the living water is still on offer, water that will purify our minds and bodies and make virtue a by-product of joy.

A prayer

Lord, I know you will not be soft with me when straight speaking is needed. Let us meet and talk. You will tell me what is not clean in my life, and I shall ask you for living water to wash it away.

He lives in our hearts

John 4:19–26 (NJB)

'I see you are a prophet, sir,' said the woman. 'Our fathers worshipped on this mountain, though you say that Jerusalem is the place where one ought to worship.' Jesus said: 'Believe me, woman, the hour is coming when you will worship the Father neither on this mountain nor in Jerusalem. You worship what you do not know, we worship what we do know, for salvation comes from the Jews. But the hour is coming—indeed is already here—when true worshippers will worship the Father in spirit and truth: that is the kind of worshipper the Father seeks. God is spirit, and those who worship must worship in spirit and truth.' The woman said to him, 'I know that Messiah—that is, Christ—is coming; and when he comes he will explain everything.' Jesus said, 'That is who I am, I who speak to you.'

The Samaritan woman's religious understanding was sketchy and intuitive, but on one point she was quite clear. 'The Christ is coming and he will explain everything.'

One summer holiday we entertained seventeen Russians to a barbecue in our garden on a Saturday evening. Our guests were in a party mood. They had come to England as tourists, but, because of a breakdown in communications at an early stage, the local man who had organized the trip mistakenly believed them to be seventeen youth leaders on a fact-finding tour. Frequent, inexplicable trips to scout troops, schools and youth clubs had left the Russians completely bewildered and just a little resentful.

Now, with their host's eccentricities explained, they danced and sang under our apple trees, determined to enjoy themselves.

'What do you think about God?' I asked one of them through an interpreter, thinking that I could predict his answer.

'We have no education in God,' he replied, 'but'—and he thumped his barrel chest—'he lives in our hearts.'

Can you understand what I mean when I say that I envied that man slightly? In this part of the world it may be that we have too much education in God, and not enough simple awareness of his presence with us. Like my Russian, the Samaritan woman was in possession of one simple, certain truth: 'The Christ is coming...'

Imagine the heart-stopping amazement that this woman must have felt when the man who had already proved his power to her said, 'You're right, and I'm him—I've come.'

A thought

Is there such a thing as a more sophisticated faith? How does the tension between intelligence and simplicity help or hinder us? Are we too ready to assume that some groups, races or religions know nothing of Jesus?

Come and see Jesus

John 4:27–32 (NJB)

At this point his disciples returned and were surprised to find him speaking to a woman, though none of them asked, 'What do you want from her?' or, 'What are you talking to her about?' The woman put down her water jar and hurried back to the town to tell the people, 'Come and see a man who has told me everything I have done; could this be the Christ?' This brought people out of the town and they made their way towards him. Meanwhile, the disciples were urging him, 'Rabbi, do have something to eat'; but he said, 'I have food to eat that you do not know about.'

We are told that when the food-buying committee came back from the Samaritan equivalent of Tesco's, they were surprised to find their master talking to the Samaritan woman, but that they declined to comment. Some people suggest that this indicates sensitivity and tactfulness on the part of the disciples, but I doubt it. We hear in another part of the Gospels that they were afraid to tell Jesus what they were discussing because it might make him angry. It seems much more likely that they were simply beginning to learn that if he was doing something, however strange, it must be worth doing, and the best thing they could do was to cooperate.

The principle holds good today. Find out what God is doing and join in, as a friend of mine once put it, and don't ask unnecessary questions.

The Samaritan woman, in defiance of many modern three-point sermons on outreach, now rushes off full of excitement to evangelize before she gets round to repenting. Whenever and wherever the power of Jesus is genuinely manifested we are bound to see this kind of natural, spontaneous spreading of the good news that Jesus has come. She simply could not contain herself, and soon the sheer infectiousness of her enthusiasm brought a congregation out to the well.

We talk a great deal about evangelism (a fact which must excite God greatly!) but if what we are doing is devising and organizing events, then asking God if he would care to help with the chairs or the refreshments, or some other little task not yet allocated, we shall get nowhere. Jesus himself, his power and his love, must be at the very centre and forefront of our efforts, exciting people so much that they rush off to tell others.

A prayer

Help us to follow you unquestioningly, Lord, and to keep you at the front of all we do.

Passion and privilege

John 4:33–38 (NJB)

So the disciples said to one another, 'Has someone brought him food?' But Jesus said: 'My food is to do the will of the one who sent me, and to complete his work. Do you not have a saying: Four months and then the harvest? Well, I tell you, look around you, look at the fields, already they are white for harvest! Already the reaper is being paid his wages, already he is bringing in the grain for eternal life, so that sower and reaper can rejoice together. For here the proverb holds true: one sows, another reaps. I sent you to reap a harvest you have not laboured for. Others have laboured for it; and you have come into the rewards of their labour.'

I have never been very good at talks that are based on three points beginning with the same letter, but this passage is about priorities, passion and privilege.

Fired by this productive encounter with the Gentile world, Jesus refuses the food that the disciples have brought, and reasserts his chief priority, which is obedience. Notice that his 'food' is not seeing thousands of people converted, or sick people healed, but simply to do the will of the one who sent him. It is about relationship. What is our priority?

The passion in this section is unmistakable. The time has come for the harvest to be brought in, and Jesus is filled to the brim with Holy Spirit excitement at the urgency and the wonder and the power and the splendour of God's salvation plan nearing its climax. What is our passion?

The privilege is for the disciples and for us. We are fellow-labourers with Jesus himself in the fields that have been planted and tended by the prophets, and died for by our friend, brother and king. An immense amount of work has been done by others. Now it is our turn. Into our hands is placed a shining sickle of love and truth and judgment. The harvest is waiting for us. Does it feel like a privilege?

The challenge of this passage is immense. If we are only playing at Christianity, it will have no appeal for us at all. There is a powerful symbolic message in Jesus' refusal of earthly food in favour of spiritual sustenance. It suggests and invites a commitment that will remove our fundamental dependence on the things of this world. I find that quite frightening, don't you?

A prayer

Lord, we want to share your passion and your priorities. We are weak and blind. Open our eyes to your power and our great privilege.

She told them about Jesus John 4:39–42 (NJB)

Many Samaritans of that town believed in him on the strength of the woman's words of testimony, 'He told me everything I have done.' So, when the Samaritans came up to him, they begged him to stay with them. He stayed for two days, and they said to the woman, 'Now we believe no longer because of what you told us; we have heard him ourselves and we know that he is indeed the Saviour of the world.'

This Samaritan woman must have been quite something! She obviously set up a very dynamic little one-woman mission team, probably standing on a Samaritan soapbox in the market-place and describing her vivid encounter in graphic detail. If present-day Christian publishers had been around at the time, she would undoubtedly have been snapped up to write one of those testimony paperbacks that begin with the old life (five husbands) and end with the new life (one-woman mission team... and so on). Clearly her audiences did not condemn her on hearing about her lurid past, so presumably the new life in her was powerful indeed.

Nor did she make the mistake that many evangelists and church leaders do nowadays, of drawing her listeners to herself instead of to Jesus. They insisted on seeing for themselves, and having seen him, they wanted to keep him, as I am sure we all would. They were then able to say, as one hopes and prays that *all* converts will be able to say eventually: 'You told us about him, but now we've met him for ourselves, and we know who he is.'

The most any of us can hope for, whatever our dreams of spiritual progress may be, is to become an effective signpost pointing to Jesus. Generally speaking, signposts are not required to pontificate about means of transport or the way in which passengers should position themselves. They simply point the way.

I cannot help feeling that this little period of time spent in a Samaritan town must have been a pleasant respite for Jesus. He had left Judea to avoid the Pharisees, and here, in the middle of a country that the Jews despised, he found acceptance and a warm response among Gentiles. Perhaps it is not surprising that, in a certain parable, the hero was a Samaritan

To reflect

Is our new life more dynamic than the old one? Do we draw people to us or to Jesus? Do we mind our own business after that? Could Jesus relax with us for a while?

Woe to him that claims obedience when it is not due; woe to him that refuses it when it is!

Thomas Carlyle

OBEDIENCE —AIMING FOR THE PLANNED DESTINATION

The sticky, sulky, salutary story of Jonah

Just about every discussion I've ever had about the authority of scripture (and we've had some crackers around our kitchen table, I can tell you!) has, at some point, concerned itself with either Job or Jonah, or both. Why? Well, I'm no biblical historian, but I gather that these two wonderful accounts of the dealings of God with man are, to the objective and knowledgeable eye, clear examples of a particular type of contemporary storytelling.

I shall never forget the outrage I felt at the age of eighteen or nineteen when a close Christian friend of mine went away to study theology, and, returning after his first term, announced, with the calm insouciance that so often accompanies newly acquired knowledge, that Jonah was a 'typical Jewish folk tale'. Time to bring in the Spanish Inquisition! How could he have been *so* corrupted in *such* a short time? After all, he knew as well as I did, because we'd been taught it at the church youth-group, that every last semicolon in the Bible had been installed carefully into scripture by God himself, and that the whole edifice of our belief in that fact would have to be condemned and demolished if one small brick was found to be faulty. The curate had said so, for goodness' sake! So necessary was it for us to feel sure in those early days, that we preferred to wear such 'certainties' like ill-fitting uniforms, rather than face the chill of a difficult world with the scanty, individual rags of honest enquiry and constructive doubt. At the time, my friend's statement sounded like the worst kind of heresy.

Nowadays, of course, I know that God may admit into heaven even those who, when asked about doctrine, suggest that it might be 'what they do up at the Health Centre'. He is mainly concerned with heart and relationship. In any case, we grow into some of those badly-fitting clothes as the years go by, don't we?

What is my view of scripture today? Forgive me if I repeat myself, but it does seem very important to make this plain. I regard the Bible as a letter from God to me. He has personally supervised every aspect of its contents, and there is nothing in it that should not be there. It includes every kind of writing that you can imagine, including poetry, history, storytelling, prophecy and teaching. This long letter begins with 'Dear Adrian' and ends 'Love, God', and I am very grateful for it.

As for the book of Jonah in particular, it is without doubt one of the most entertaining narratives in the Bible, and, frankly, it doesn't matter a jot to me whether it describes a historical event or not, because, like the parables of Jesus (are *they* true?), it contains so much information and truth about God and man that I am quite sure the Holy Spirit inspired its inclusion in the Old Testament.

So what does this authoritative piece of scripture have to say to us? Perhaps the major theme of the book is obedience, a feature of Christian living that Jesus returned to again and again. I find obedience extremely difficult, not least because it is in the (apparently) small things that God challenges us most directly and intrusively. Okay, I know people often say that sort of thing about small things, but I really mean it. Let us suppose that the phone were to go right now, even as I was typing these words, and someone from America or Africa or Australia asked if it was possible for me to drop everything and fly out immediately to speak to five thousand people. I would find it much easier, in the most important sense, to be obedient to that sort of call, assuming it was from God as well as from some frantic organizer, than to adapt my normal responses in a purely domestic situation.

Only last night (you're going to think this sounds *so* daft) I was in the kitchen doing something or other, and I said to myself, 'I think I'll have a cup of tea.' The only other person in the house was one of my teenage sons, who was watching television in the sitting room. He and I usually get on very well, but that day we'd had a pretty stormy row and I wasn't feeling very charitably disposed towards him. We hadn't spoken for a couple of hours. As I filled the kettle and put a teabag into my cup it occurred to me that the most generous—and helpful—thing I could do, would be to offer him a cup of tea as well. But I didn't want to. Why should I? He hadn't been very reasonable with me earlier on. Why should I make him a cup of tea? Let him make his own cup of tea. After all, it wasn't as if he'd even know I'd made myself a cup of tea without offering him one, because I'd drink it in the kitchen. So, there!

It's at times like this that being a Christian is so very annoying and so very rewarding. My son wouldn't know, but God's Son would. It was an opportunity to begin the peace-making process, and I could either take advantage of it or waste it. I made a second cup of tea, and suddenly we were talking again.

I know that sounds like a trivial little incident, but the fact is that genuine change in behaviour and attitudes, as opposed to the theoretical total transformation that we are sometimes promised by certain sections of the Church, usually grows in the good soil of moral self-confidence resulting from these tiny experiences of victory in obedience. God is very clever, you know.

It was rather similar for Evie, a lady I met in South Africa, who worked as a housemaid for a Christian doctor friend of mine called Jane. Jane often talked to Evie about Jesus, and eventually Evie herself became a believer. Asked what difference being a Christian had made to her life, she replied that she now dusted the space behind the furniture as well as the bits you could see, because, whereas Jane didn't often check those hidden places, the Lord always did, and he demanded her obedience in such things.

I would like briefly to mention two other important things about the Jonah story.

First, Jesus used it as a picture or parallel of his own death and resurrection, hence the connections with the Easter story that I have made in some of the notes.

Secondly, the story offers us a quite fascinating and challenging insight into what is possible in terms of a relationship between God and one of his people.

I promise you, there is much to learn from dear old Jonah.

Prayer

Father, may we have a whale of a time with Jonah. Amen.

Where now?

Jonah 1:1–2 (RSV)

Now the word of the Lord came to Jonah the son of Amittai, saying, 'Arise, go to Nineveh, that great city, and cry against it; for their wickedness has come up before me.'

When I became a Christian, in the sixties, guidance was one of the items included in a sort of invisible evangelical kit-bag that was issued to all new recruits. From in front or from behind (depending on which scripture was quoted) God would direct every step that we took. We would always know where to go and what to do because he would tell us.

I can't speak for others, but this subtle mis-teaching left me frequently paralysed (when God seemed to be saying nothing) and sometimes neurotic and twitchy (when a random thought invaded my mind). Did the Lord really want me to get a train to Walsall and give a blue cardigan to the first person that I met?

It was during this period that a friend told me he was being led to work in the Holy Land because every time he opened his Bible he found a reference to Israel.

It is precisely because the Holy Spirit *does* guide people clearly and specifically when necessary that we need to avoid the rather superstitious view of God's leading that prevails in many parts of the Church.

God's communication system is not based on some mouldy old hand-operated printer that produces documents too fuzzy to read. If he speaks to you—you'll know it!

Paul the apostle is a good model. He prayed constantly, made common-sense decisions, and was always ready to change his plans when a dream or a vision or a direct word from God told him he'd got it wrong.

Of course God is concerned with every step we take, but we're not involved in some ghastly spiritual version of *Come Dancing*. Jonah knew *exactly* what God wanted him to do. That's why he cleared off. On Palm Sunday Jesus knew exactly what God wanted as well. He didn't clear off, though. He entered Jerusalem knowing that death was inevitable.

A prayer

Lord, help me to stay close to you in prayer and study, so that our relationship affects all the decisions that I make. I trust that I will hear you clearly and specifically when necessary.

Not my will...

Jonah 1:3 (RSV)

But Jonah rose to flee to Tarshish from the presence of the Lord. He went down to Joppa and found a ship going to Tarshish; so he paid the fare, and went on board, to go with them to Tarshish, away from the presence of the Lord.

I wonder what Jonah did when he was not out being a prophet? Perhaps there was a sign over his door saying: AMITTAI AND SON—STICK WHITTLERS. Every now and then, as Jonah sat happily at home, whistling through his teeth and doing a spot of bespoke whittling, the Spirit of God would whisper in his ear and his heart would sink as he realized that it was time to move into prophet mode once again. Why had he got so fed up with it? What was the reason for his deliberate act of disobedience when he was told to go to Nineveh? We can't be sure—but we can guess.

My guess is that his lack of enthusiasm dated from the time when he began to realize that he would never be anything more than a messenger. It would have been quite exciting at first—rather exhilarating. How powerful it must have felt to threaten the enemies of Israel with the hammer of God as a consequence of their evil ways. Perhaps the first one or two failed to repent and suffered destruction as a result.

Then (as far as Jonah was concerned, anyway) the rot began to set in. Following the prophet's impressive forecast of doom and gloom, people repented, and Jonah began to sense that the God whose message he had delivered much *preferred* to forgive sinners. I guess Jonah felt a bit of a twit when this happened. All that ranting he'd done, and now God had changed his mind. Very hard to walk away keeping your back view dignified in those circumstances.

Unlike Clark Kent and Bruce Wayne, Jonah was not at all keen to don his super-prophet costume, not if he was going to end up feeling an idiot yet again.

God reserves the right to follow up our obedience in any way that seems fit. If we don't like it we can try to run away, but, as Jonah was about to discover, that doesn't always work.

A thought

Am I willing to have my cake but give up the right to eat it?

Trouble for others

Jonah 1:4–6 (RSV)

But the Lord hurled a great wind upon the sea, and there was a mighty tempest on the sea, so that the ship threatened to break up. Then the mariners were afraid, and each cried to his god; and they threw the wares that were in the ship into the sea, to lighten it for them. But Jonah had gone down into the inner part of the ship and had lain down, and was fast asleep. So the captain came and said to him, 'What do you mean, you sleeper? Arise, call upon your god! Perhaps the god will give a thought to us, that we do not perish.'

I find these verses a little disturbing. If I weren't doing these notes for you I'd skip this bit and go on to something more comfortable. Can it really be true that my disobedience could cause a whole lot of trouble for folk who've done nothing wrong? Honesty compels me to admit that I know it to be true in my own life. I haven't gone down to Newhaven and taken ship to Dieppe to flee the will of God recently, but I have quite deliberately failed to tackle problems, heal relationships or perform tasks that should be top priorities in my life. The innocent fellow-travellers who suffer as a result are usually members of my family. Guilt makes me grumpy. Failure makes me fret. I become a little cloud, inflicting bad weather on my small part of the world.

In this account the little cloud called Jonah is lying, like a baby in its womb, down in the depths of the ship, hoping perhaps to hide in unconsciousness as so many of us do when we feel like fugitives.

What an awakening! The sensation of being dragged violently back into reality must have been dreadful—it always is. The fear and panic in the captain's voice, the sounds and movements of the storm, and the inescapable knowledge that God had taken the situation by the scruff of the neck and was shaking it until his disobedient servant fell out—all these things must have combined to become a waking nightmare for the prophet. The crew had dumped the cargo, a multi-faith prayer meeting had been held, everyone was quite terrified, and it was all Jonah's fault!

A question

Will I do what I'm told at last?

Owning up

Jonah 1:8–9 (RSV)

Then they said to him, 'Tell us, on whose account this evil has come upon us. What is your occupation? And whence do you come? What is your country? And of what people are you?' And he said to them, 'I am a Hebrew; and I fear the Lord, the God of heaven, who made the sea and the dry land.'

Isn't it difficult to own up sometimes? When I was about nine years old my father made a bow and arrow for myself and my brother, Ian, who was two years younger than me. He spent hours hunting in the woods for the right—absolutely straight—lengths of hazel, and then sat outside the shed on our allotment, trimming, cutting, tying, sharpening, and fashioning flights out of cardboard. Ian and I tried the weapon out. It worked marvellously. Later that day, when no one else was around, I did what I'd been wanting to do ever since I saw the completed implements. I fired the arrow as far as I possibly could. It was inexpressibly wonderful to draw back the string and feel the potential power in that strong, flexible length of hazel. When I released the arrow, it flew in a majestically huge and regular arc, curving up towards the sun, and curving down into a thick and impenetrable mass of undergrowth. That beautiful arrow was lost. I didn't tell anyone.

For some reason my father got it into his head that it was Ian who had lost the arrow. When I got to the allotment next morning Ian was in tears, and my father was angrily trying to make him confess. A block of ice gripped my heart as the crying and shouting escalated. Words crouched miserably just inside my mouth, too frightened to come out. Then my brother was clipped round the ear and I couldn't stand it any more. The smallest voice you ever heard in your life said, 'Dad, it wasn't Ian who lost the arrow, it was me.'

My father had used up all his anger on Ian, so I didn't get shouted at, but the ice took a long time to melt.

Poor old Jonah Poor old Ian.

A prayer

Lord, if there are things lodged in our hearts that chill us when we remember them, give us the courage to confess to the right person at the right time.

Overboard

Jonah 1:12–15 (RSV)

He said to them, 'Take me up and throw me into the sea; then the sea will quiet down for you; for I know it is because of me that this great tempest has come upon you.' Nevertheless the men rowed hard to bring the ship back to land, but they could not, for the sea grew more and more tempestuous against them... So they took up Jonah and threw him into the sea; and the sea ceased from its raging.

This is a very heart-warming story, don't you think? I like the sound of the fellows on this ship. The whole of their profits had gone overboard with the cargo, they'd been buffeted and terrified by an appalling storm, but they still tried as hard as they could to avoid throwing the author of their misfortunes into the sea. Of course, they must have been a little puzzled. Did this powerful, weather controlling God *really* want them to throw his prophet into the ocean? Wouldn't he be angry with them? They failed to understand, just as Peter failed to understand when he provoked the famous 'Get thee behind me, Satan' speech from his master, that, in the context of God's planning and special knowledge, negative events and circumstances are sometimes essential. As we think about Jesus' horrendous death on the cross, this central truth becomes very evident, but enlightenment usually comes only by hindsight.

I got thrown overboard when illness left me with no job, no church, and no prospects. If you had suggested to me then that this was all part of God's plan for me I would have gone for your throat. I guess that as Jonah travelled the short distance from the ship's rail to the boiling sea, he must have reflected that he had known better days. But he knew God better than I did when my crisis happened. I don't doubt that he was very frightened, but there is a sort of wry awareness in his brave assertion that the tempest would abate if the sailors threw him over the side.

'Maybe I'm going to drown,' he might have said to himself as he hit the water, 'but I have an awful feeling that I'm going to Nineveh...'

A reflection

We are not really capable of assessing the divine perspective on any situation or circumstance. Perhaps its more useful to develop trust and obedience than insight.

The screaming moment Jonah 1:17—2:3 (RSV)

And the Lord appointed a great fish to swallow up Jonah; and Jonah was in the belly of the fish three days and three nights. Then Jonah prayed to the Lord his God from the belly of the fish, saying, 'I called to the Lord, out of my distress, and he answered me; out of the belly of Sheol I cried, and thou didst hear my voice. For thou didst cast me into the deep, into the heart of the seas, and the flood was round about me; all thy waves and thy billows passed over me.'

When the scribes and Pharisees asked Jesus for a sign, he told them that the only sign they'd be given was the sign of the prophet Jonah.

On the day that we call Good Friday, Jesus allowed us to 'throw him overboard' so that the storm of God's displeasure would not destroy us. He spent three days in a place that was far darker and more dismal than the belly of a whale. From the cross he cried out his desolation and anguish to his Father, whose back was turned on his son for that one screaming moment in eternity. Unlike Jonah, Jesus was innocent. He went where he was told, said what he was told, and died when he was told.

I have to say that I don't understand the crucifixion. I accept that this is more a measure of my understanding than a comment on the crucifixion, but I suspect that many others will identify with my lack of comprehension. I don't mean that I can't see the basic logic of somebody taking the blame and being punished for what I have done and not done; nor am I saying that I don't accept or appreciate the power of what Jesus did. How could I? The wordless truth and significance of the cross is in my bones, and in the bones of every suffering body or situation that ever was. I think I mean that there is a great mystery enshrouding that strange, cosmic event, and that I prefer the mystery to half-baked, glib explanations of what was going on.

What about Jonah? I wonder if he knew what this dark, wet, heaving environment was. We shall never know for certain, but one thing's clear enough from the prophet's impassioned prayer—there's nothing like being swallowed by a whale to stimulate revival!

A prayer

Thank you so much, Jesus, for being obedient.

Raging at God

Jonah 2:5–6 (RSV)

'The waters closed in over me, the deep was round about me; weeds were wrapped about my head at the roots of the mountains. I went down to the land whose bars closed upon me for ever; yet thou didst bring up my life from the Pit, O Lord my God.'

I sometimes find myself thinking rather dark thoughts, especially on the day before Easter Sunday. When I read these words of Jonah, spoken from the belly of the whale, I suddenly remembered that horrible incident (widely covered by the media at the time) when a young Italian boy was trapped at the bottom of a disused well. Attempts to rescue the poor lad went on for days with the whole world watching via newspapers and television. Everywhere people prayed that he would be brought up alive from the pit. But he wasn't. He died at the bottom of the well while his mother wept at the top.

I raged at God. I hated God. I told God what I thought of his weakness or his cruelty or whatever it was that prevented him from doing something so obvious, especially in the face of such a barrage of prayer from every corner of the globe.

'You must have seen him!' I raved. 'How could you watch him go through that and not do anything about it? How? Tell me!'

I won't bother trotting out the statutory answers to these questions. I know them. I've used them when others have asked me about such things, and they're not really satisfactory. Two things help me.

First, the God I meet through Jesus weeps and hurts and cares and loves. I've grown to trust him despite getting so angry with him. That isn't an answer—it's a relationship.

Secondly, I take heart from the experience of the disciples on the night following Jesus' death. I believe that they too must have raged at God, unable to believe that he could have allowed such a cruel, pointless, waste of a life that had so much to offer. How could a loving Father stand by and watch as his Son was nailed to a piece of wood between two criminal scum? What a mess! What a waste! What a dark night of tears. Nothing would ever mean anything again.

Then came the dawn.

A prayer

Hold my hand, Lord, it's dark.

Solid ground

Jonah 2:10 (RSV)

And the Lord spoke to the fish, and it vomited out Jonah upon the dry land.

As soon as God had had a chat with this very cooperative whale the creature obligingly deposited Jonah on dry land, and, for the first time since leaving Joppa harbour, the prophet felt solid ground beneath his feet.

This is what Easter is all about. Until Jesus rose quietly but triumphantly from the dead, the world was an island in creation that sank beneath the feet of every man and woman as soon as their mortal bodies became too old to function. The resurrection redefined solid ground. Now, death is no longer relevant, because we can be admitted into the true reality of eternal life with Jesus in the place where he lives with his Father. As soon as death had been overcome, a return to Eden—spiritual and physical—became possible.

All that and chocolate eggs as well!

I've rarely been able to celebrate Easter on Easter Day, but I do celebrate it on all those occasions when, like Jonah, I am rescued yet again from some whale of a problem that is about to digest me into nothingness. I know I am saved once and for all, but every now and then the resurrection principle acts as a structure within my confusion and I know I'm saved all over again.

One of the few occasions when my mood matched the day was an Easter Sunday when I attended the morning service in Norwich Cathedral, one of my all-time favourite buildings. It was one of those incomparable spring mornings full of rippling light and hope. The place was packed, the singing was wonderful, and the prayers seemed to buzz and resonate with the will of God. The deep bass note of tradition and the high and beautiful living presence of the Holy Spirit made my heart soar. Tears filled my eyes and I, who have almost never raised my arms in worship in the most informal situations, suddenly wanted to thrust my open hands as high into the air as high as they would go in the middle of a formal Anglican cathedral service. I didn't. I wish I had done. I was an Easter chicken. I bet, if the truth were told, there was a whole flock of us there that day.

A prayer

Thank you for setting our feet on the mainland. May Easter be always in us.

Completing the loop

Jonah 3:1–2 (RSV)

Then the word of the Lord came to Jonah the second time, saying, 'Arise, go to Nineveh, that great city, and proclaim to it the message that I tell you.'

Poor old Jonah! If he had gone to Nineveh when he was first told to, he wouldn't have ended up in the mess he found himself in and having to hear God give him exactly the same order as before. The prophet's personal rebellion had been nipped in the bud before it had the chance to get going. No doubt he was relieved and grateful to be saved from a blubbery death, but as he squelched off in the direction of this stronghold of the national enemy, all the old misgivings must have fallen over him like a shadow.

But how thankful we should be that God *does* organize and allow these 'loops' in our lives. Have you done a loop? I have. On at least one occasion in my life I have deliberately taken a direction that is opposed to the will of God. One day I shall write a book with the title, *Life in the Loops*. These little drifts and diversions are almost always interesting (ask Jonah!) but they become progressively more hollow, unsatisfying, or just plain dangerous—more dangerous, indeed, than those things that the world fears most. I don't know if Jonah really believed that he could escape God by changing his geographical position, but a greater and more horribly permanent fate would have resulted from real separation from the creator.

Yes, the good news is that God will sort our mistakes and wrong turnings out. He would never have taken us on in the first place if he wasn't prepared to cope with the inevitable dips in our behaviour and response. (Most of the prophets were temperamental, awkward, passionate people who wouldn't last two minutes in most of our modern churches.)

The bad news is that the job we've been given doesn't change. As far as God is concerned, completing the loop means 'business as usual'.

Off to Nineveh!

A prayer

Thank you, Lord, that you rebuke us when we get in a mess, but that you don't give up on us.

Into action

So Jonah arose and went to Nineveh, according to the word of the Lord. Now Nineveh was an exceedingly great city, three days' journey in breadth. Jonah began to go into the city, going a day's journey. And he cried, 'Yet forty days, and Nineveh shall be overthrown.'

Do you get the impression, as I do, that Jonah slipped straight into top prophesying gear as soon as he actually reached Nineveh? Prophets and evangelists are like that in my experience. They may moan or complain or even become sullenly uncommunicative at times (modern ones as well as Old Testament ones) but as soon as they start to do what they are called and born to do there's no stopping them. A sort of spiritual professionalism takes over. Vanity and vulnerability take a back seat as God drives his message into the listeners. I'm quite sure that Jonah's warning to the citizens of Nineveh was not even slightly diluted by his reluctance to be there. His 'ministry' was part of him, which is more than can be said for many of us.

I know at least two people who have spent most of their lives denying (or trying to deny) a part of themselves that God has almost certainly been wanting to use for years.

One of them is a very talented artist who, when he became a Christian more than thirty years ago allowed the climate of Christian disapproval that befogged art at the time to dissuade him from continuing with his career as a painter. He has recovered from this foolishness now, but many years were wasted as he tried to pretend that this essential part of him had been painlessly amputated, and that he didn't care. God cared. If Jonah had been ordered to paint pictures he would have been wasting his time at Nineveh.

My other friend is a musician—a cellist. This chap has wanted to 'do something for the Lord' for ages. He gets quite depressed when things don't seem to work out. He's just beginning to realize—with some amazement—that what the Lord wants is some really good cello-playing, and not just 'Christian stuff'.

Painting, prophesying or playing the cello—whatever is right is all right.

A question

Are we doing what we are?

And the power of fear

Jonah 3:5–9 (RSV)

And the people of Nineveh believed God; they proclaimed a fast, and put on sackcloth, from the greatest of them to the least of them. Then tidings reached the king of Nineveh, and he arose from his throne, removed his robe, and covered himself with sackcloth, and sat in ashes. And he made proclamation and published through Nineveh, 'By the decree of the king and his nobles: Let neither man nor beast, herd nor flock, taste anything; let them not feed, or drink water, but let man and beast be covered with sackcloth, and let them cry mightily to God; yea, let every one turn from his evil way and from the violence which is in his hands. Who knows, God may yet repent and turn from his fierce anger, so that we perish not?'

How could one disobedient little prophet have such a dynamic effect on such a huge community? In scale and depth of response this mission of Jonah's makes a Billy Graham rally look like a Quaker meeting in a telephone box. How did he do it? Well, first of all, of course, he didn't do it. His threat of destruction after forty days carried the authority and authenticity of the Holy Spirit, yet another lesson for all of us that it is both pointless and perilous to claim that we speak for God when we are only guessing.

Secondly, and precisely because the prophecy was so convincing, the citizens of Nineveh were clearly terrified. Modern evangelism tends to major on the attractiveness of God's love for us, and the logical desirability of being reunited with our creator, and we need those emphases to counteract the influence of the Pharisees who surround us, but fear has a long and respectable pedigree in the history of God's dealings with men and women. Why? Quite simply because God knows that for those who do not belong to him there is a lot to be frightened of. If someone whom you love is in danger you warn them, and you hope against hope that they will save themselves.

The people of this city threw themselves into repentance wholeheartedly, inspired and commanded by their king, who ordered a suspension of all normal activities while everybody turned to God.

A question

This kind of head-heart-body repentance is rare today. Why?

Unless you become... Jonah 3:10 (RSV)

When God saw what they did, how they turned from their evil way, God repented of the evil which he had said he would do to them, and he did not do it.

In a magazine article my wife described an occasion when, after working in Germany for a few days, I flew into Heathrow, arriving at about seven o'clock in the evening. Bridget drove up to meet me, bringing our two younger sons with her. Joseph, aged twelve, and David, aged eleven, knew how much I would be looking forward to seeing them. They pushed to the front of the waiting crowds so that their shining faces would be the first thing I saw as I came out of the green channel with my luggage. It was such a pleasure for me to see them there.

The God who so freely forgave these Assyrian penitents, and who describes himself through Jesus as a Father, takes a similar pleasure in our confident awareness that he wants to see us. Not because we have earned his affection, nor for any other motives of personal pride, but because, like Joe and David at the airport, we know that he loves us with a passion that is graphically illustrated in the story of the prodigal son. Let's not get smug about the rotten old sinners in Nineveh. We all need to go through the repentance door if we want to be hugged by God.

What sort of door is the repentance door? I found a clue once. A few miles along the coast from us there's a place called Jungle Tumble. It's a highly coloured maze of tunnels, ladders, netting and plastic balls—a little paradise for children who want to enjoy the ecstasy of physical abandonment. When Katy was four and David was eleven we visited this place that we'd heard so much about. On arriving we discovered that only children under a certain fixed height were allowed. Katy was little enough. David was too big. What to do? Fortunately the lady in charge invited David to duck his head under the bar. 'Look,' she said, 'now you're small enough!'

We bow our heads and become a bit smaller before we enter joy.

A reflection

Chesterton said, 'A man is never so tall as when he bows.'

Getting cross with God **Jonah 4:1–3 (RSV)**

But it displeased Jonah exceedingly, and he was angry. And he prayed to the Lord and said, 'I pray thee, Lord, is not this what I said when I was yet in my country? That is why I made haste to flee to Tarshish; for I knew that thou art a gracious God and merciful, slow to anger, and abounding in steadfast love, and repentest of evil. Therefore now, O Lord, take my life from me, I beseech thee, for it is better for me to die than to live.'

Well, who's an angry little prophet, then? Jonah is very bold with God, isn't he? Mind you, he must have known him very well. It reminds me of the way one of my sons used to respond to being told off when he was very small. After a minute or two of my parental raging he would look me in the eye and say triumphantly, 'Anyway, you love me, so you'll be nice to me in a minute...' I wouldn't recommend that as a way of responding to the wrath of God, but I'm glad David knew I loved him, and I find the interchange between Jonah and God a refreshingly real and familiar one. The prophet is doing a real Basil Fawlty here, furious that God has done exactly what he feared he would do. He's forgiven them! Huh!

It's interesting to note that God did not insist on Jonah sharing his intention or motivation as far as Nineveh was concerned. He simply wanted him to do as he was told. Jesus made exactly the same point in his parable of the two sons. One said he would do what was asked of him, but didn't. The other got stroppy and refused to obey, but then went and did what he'd been told. Similarly, when Jesus called Zacchaeus down from his tree, the little man wasn't required to sort his attitudes and behaviour out before nipping home to sort a meal out. Again and again throughout scripture the same point is made. Those who love God are those who obey him.

Now it was time for Jonah's little attitude problem to be sorted out.

Questions

Do I trust God enough to get cross with him? Do I love him enough to obey him?

The incredible sulk **Jonah 4:4–5 (RSV)**

And the Lord said, 'Do you do well to be angry?' Then Jonah went out of the city and sat to the east of the city, and made a booth for himself there. He sat under it in the shade, till he should see what would become of the city.

I really like God in this story. I don't like him in all the Old Testament accounts, particularly the bits where mass killings are ordered, but I shall understand what that was all about one day. The thing I like in this story is that, having shown such compassion and taken such trouble with the enormous community at Nineveh, God now concentrates on one confused individual—Jonah.

If the prodigal son's elder brother is the heavyweight sulking champion of the New Testament, Jonah must be a front-line candidate in the Old. There he sits on the hillside, probably muttering about Joppa and ships and storms and whales and people not doing what they say they're going to do...

God tries to talk to him about it, but it seems that Jonah is one of those people who just can't understand anything without concrete examples or visible object lessons. The whale was the first and most dramatic one, but now it was time for something a little more agricultural. It has been most refreshing over the last few years to find that God does not have a set of unvarying procedures that he applies to anyone who comes within his orbit. In my own case, for instance, there have been times when my rather negative expectations led me to predict a divine clip round the ear as a response to less than wonderful behaviour. In fact, because he knows and loves me, God has used encouragement and humour to lift me out of my lower self. Mind you, when the aforesaid clip round the ear is necessary he doesn't seem to have any qualms about applying it, and that's as it should be, even if I don't like it much at the time.

Jonah and you and I may be very different in outlook and personality, but don't worry—although we shall all finish up in the same place, a very individual and carefully designed route has been prepared for each of us.

A prayer

Thank you, Father, for loving me as an individual and planning things specially for me.

The final lesson

Jonah 4:6–11 (RSV)

And the Lord God appointed a plant, and made it come up over Jonah that it might be a shade over his head, to save him from his discomfort. So Jonah was exceedingly glad because of the plant. But when dawn came up the next day, God appointed a worm which attacked the plant, so that it withered. When the sun rose, God appointed a sultry east wind, and the sun beat upon the head of Jonah so that he was faint; and he asked that he might die, and said, 'It is better for me to die than to live.' But God said to Jonah, 'Do you do well to be angry for the plant?' And he said, 'I do well to be angry, angry enough to die.' And the Lord said, 'You pity the plant, for which you did not labour, nor did you make it grow, which came into being in a night, and perished in a night. And should not I pity Nineveh, that great city, in which there are more than a hundred and twenty thousand persons who do not know their right hand from their left, and also much cattle?'

My sulks are fairly fragile. If someone tickles me or says something absurd, my glum expression is likely to crack, and once I've smiled my sulk is usually ruined. Jonah, on the other hand, is so determined not to give an inch to God that he walks straight into the logical trap that is set for him. The writer of this book fails to record the prophet's response to the final, telling argument that one hundred and twenty thousand people must be as important as a plant, but I have no doubt that Jonah got the point. Perhaps the mention of cattle swung it in the end. A real waste!

A sad footnote to this story, recorded a few pages further on in the Old Testament in the book of Nahum, is that the people of Nineveh learned very little from their great deliverance. As far as we can tell they returned to their sins and were destroyed.

Jonah teaches us that obedience is essential; that God would rather forgive than punish; that he takes as much trouble with individuals as whole communities; and that he can be very humorous and nice.

A question

Do I share these attributes of God?

The way to heaven out of all places
is of like length and distance.
Thomas More

HEADING FOR HEAVEN —WHY DID WE LEAVE IN THE FIRST PLACE?

1 Corinthians 15

After my mother died and her body had been cremated we were left with a smart, polished wooden urn that, according to the undertaker, contained her ashes. Someone told me once that these urns often do not contain the actual remains of one's relative, but a mixture of the ashes of all those cremated on that particular day. I have no idea if this is true, but it didn't really matter to me. That sealed box was more of a symbol than anything else, a mini-coffin that we could lodge in a place that might help us to focus our memories of Mum in the future.

There was even a hint of humour in our response as a family to this sombre object. Ian, my younger brother, was the one who collected it from the undertaker's office in Tunbridge Wells, and when Bridget and I visited his home a few days later he said, 'Mum's in the back room.' For some reason this made us both slightly hysterical, not least because Mum herself would have been highly amused by the idea that she was stored in a small container on the sideboard. My mother was too large a character to be contained in a small anything.

What were we to do with the urn?

After some discussion it was agreed that Mum's preference (we may have been wrong, but she could hardly argue with us now) would have been burial in the same grave as her parents in the graveyard of a little non-conformist chapel near Rushlake Green in East Sussex. None of us had been to this place since we were children, and although church records indicated that a stone had been placed at the head of the grave, we found no trace of it on the plot where Mum's parents had been buried many years ago.

Digging at one end of the grave to make a hole for the urn on the day before the burial, Ian's spade suddenly came up against something hard and unyielding. Careful excavation revealed the missing gravestone which must have sunk gradually into the soft earth over the years, until it had disappeared altogether beneath the grass that covered the grave. After a sluice-down, the names of John and Kitty Baker, my grandparents, were visible once more. I never knew my grandfather, but I loved Nanna with that special variety of openly excited passion that I find so endearing in small children nowadays. Travelling on the bus to visit her house in Heathfield had always been a trip to heaven. I liked the idea that my mother would, in a symbolic sense, at least, be reunited with her mum and dad, here on this quiet Sussex slope, overlooking a view which happened to be her favourite one in all the world.

Next day, the day that we had chosen for the burial of the urn was the windiest, wettest day of the year so far. It seemed as if the whole world was weeping in sympathy with us as we huddled around that oblong of turf with the little patch of newly turned earth at one end, trying to turn a wild, ragged experience into something that had a shape. Turning away at the end seemed like a form of treachery. Silly though it was, both Bridget and I, and probably the others as well, found it hard to leave Mum alone on that hillside in the wind and weather. We wanted to take her home with us.

On St Patrick's day, Mum's birthday, we returned to put some daffodils and greenery on the grave. This time the feeling was quite different. Spring sunshine bathed the hillside in bright hope, and in the field next to the graveyard two horses rolled and galloped and sported out of sheer high spirits. Mum loved horses. In the clear March air the view across the valley was spectacular, and I remained for a while after the others had gone back to the car, just gazing out towards the far horizon. I felt no less sad about Mum's absence from our lives—I'm still trying to deal with it on the most basic level—but I knew in my heart, as I stood there, that we who follow Jesus must not betray him and his death and resurrection by accepting death as a finality. We come to terms with our temporary loss because normal living demands that we must, but, as David Watson said repeatedly as he approached his death, the best is yet to come. As I walked away from the place where I am sure we shall often come to remember my mother, I knew, with rare conviction, that, as surely as that stone in my grandparents' grave re-emerged when it seemed no longer to exist, I shall meet her and my grandmother again, and we shall have new bodies and new understandings, but those two people who loved me will undoubtedly be themselves, and I shall certainly be me.

If that is not so, we are wasting our time, and that is primarily the subject of this great chapter from the New Testament.

Prayer

Father, it is agony to lose people whom we love, but we know that Jesus died in order that we can be reunited one day. Help us to be properly balanced in the way that we deal with death. We can't help mourning, because we miss those we've lost so much, but let us keep in mind the hope that we have in you, not just as an airy-fairy, abstract thing, but as an excited anticipation of genuine contact with people who will be equipped with new bodies that cannot ache as my mother's did, because they are eternal bodies. Thank you for lending us those who have loved us. Help us to hand them back to you with as good a grace as we can. May the sense of heaven-waiting be strong and evident in us so that others can take heart from our example, and truly believe that the rising of Jesus from the tomb guarantees that all those who follow him will rise in exactly the same way. Amen.

The right direction

1 Corinthians 15:1–8 (NIV)

Now, brothers, I want to remind you of the gospel I preached to you, which you received and on which you have taken your stand. By this gospel you are saved, if you hold firmly to the word I preached to you. Otherwise, you have believed in vain. For what I received I passed on to you as of first importance: that Christ died for our sins according to the Scriptures, that he was buried, that he was raised on the third day according to the Scriptures, and that he appeared to Peter, and then to the Twelve. After that, he appeared to more than five hundred of the brothers at the same time, most of whom are still living, though some have fallen asleep. Then he appeared to James, then to all the apostles, and last of all he appeared to me also, as to one abnormally born.

Paul is determined to put the erring Corinthians firmly back on track. There is only one right way to go and here he reminds them what it is.

I remember making one of those interminable tube journeys from central London to some nameless suburb in the middle of nowhere. Two businessmen of the thrusting executive type got on at Baker Street and began talking in fruity, overloud voices. They spoke of 'oil' and 'productivity' and 'corporate industry' and 'international awareness'. As I listened to their confident tones, and admired their advanced strap-hanging techniques, I felt slightly inferior. Here were these hugely competent captains of industry on their way to clinch some multi-million pound deal, while I trundled off to my latest speaking engagement with a suitcase full of books for sale. My reverie was interrupted when the train arrived at about the third stop since Baker Street, and one of the two men peered out at the platform in sudden alarm.

'We're going the wrong way!' he bleated.

The two high-flyers ducked out of the train, leaving me to reflect on the fact that while I might be a bit of a twit, at least I was going the right way.

Paul is reminding his readers of the basic truths of Christian faith. Jesus is the way, and everything else depends on following his lead. This requires obedience rather than talent.

Thought

Am I still on board?

Boasting

1 Corinthians 15:9–11 (NIV)

For I am the least of the apostles and do not even deserve to be called an apostle, because I persecuted the Church of God. But by the grace of God I am what I am, and his grace to me was not without effect. No, I worked harder than all of them—yet not I, but the grace of God that was with me. Whether, then, it was I or they, this is what we preach, and this is what you believed.

I have heard Paul described by some critics as a conceited evangelist. Quite apart from the fact that this is an obvious tautology, I believe that it shows a complete misunderstanding of the man. Paul's real problem is that he believes in the power of God and he isn't afraid of telling the truth. The result is that he can say 'I worked harder than all of them' without any self-consciousness at all because he honestly believes that any success he achieves is attributable to the grace of God working in him. There is a right kind of bold assertiveness, and we see too little of it in this age. Very few people are broken and humble enough to boast about God as naturally and loudly as Paul.

I once spoke at a meeting in the north-west of England, under the title 'Wounded in Action'. I talked about my own experience of suffering, the way in which genuine friendship had helped, the perils of looking for quick-fix solutions to long-term problems, and the dreadful (and inaccurate) feelings of spiritual failure when depression or breakdown occurs. As soon as I stood up to speak I could sense the pain in many of those present and by the time I had finished the air was heavy with need.

Then the organizer of the meeting stood up. 'I'm sure we've all enjoyed listening to Adrian,' he said, 'and of course we know that all these questions and problems are answered when the Lord Jesus Christ comes into our hearts...'

Saying that probably made the organizer feel a lot better, but down in the body of the hall a lot of very miserable people (who had asked Jesus into their lives a long time ago) were feeling much worse. I know that I should have offered to pray with the people then, or at least invited them to pray with each other. I didn't because I felt inadequate and not 'spiritual enough'.

I was refusing to believe that God could use me until I was good enough. Now *that's* conceit!

Prayer

Sorry, Lord. Use me.

Silly sheep

1 Corinthians 15:12–15 (NIV)

But if it is preached that Christ has been raised from the dead, how can some of you say that there is no resurrection of the dead? If there is no resurrection of the dead, then not even Christ has been raised. And if Christ has not been raised, our preaching is useless and so is your faith. More than that, we are then found to be false witnesses about God, for we have testified about God that he raised Christ from the dead. But he did not raise him if in fact the dead are not raised.

Christians are like sheep. I suppose that's a good thing really, isn't it? The metaphor was selected at a rather high level, after all. But problems arise when false or misguided shepherds appear and lead the bleaters into poisoned pasture. It seems almost beyond belief that these Corinthians allowed themselves to be persuaded that a lifetime of faith and discipline would be followed by oblivion. What sort of pressures resulted in their acceptance of such a foolish distortion?

I have a young friend who attends a very lively and ultra-charismatic fellowship in the West Country—the sort of church where you can't own a canary unless it's been hatched-again. David described how a north-European evangelist had visited the church for a fortnight, bringing with him a conviction that God wanted to miraculously change his followers' dental fillings from dull grey to solid gold. Wide-eyed, the congregation listened to this message, and then submitted themselves as a body to the evangelist's prayer that God would touch their gums like a sort of divine Midas. This was followed by much celebration as the speaker announced that God had indeed worked in the mouths of many. So intensely positive was the feeling in the church that on the following day David was persuaded to publicly testify to the metamorphosis in his own fillings—this despite the fact that his bathroom mirror showed clear evidence to the contrary.

Much ashamed, he subsequently got a (very close) friend to check his fillings, and confessed to the church that his previous testimony had been false. Strangely, he discovered that he was not alone...!

Beware! God is quite capable of doing whatever he likes with teeth, but technique and cultivated atmosphere are no substitute for spiritual reality.

Thought

Sheep need to be serpents and doves. What a menagerie!

What if...? 1 Corinthians 15:19, 29–34 (NIV)

If only for this life we have hope in Christ, we are to be pitied more than all men... Now if there is no resurrection, what will those do who are baptised for the dead? If the dead are not raised at all, why are people baptised for them? And as for us, why do we endanger ourselves every hour? I die every day—I mean that, brothers—just as surely as I glory over you in Christ Jesus our Lord. If I fought wild beasts in Ephesus for merely human reasons, what have I gained? If the dead are not raised, 'Let us eat and drink, for tomorrow we die.' Do not be misled: 'Bad company corrupts good character.' Come back to your senses as you ought, and stop sinning; for there are some who are ignorant of God—I say this to your shame.

This part of Paul's letter challenges me in a dark and dangerous part of myself, and I would like to share that challenge openly because I believe that many others will identify with my experience. It is about the final barrier between partial and total commitment to the demands of Jesus on the very centre of my will. Paul no longer cares about preserving his life in the worldly sense. Why should he, when he has encountered a dynamic, joy-inspiring God who beckons him on to an eternity of unspeakable rightness? He experiences terrible physical hardship and will eventually be executed because he pursues the path of obedience. It doesn't matter—he's not troubled. He's going to live with Jesus. It is this certainty that causes his incredulity over the Corinthians' acceptance of Christianity without resurrection. Why bother?

Sometimes a chill fear creeps over me. 'What', I ask myself, 'if I've got it all wrong? What if I'm giving my energy and time and concentration to something I've dreamed up—something that will collapse in darkness when the end comes? What if there *is* no resurrection?

These fears (or lies, if you like) don't inhabit me constantly, and I do have great faith in Jesus, but I know that a little part of my will stands back from the precipice of total trust, afraid that if I step out, I may not be caught.

Prayer

Father, help us to give up the world, and thereby gain everything. Forgive us for not trusting you.

New bodies for old

1 Corinthians 15:35–38, 42–44, 49 (NIV)

But someone may ask, 'How are the dead raised? With what kind of body will they come?' How foolish! What you sow does not come to life unless it dies. When you sow, you do not plant the body that will be, but just a seed, perhaps of wheat or of something else. But God gives it a body as he has determined, and to each kind of seed he gives its own body... So will it be with the resurrection of the dead. The body that is sown is perishable, it is raised imperishable; it is sown in dishonour, it is raised in glory; it is sown in weakness, it is raised in power; it is sown a natural body, it is raised a spiritual body. If there is a natural body, there is also a spiritual body... And just as we have borne the likeness of the earthly man, so shall we bear the likeness of the man from heaven.

I'm afraid I would have made a rather good Corinthian—I mean in the sense that I can easily identify with their problems. Paul is dealing with their worries about life in the hereafter in this passage. What kind of bodies will we have? The same? Different? Will we know each other? Will we be able to talk to each other? The apostle suggests that our heavenly bodies will be like blooms that have grown from seed that has died (our earthly bodies) and that the contrast between the one and the other will be as dramatic as a sunflower emerging like magic from a scrap of parrot food. Now, we are like Adam. Then, we shall be like Jesus.

I must confess that when I look at my own body (an experience to be avoided whenever possible) I am very glad that the responsibility is God's and not mine.

I shall never forget hearing about a girl called Jayne, who had cerebral palsy. Jayne was a devout Christian who brought joy into many lives. She died at the age of sixteen after a totally wheelchair-bound life. Shortly before her death she had a vision of herself entering heaven.

'Oh, mummy,' she said, 'I'm walking through the gates of heaven! Mummy, I'm dancing with Jesus!'

Let's get excited—I think it's probably going to be wonderful.

Prayer

Father, show us more of Jesus so that we will want to be like him.

Is it worth it?

1 Corinthians 15:56–58 (NIV)

The sting of death is sin, and the power of sin is the law. But thanks be to God! He gives us the victory through our Lord Jesus Christ. Therefore, my dear brothers, stand firm. Let nothing move you. Always give yourselves fully to the work of the Lord, because you know that your labour in the Lord is not in vain.

How we need our dulled eyes to be opened and brightened by Paul's enthusiasm and certainty. He carries through his earthly life a cosmic view of existence that seems to be denied to most Christians. In my travels around the country and the world I meet so many believers who are weary, or disappointed, or disenchanted, and sometimes I am one of them. There are times when I yearn with all my heart for some clear sign that my labour in the Lord is not in vain. Every now and then, God graciously gives me such a sign.

A few weeks ago a friend visited from London. He quite often drives over for a morning—there's nothing unusual about that. But, on this particular morning, as we walked the dog in a nearby field, something different happened. A ripple of pure excitement passed through me, and the colours around us seemed to acquire a new intensity and brightness, rather like the effect of sunlight suddenly shining through a crack in a leaden sky. I knew that God was crowning the moment with significance, but I didn't know any details. Not many years previously I would have crinkled my eyes into the classical smile of evangelical concern and insight and said, 'I think the Lord wants to speak to you, brother.' Instead, I said, 'Something's going on, Steve. God's involved in our meeting today, but I don't know what it's about. Is there anything you ought to say to me?'

There was something Steve had to say to me, and it *was* significant.

The point I want to make, though, is that in that short period when the Holy Spirit was so evidently in command, all problematic issues became totally irrelevant, and it was impossible to doubt the benefits of walking in the Lord. I would like to live in that experience for ever—and I will. Jesus has risen.

Prayer

Remind us of reality, Lord.

The letter killeth, but the spirit giveth life.

2 Corinthians 3:6

COMFORT FOR WEARY WALKERS

The Holy Spirit

As I sit down to write the introduction to this section, it is just after seven o'clock in the morning. I was the first one to get up, because I'd booked an alarm call for six-fifty, and I had to leap out of bed and sprint to the phone before it woke everybody else up. The phone in our bedroom was over on the piano by the door. It could have been placed nearer to the bed had it not been for the fact that I am quite capable of reaching a hand out, lifting the receiver, saying 'thank you very much', replacing it and going back to sleep. Nowadays, Bridget and I are usually recalled to consciousness by our new automatic tea-making device (bought last Christmas as a brave declaration that we are beginning to accept middle-age), but Bridget's parents are staying for a few days so we've lent it to them.

After having a shower (our shower has only two settings—'boiling' and 'arctic'), I went back to the bedroom to dress, observing when I arrived that Bridget was also up now. 'Last one up makes the the bed' is the rule in our bedroom. This tradition has occasionally resulted in an unseemly scramble to be the first one to actually get a foot on the floor, but this morning I had won by a mile, and the bed was already made. On the sofa at the other end of the room a small form was still enjoying the relaxed sleep of the innocent. Katy, aged ten, has relinquished her room for a few days so that her brother, David, can sleep in her room, in order that their nanna and grandpa can sleep in *his* room. It sounds complicated but it works, not least because Katy would much rather sleep on the sofa in our room than in her own bed. As I finished dressing I leaned down and kissed my daughter gently on the cheek. She stirred and peered balefully at me through one half-opened eye before settling down to go back to sleep. Downstairs my wife had ensured that the kettle was performing its accustomed task, and soon the first cup of tea of the morning, the one that truly resurrects, was in my hand.

Now, I am sitting at the computer typing these words. Katy is up, and commencing the crucial daily battle to make her hair look exactly as she wants it to; Joe, who has got an agency job for the Easter holidays, has crawled out of his bed on the third floor and is making low but resonantly penetrating groans of despair as he contemplates another eight hours spent in the incessant noise and tedium of the plastics factory; Bridget is trying to make sandwiches for Joe and lay the table for breakfast and find a hair-band for Katy all at the same time; Bridget's mother has just called down the stairs to ask if it's all right for them to use the bathroom now, and David is still dead to the world in Katy's bedroom upstairs. Through the window beside me I can see that one of those super-fresh early spring days is gathering itself delicately together, and I find myself wishing that I wasn't disciplined enough to stay in this chair until I've produced my daily quota of one thousand words.

Katy has just come in and leaned on my shoulder to ask what I'm writing about, then gone away disgusted because I said I was going to write about what she'd just said.

An average day in the Plass household is under way.

Where does the Holy Spirit fit into all this? Well, more to the point is that if he doesn't fit into this everyday ordinariness, then he doesn't really fit into any situation. Interpersonal relationships in a family like ours are filled with complexities, tensions and subtleties that have been shaped, controlled or altered by the practical ministry of the Holy Spirit. In case that sounds too vague, I mean that, over the years, Bridget and I have prayed for our children and each other a million times, sometimes in tears; we have implored his help to fight against impulses in ourselves that would assuredly have had very negative effects; we have tried to allow the direct and immediate influence of the Spirit to change very specific situations, occasionally with dramatic results; it would not be an exaggeration to say that we have survived as a family because the Holy Spirit is here with us as Jesus was with his disciples.

Much of the confusion and disappointment that one encounters among Christians seems to spring from a reluctance to allow that it is in the ordinary circumstances of life that we are most likely to see God working out his purposes. As a young Christian I went through agonies because it seemed so very difficult to transfer all the life and vibrancy of formal situations to the place where I actually was, to the dark space of solitude, the *at home* part of myself where religion meant nothing and I needed a God who was willing to become a small friendly person who would tolerate my weakness and just be with me. Today, I have moved very much closer to understanding that he was there—and he was there, all the time—but the clearing of my sight and perceptive faculties has taken—is taking—all my life. What I can say for sure, though, is that the Holy Spirit, in his most influential role, is a house-guest.

Prayer

Father, we want the Holy Spirit to be involved in the very centre of our lives. We invite him to join us when we are at our most ordinary and defenceless, and we thank you that you have provided us with a comforter to be with us in the same way that Jesus was with his followers 2,000 years ago. May we not be afraid to seek his help at the most dismal, despairing times, those times when religion means nothing, and we just need a friend. Amen.

Divine triviality

Acts 1:14–18 (NIV)

They all joined together constantly in prayer... In those days Peter stood up among the believers... and said, 'Brothers, the Scripture had to be fulfilled... concerning Judas...' (... Judas bought a field; there he fell headlong, his body burst open and all his intestines spilled out.)

I have written elsewhere about the ease with which the apparent ordinariness of life can seduce us into doubting the reality of a spiritual dimension. When you come back from an uplifting Christian meeting to find that the dog has messed in the middle of the living-room carpet, or the children have done something so unspeakably awful that you lose your temper and respond in equally unspeakable ways—or both—it is easy to believe that the uplift was caused by religious falsies of some kind.

In fact, God is more ordinary than the most ordinary thing that we can imagine. He made this world, and he inhabits it in a much broader and more secular way than the churches do. One of the most effective deceptions of the devil is the idea, fixed firmly in the minds of many Christians, that certain arenas are spiritual ones, while others are not. Couple this with subtly false teaching about the Holy Spirit working in us without any cooperation on our part, and you have the dismally frequent phenomenon of the paralysed Christian. When the Spirit works in us it will never be without our assent. That assent will require the virtue that Jesus rated so highly—obedience. Doing what you're told can be very tough indeed.

Peter stands up, filled with the Spirit, at this early and highly dramatic stage in the history of the Church, to perform obediently the job that is required at that particular moment, but let's not kid ourselves. The Holy Spirit does not confine himself (unlike some speakers) to large meetings. We might not have experienced tongues of flame, and we may never be called upon to act as the hinge upon which the history of the Church turns, but the Holy Spirit is just as keen to find arenas in our personal lives where, given our obedient cooperation, he can change a life or a situation for the better, however trivial or ordinary that situation may seem to us.

'And Adrian, filled with the Spirit, stood up in the kitchen, and did not get irritable and sulk as he would normally have done, and those who saw this were amazed, and said, "Surely this man has been drinking." But he hadn't (not this time). He was just doing what he was told for once...'

Prayer
Holy Spirit, inspire me in the ordinary things.

Least of the gifts

1 Corinthians 14:39–40 (NIV)

Therefore, my brothers, be eager to prophesy, and do not forbid speaking in tongues. But everything should be done in a fitting and orderly way.

I've written little about speaking in tongues, despite the fact that this gift has become a very important part of my life. There are two reasons for this reticence, one quite unworthy, another that springs from genuine concern.

The unworthy reason is connected with the look one sometimes gets when this subject arises. 'Here's another one for the funny-farm' just about sums it up. This negative response has been intensified by the unfortunate way this gift has been elevated to a status that it was never supposed to have. How foolish to suppose that Christians must have this gift. I confess that there were times in the past when I kept my mouth shut during discussions about 'The Gifts', just to avoid being thought a loony. I should have spoken up, and didn't.

The more sensible reason for restraint (even now, when being thought a loony is the least of my problems) is an awareness that love is the gift of gifts and I would rather talk about that great sea of generosity than one little drop of benefit, however shiny it may be. An unhealthy appetite for 'magic' has caused a lot of trouble in the past.

Having said all that, I am glad that, on a Thursday night more than twenty-five years ago, a Christian friend called Marian nervously demonstrated the new gift she had received, so I could begin to understand what she was talking about when she said that the Holy Spirit was doing new and unexpected things in her life. Since that time I have spoken to God in a language that I don't understand on countless occasions, always (apart from one notable and alarming occasion which is recorded elsewhere) in private.

How can I describe this experience? Well, all I can say is that there are times when I run out of prayer and understanding and intelligence and just about everything else. When that happens a child—a baby perhaps—cries out to his daddy from inside me, and the language, or baby-talk, is what we call tongues. Sometimes—not often in my case because I'm a miserable beggar—it is an overflowing of sheer joy.

I remain sceptical about many tongues that I hear in churches, and about my own occasionally, and I know it's only another tool in the spiritual kit-bag, but it really has been such a helpful gift and I thank God for it.

Prayer

Lord, if you want to add this gift to the ones I've already got, help me to take it. If not, help me to be happy for those who have received it.

A little wine?

Ephesians 5:17–18 (NIV)

Therefore do not be foolish, but understand what the Lord's will is. Do not get drunk on wine, which leads to debauchery. Instead, be filled with the Spirit.

The prospect of being in a state of continual spiritual drunkenness appeals to me immensely. The fact is, though, that quite a lot of us Christians are leaning on the prop of alcohol as opposed to the power of the Spirit. In our zeal not to be governed by petty rules, could it be that we have gone too far? A robust wine-drinking culture has developed among many believers I know. Indeed, I'm sure that I have aided this development. I really do enjoy eating good food and drinking good red wine with good friends. There's nothing wrong with that, but there are times when, however jovial the situation, a little voice seems to whisper, 'You had enough some time ago—the small amount of control you've lost is too much.'

Why is the stimulation of contact with the Holy Spirit not sufficient sometimes? Let's have a little honesty here, shall we, as we examine the rival merits of these two sources of intoxication?

Well, you can buy the liquid sort up the road for quite a small amount of money. You don't have to be in a special state of mind or virtue, or believe anything specific in order to procure wine. You just have to be over eighteen and have enough money. It can be shared with friends without having to establish that they are in a like spiritual state, and you can always go and get more if you run out. It's an easy, perhaps lazy, way of achieving a quick buzz and a convivial atmosphere. Drawbacks are (speaking personally) that if you do drink a bit too much you end up with a headache and a dry mouth in the morning, and possibly the memory of saying things that have no chance of surviving scrutiny in the cold light of day. Worst of all, though, is the sense that you have been conned into accepting a counterfeit, because it was, or appeared to be, more readily available than the real thing.

The real thing—being drunk in the Spirit—is the purest experience that I have known, although I've only experienced it a few times. It has happened to me when I have been walking closely with Jesus, and there is no hangover, no trace of regret, no headache and no feeling of being conned. It's a taste of joy and eternity. Why do I ever settle for anything else? Too much like hard work? Too expensive? Ah, those are the questions that are being put to me even as I write...

Prayer

Stick with me, Father. Help me to grow up and grow towards you.

Whose agenda?

Revelation 1:19–20 (NIV)

'Write, therefore, what you have seen, what is now and what will take place later... The seven stars are the angels of the seven churches, and the seven lampstands are the seven churches.'

At a big Christian festival over in Europe recently, a friend told me, the number of people requesting counselling from the on-site team (of which he's a member) was considerably less than in recent years. My friend couldn't explain the change, but as I listened to a variety of festival speakers I felt that I'd found a clue. The fact was, that if you picked the right seminar or discussion, and carefully avoided others, you would be able to hear justification for just about any point of view you wished to take.

Gay Christianity is a good example. A large proportion of those who used the counselling team in the past were seeking help with problems relating to that issue. Many of them felt that scripture, and the Church, had established a norm of disapproval towards homosexual practice, sometimes seasoned with non-judgmental love and compassion, but, sadly, very often not. Those gay Christians who accepted this view as an expression of the mind of God experienced agonies of guilt and resentment, often expressed to members of the counselling team. Now, however, with the climate of opinion in the Church changing so quickly, it was possible to hear one speaker stating categorically that homosexual practice is perfectly compatible with Christian belief, while in the next tent but one the opposite view was being put, less dogmatically (politics creep in everywhere, don't they?), but with an equal underlying conviction. Why should you need counselling about something that is openly and unequivocally given the public seal of approval?

The same dichotomy of view was evident in the general area of sex outside marriage. I'm not concerned here to express my view on these matters. I just want to say two things. First, how much we need to hear what the Spirit says to the churches in this age, as opposed to what we concoct to support our own inclinations. I would like God to lay it on the line. Where are the mad, brave, genuine, unpopular, effective prophets of this age? Secondly, are those who stand and claim to speak for God—on whichever side of whichever argument, myself included—prepared to change, adapt or totally dump their ideas when the Spirit tells them they're wrong? If not—what's the point of it all?

Prayer

Holy Spirit, speak truth into the Church. Give us the grace to listen and respond.

Using the gifts

John 15:12; 16:7 (NIV)

My command is this: Love each other as I have loved you... But I tell you the truth: It is for your good that I am going away. Unless I go away, the Counsellor will not come to you; but if I go, I will send him to you.

A man called Bill had two grown-up daughters, whose names were Imogen and Sally. Imogen, a handsome, impractical girl, gifted with a powerful imagination, was perhaps just a little too intense for her own or other people's good. Sally, the younger sister, was a relaxed, intelligent creature with a homely smile and a lot of common sense. She annoyed Imogen from time to time by being, not only right, but nice as well.

One day Bill had to go away. He got up early, got ready, then woke his daughters and spoke kindly to them.

'Girls, I have to go away for a while, and I have two things to say before I leave. Most important, I want you to be nice to each other. Nothing matters much compared with that. Okay?'

Both girls nodded, but only Sally was able to be upset and take in what her father was saying.

'The other thing,' continued Bill, 'is that, in the kitchen, you'll find a present, or rather some presents, that should make it easier for you to remember me and do what I've asked. Now I must go.'

A little later the girls crept excitedly into the kitchen to discover a brand-new set of pots and pans on the table.

'Oh, Sally,' cried Imogen, 'what a wonderful way to remember Father! Every day we'll put the pots and pans on the table and look at them and think about how much we love him, and then, after giving them a good polish, we'll put them away until the next day.'

'You're joking,' laughed Sally. 'We're not going to just look at them—that's not what they're for.'

'Well, what are they for, then, clever-clogs?' grumped Imogen.

'They're for cooking with, of course. That's what Father meant. He wants us to prepare lovely meals for each other every day. We're supposed to use them, not sit and look at them! You are funny.'

Imogen was horrified. 'Mess up these beautiful things Father has given us with horrible, dirty old food, and then have to wash them up? Never!'

'Come on,' coaxed Sally, 'let me make you something tonight.'

But Imogen cradled the set of utensils and glared at her sister. 'Get out of the kitchen!' she shouted, 'You don't belong here—you'll cook with these over my dead body!'

Thoughts

What happens when Bill gets back?

When a church has gifts but lacks love, it may be a dead body.

Threesome

2 Corinthians 13:14 (NIV)

May the grace of the Lord Jesus Christ, and the love of God, and the fellowship of the Holy Spirit be with you all.

How do you imagine the members of the Trinity? Do you think it matters if we picture them in a human setting? I don't see how it can. After all, two thousand years ago it actually happened. God became man. Those are the three words that changed the world. If you do think it matters—well, you'd better not read any more of this note. Bye!

It's late at night. Three figures are sitting around a camp-fire on the banks of the sea of Galilee, enjoying the way the sparks fly, and the smell of freshly-caught fish sizzling over the flames. It's not a bottle party. Instead, the trio have contributed large measures of the grace, love and fellowship that are specialities of this particular house. The Father is an older man (well, be fair—he's got to be, hasn't he?), a bearded, deep-eyed, still personality, rich with potential for earth-shattering anger, or extravagant, all-embracing love. He gazes into the flickering tongues of orange and red, his head filled with an eternity of thoughts.

Poking the embers with a long stick on the other side of the fire, in charge of the fish as usual because he has previous, hands-on experience, sits Jesus, the Son, the only one who has ever known or ever will know how it feels to be God with a real human skin. The marks of death are still on that skin, and will stay there until the victory that is already won has been claimed by the least, lost soul. He has a wonderful smile, laced with pain.

The third member of the party is more difficult to describe, except that he is like one of the flames in the fire—vital and restless, beautiful, moving, constantly changing shape, alternately reflecting light and seeming to disappear into the shadows. The Holy Spirit is the one who is out and about and doing—but he does enjoy fish as well.

So, when the meal has been cooked and eaten, and the family gets down to business, what is the subject of their intense, concerned conversation? The answer, believe it or not, dear reader, is that they are talking about—you.

Prayer

May the grace of our Lord Jesus Christ, the love of God, and the fellowship of the Holy Spirit be with us all, evermore. Amen.

Transported

Acts 8:39–40 (NIV)

When they came up out of the water, the Spirit of the Lord suddenly took Philip away, and the eunuch did not see him again, but went on his way rejoicing. Philip, however, appeared at Azotus and travelled about, preaching the gospel in all the towns until he reached Caesarea.

What an amazing period of Church history this was. And for someone like me who spends hours on trains and in cars, the speed and simplicity of Philip's transport after finishing his task is highly enviable. But as I read this story I find myself asking one of those questions to which you never really expect to find a totally satisfactory answer.

Why, if the Holy Spirit is capable of such dramatic activity—activity moreover that appears easily to bypass the limitations of nature—doesn't he simply sort out all the problems of creation with a series of divine conjuring tricks? The usual answer is, of course, that human beings have been given free will, and God would never use his power to change people who don't want to be changed. I don't dismiss this argument—it's the best one I've heard—but it still doesn't really explain why God doesn't intervene frequently, dramatically and miraculously in order to provide all the information people need to make the sort of changes in their thinking and behaviour that the Bible tells us they so urgently need. Why not organize thousands of Damascus Road experiences for people who are unsure and wavering, or, like Saul, desperately resisting the awareness that faith is developing inside them. What about huge messages inscribed across the sky by a giant hand, like Daniel's writing on the wall? Why not chuck a thunderbolt or two at well-known evildoers? Some significant public healings? I've got lots of ideas. For instance, what about—

'Enough!' says the small, definite voice that heads off some of my less productive mental indulgences. 'My ways are not your ways. My solutions are not your solutions. You're not even asking the right questions—I don't know how you expect to understand the answers. You'll end up putting other people off. Tell them something you do know for sure, like the fact that I forgive you every time you're not available to do the things that might bring someone a bit nearer.'

'Sorry.'

'It's all right.'

Prayer

Thank you for the things that we do know. We'll go on asking questions, but help us to accept that sometimes the answers will be beyond us.

Each to his own

Galatians 2:11 (NIV)

When Peter came to Antioch, I opposed him to his face, because he was in the wrong.

'You wouldn't mind if I made a comment, would you?'

After hearing me speak, folks had lingered for a chat. Now there were two left, a man, and the woman who'd asked the question.

'No,' I adopted my always-willing-to-accept-constructive-criticism expression, 'of course I wouldn't mind. Go ahead.'

'Well,' she said, 'I just want to say I think it's not a good idea to trivialize sin like you do. Adultery's nothing to joke about. A lot of people get very hurt when something like that happens.'

I knew what she was referring to. I'd talked about the adulterous relationship between David and Bathsheba, and David's subsequent confrontation with Nathan the prophet. Nothing trivial about that, but then I said something like this:

'Right, anyone who's committing adultery at the moment raise a hand—no, don't! I didn't mean it!'

I could see how she might have thought I regarded this sin as trivial, but experience has shown that, as far as my own work is concerned, this kind of approach is far more effective than simply telling people off. Still, perhaps this lady was right—perhaps I had got it all wrong.

'Thank you,' I said (humble, eh?), 'I'll certainly think about that.'

I could sense that the man who was waiting to speak to me was getting rather agitated. The woman left and I turned to him.

'Hello,' I said.

'Hello,' he said, 'I've been committing adultery with my neighbour's wife,' and he burst into tears.

We prayed together and he went off with Jesus to wrestle with the world, the flesh and the devil. I tell this story because it further confirms my growing conviction that God takes a Peter, a Paul, a Felicity, an Agnes, a Bert or an Adrian, and says, 'The Holy Spirit shall work through the personalities of these people, and though the style of that work may vary from person to person, the fruits will not. Lay off each other.'

Prayer

Father, I don't like criticism, but I need it. Help me to listen and learn from what other people say to me. But help me also to be true to the task you have given me, and to do it in a way that honours you. I will try to respect the way in which my brothers and sisters work for you, however strange or different it may appear.

Lies and damned lies Acts 5:3–5; 7–10 (NIV)

Then Peter said, 'Ananias, how is it that Satan has so filled your heart that you have lied to the Holy Spirit and have kept for yourself some of the money you received for the land?... What made you think of doing such a thing? You have not lied to men but to God.'... Later his wife came in, not knowing what had happened. Peter asked her, 'Tell me, is this the price you and Ananias got for the land?' 'Yes,' she said... Peter said to her, 'How could you agree to test the Spirit of the Lord?...' At that moment she fell down at his feet and died.

Good bit this, isn't it?

'No,' you reply, 'it's not a "good bit", it's a horrible bit. These two people get bumped off for telling a fib. Horrible!'

Nobody likes this story much. I've sat in many Bible studies watching people wrestle with the idea that the God whose name is love could be capable of causing someone's death because of a lie. That aspect doesn't actually trouble me too much—I do moan about God occasionally, but, deep down, I trust he knows what he's doing. What interests me is an idea I have that most of us tell many more lies than we care to face. Maybe that's what makes this story so unpopular.

Take me, for instance. I've practically made a living out of telling the truth, and I do try to be as honest as possible whenever I write or speak, but, as with many others, there are some shadowy areas that just don't get talked about. And the way in which wives and husbands cover for each other is a good example. It's become a habit over the years for my wife and I to shade or bend the truth, if necessary, when one of us is particularly vulnerable or under attack from the 'outside world'. Do all couples do this? I've no idea. Is it wrong? Well, I've always told myself that it's a sort of special case—dishonesty made honourable by the fact that we are protecting each other. But is this what happened with Ananias and Sapphira? We're told that she knew exactly what was going on and quite readily, almost automatically perhaps, supported his attempt to cheat the Holy Spirit. Maybe she was just being loyal, but it came to the same thing in the end.

I suspect that there may be an area of subtle danger here. We are certainly taught that husband and wife become one flesh, but the neglect of individual development and responsibility can result in corporate acts of dishonesty that may seem comparatively small and reassuringly domestic at the time, but—well, read the story again.

Prayer

Father, help us to remember that we are accountable to you before anyone else.

The bottom line **Romans 8:12–17 (NIV)**

We have an obligation—but it is not to the sinful nature, to live according to it... For you did not receive a spirit that makes you a slave again to fear, but you received the Spirit of sonship. And by him we cry, 'Abba, Father.' The Spirit himself testifies with our spirit that we are God's children. Now if we are children, then we are heirs—heirs of God and co-heirs with Christ, if indeed we share in his sufferings in order that we may also share in his glory.

One criticism levelled against the Church in Victorian England is that it dulled the edge of resistance among the poor. Preachers exhorted worshippers to look forward to an eternity of joy that would totally eclipse the misery and hardship of this life, one minister whose sermon I read even claiming that the death of a young boy through starvation was actually a form of healing. Of course, the pendulum has swung violently since then, partly for the very good reason that many Christians are now aware that social issues are not just secular concerns, and partly for the very bad reason that people are frightened stiff (an apt expression) of dying, and are looking for a faith that focuses on this life rather than the life to come. This pendulumic swing has sometimes resulted in an odd form of Christianity. It might be best expressed by slightly rewriting a famous portion of scripture.

'For God so loved the world that he gave his only Son, that whosoever believes in him, keeps his nose clean and makes a significant but sensibly balanced contribution to church life in terms of time and cash, shall have a reasonable expectation of material comfort, physical good health and ongoing prosperity in the fields of business and emotional relationships, with guidance provided as and when necessary so that opportunities in all these areas shall not be missed or wasted. Oh, yes—and eternal life gets thrown in as well.'

Have you noticed how ratty some Christians can get when their lives stop running smoothly. I know, because I've done it myself. How could God let this happen to me? I've had to sell the car. I'm eating into my capital...

I don't want to minimize these problems, but perhaps the pendulum has swung too far. Jesus died so we could 'share in his glory'. That's what he bought for us—not a semi-detached in Bromley. The bottom line for those of us who, by the Spirit, cry '*Abba*, Father', is that we shall be with him for ever in paradise, and then we shall find out what that 'glory' really means.

Prayer

Thank you for eternal life. I prioritize it—help my unprioritization.

The most important thing

Matthew 7:21–23 (NIV)

'Not everyone who says to me, "Lord, Lord", will enter the kingdom of heaven, but only he who does the will of my Father who is in heaven. Many will say to me on that day, "Lord, Lord, did we not prophesy in your name, and in your name drive out demons and perform many miracles?" Then I will tell them plainly, "I never knew you. Away from me, you evildoers!"'

Here is perhaps the most ominous warning of all, from Jesus himself, that what is generally called 'Holy Spirit' activity is utterly useless if it is not accompanied or motivated by love. Not only is it useless—it can be very dangerous.

An elderly friend of mine, a devout Christian who has most unusual spiritual vision at times, told me of a visit she paid many years ago to a spiritualist meeting led by a famous 'healer' who was a close acquaintance of hers. My friend had no illusions about the spiritualist church, and would never have allowed this man to pray for her, but she occasionally went to his meetings to pray silently for him and for all those present. On this occasion she was sitting in a row of people feeling very conscious of a back pain that she suffered from periodically. Without warning (and without previous knowledge of her affliction) the man sitting next to her placed his hand on her back and prayed for the pain to be removed. The pain did go immediately, but my friend was very angry. She hadn't asked for prayer, and certainly wouldn't have wanted it from a member of the spiritualist church in any case. Later, her concern was fully justified. She collapsed at the sink in her kitchen, unprepared by the pain that usually warned her that it was necessary to lie down for an hour or two. How did the removal of that pain come about? I don't pretend to know, but I do know that I would not want any counterfeit benefits from the same source.

The alarming thing is that similar things are happening in those churches that evangelical Christians would describe as 'sound'. Let us never tire of reminding ourselves and each other that an appetite for spiritual fireworks needs to be curbed until we have learned how to care. Heaven is not the headquarters of the Magic Circle, it's the home of love.

Prayer

May Jesus be or become the most important thing.

Cuddling fear

Romans 8:15–16 (NIV)

For you did not receive a spirit that makes you a slave again to fear, but you received the Spirit of sonship. And by him we cry, 'Abba, Father.' The Spirit himself testifies with our spirit that we are God's children.

For as long as I can remember, darkness and light have both been only a step away from the place where I am. Sometimes it feels easier and safer to stand absolutely still.

When I was little this was not just a metaphor, it was a fact as well. There were many nights when I woke to find the darkness pressing upon me like a weight. So frightened was I that I would heave the weight aside, scramble from my bed and creep out onto the landing intending to seek refuge in my parents' room. Our landing received very little light from the frosted-glass window at the top of the stairs, and there were many occasions when I simply froze, midway through my journey. When I close my eyes I can still feel the cold emulsioned wall against which I placed the palm of my left hand, and the metal radiator on which my right hand rested, as I stood, paralysed, too scared to move forwards or backwards. This, despite the fact that I knew the door of my parents' room was very close, and that as soon as I opened it the light from their big front window would illuminate the path to safety. There was an intensity of fear in those locked, motionless minutes that has not been surpassed by any experience since, but there was something else as well. How can I describe that extra sensation without sounding completely mad? There was a cosiness about the pocket of velvet black in which I stood like a human statue, that was compounded of independence and excitement because no one knew that I was there, and, ludicrous though it sounds in view of all that I've already said, a kind of safety. I wasn't anywhere, and in the sort of childhood I had, that wasn't a bad place to be.

I have always, for as long as I can remember, been just a step away from darkness and light, and I am still tempted to stay exactly where I am.

Prayer

Father, there are real dangers in cuddling our fears to ourselves. We are supposed to be free children of God, but a lack of trust prevents us from taking the step that might make all the difference. Lead us gently from the landing to the light, Lord. Lead us to the kind of security that doesn't need to play games.

Brooding Spirit

Genesis 1:1–2 (NIV)

In the beginning God created the heavens and the earth. Now the earth was formless and empty, darkness was over the surface of the deep, and the Spirit of God was hovering over the waters.

Autumn is a fierce reply
To those who still deny your brooding heart
Flaming death in fading sun
The yearly mulching of elation, sadness, pain
A branch unclothed
The tatters flying, tentatively lying
Far more beautiful for dying
Rainbowed floating rain
The final breath
Softly whispering 'enough'
But memories come down like leaves
On old uneven pathways
Such a sweetness
See my breathing stands upon the air
And you, my oldest friend, are there
As evening falls
We pass between the tall park gates
A short cut to the town
A shiver moves the children's swings
The earth is soft and dark and rich
A Christmas cake
We know the grass
Will not be cut again this year
So down the tiled streets
The peopled rivulets
Perhaps towards some tea
In places that were ours but now have changed
Though early Autumn darkness
Stares as hungrily through plate-glass windows
Velveted by bright electric embers
We are glad to be there pouring tea
And pleased that we are laughing once again
Relieved that we are us once more
I have been troubled by a fear
That everything is gone
The fingertips of friendship cold and numb
But Autumn is a season that returns
With intimations of the death of pain

And so, my friend, shall we
Spirit, you have brooded well
Melancholy Autumn beauty
And the Spring to come

Prayer

The creation is still beautiful, Father, even in its fallen state. Help us to hear the message that the Spirit offers us through the seasons. How wonderful it must have been when it was new. How wonderful it will be when it is new again.

In the resurrection everyone will receive that bodily stature which he had in his prime, even though he has died an old man.

St Augustine

POWER TO PERSEVERE

The miracle of resurrection

Have you heard of Bert Hinkler?

I was about to say, 'No, neither had I until last year'—but I expect someone is replying, 'Yes, actually, I have.' There are always a few clever Dicks around to put us all straight, aren't there? You know the sort of people I mean. They're the ones who go along to watch TV quiz shows being made, and shout out the right answer when the contestants are stumped and the question-master says, 'Let's ask our audience.' They're the ones who have been aware for years that a pregnant goldfish is called a 'twit'. They're the ones who came out of their mother's womb, not clearing their lungs with a good old vulgar cry, but reeling off the entire list of the kings and queens of England, the ones who are programmed within their genes to know that a 'pucket' is a congress of caterpillars. They're the ones who, if ever they entered for the Mastermind contest on television, would choose General Knowledge as their specialist subject.

Anyway, leaving them aside, for all those who are honest enough to admit that they do not have an encyclopaedic knowledge of Bert Hinkler, I would like to tell you how Bridget and I came to hear about him, and about the unusual act of resurrection that has been organized in his honour.

In the summer of 1996 we took three of our children on a speaking tour that involved three weeks in Australia, a week in New Zealand and a week in America. In the course of the Australian part of the tour, we made a return visit to the state of Queensland, a vast tract of country that we have come to love very much, not just because it is a beautiful and fascinating part of the world, but also because we have many good friends there (and I can nearly do the accent). One evening we were booked to speak in Bundaberg, a small coastal town where we had stayed during a previous trip. The only thing we really knew about Bundaberg was the fact that a very good ginger beer was manufactured there, one which is sold in its stubby brown glass bottles all over Australia—we've consumed many a gallon of ice-cold ginger beer during long, hot car-trips in Oz.

This particular evening was a specially significant one for Bridget and me. August the first was our twenty-sixth wedding anniversary, and the children had stayed behind for the night with a friend in the Sunshine Coast apartment that was to be our base while we were in Queensland.

A large sign over the entrance to the motel we had been booked into informed us and the rest of the world that it was called simply 'The Bert Hinkler Motor Inn'. Even as we registered and found our way to the room where we were to stay the night, I found myself idly wondering if Bert Hinkler was the owner of a whole chain of motels, or whether he was some famous ex-resident of Bundaberg whose name was likely to appear on garages and restaurants and memorial halls all over town, rather as King Arthur's does in Tintagel.

Our room was well-equipped and comfortable, except for one item, a double water-bed, something neither of us had ever experienced before. I lay down tentatively on one side, only to find that the tide immediately came in, as it were, on the other, causing it to expand and rise bulbously. I nervously anticipated, rightly as it turned out, that trying to relax on the stomach of a giant suffering from gastro-enteritis would be easier than sleeping on this thing. Bridget took one look at my overweight form encased in its deep rubber trough, and said dispassionately, 'We might as well cancel our trip to Harvey Bay to see the whales.'

Very amusing. Deciding to change the subject, I spoke from my watery grave.

'Who do you think Bert Hinkler is?'

'No idea. Who do *you* think he is?'

'No idea—that's why I asked you.'

Conversation always sparkles like that in the Plass household. That's the way it is with writers.

Our performance went well that evening. It was one of those very local events where everyone knows everyone else, and they've all set out from home with the firm intention of having a really good evening whatever happens. It was fun and friendly and we felt good.

As our host drove us home we asked him who Bert Hinkler was.

'I'll show you tomorrow,' he said.

After a passionless night spent on our water-bed (a stand-up comic would undoubtedly have felt constrained to say that we were drifting apart) we checked out and set off with our host to a different part of town, where we found an extensive, beautifully maintained area of ornate gardens devoted exclusively to the memory of this same Bert Hinkler. Right in the centre of this area stood a house, and, so strange did this building appear to my eyes, that I stood quite still for a moment, trying to make sense of what I was seeing. For this unpretentious little villa, set in the middle of a small Queensland town halfway up the east coast of Australia, and 15,000 miles away from the islands of Great Britain was, without any doubt at all, a typically English house, dating perhaps from the mid-1920s. There it was—standing there—an English house.

'Come in and have a look round,' said our host.

Inside, we found that the furnishings and decoration were of exactly the same era, and that the house itself was a sort of museum—more than that, it was a shrine—to the memory of Bert Hinkler, one-time resident of the town of Bundaberg and a pioneer of international air travel.

We found out lots of facts about him.

Born in Bundaberg in 1892, by the age of nineteen Bert Hinkler had already constructed and flown his own glider. He ate, slept, breathed and dreamed flying. Arriving in England just as war broke out he offered himself to the Royal Naval Air Service and was accepted as a volunteer. After 122 flights over France, including thirty-six night bombing raids he was awarded the DSM and demobilized in 1919, having graduated as a pilot.

Hinkler then concentrated on record-breaking flights, including, in 1928, a new record for the trip from England to Australia, when he took fifteen and a half days to fly from Croydon to Darwin. The previous record had been twenty-nine days. Other exploits, adventures and records followed until, in 1933, in the course of a further flight to Australia, Hinkler's plane crashed in the Italian Alps and he was killed on impact. The Italian nation showed great sympathy, organizing and paying for a funeral with full military honours in Florence on Monday, 1 May 1933.

During his lifetime *The Times* newspaper had spoken of Hinkler's exceptional skill, daring judgment, and genius amounting almost to a sixth sense for the discovery of navigational facts, adding that his triumphs were ones of which the 'British race' must justly be proud.

And I had never heard of him.

We moved slowly from room to room in the little house, studying the faded old photographs of Bert greeting the press, Bert standing beside one of his planes waving goodbye before yet another record-challenging trip, and Bert being presented with an award by some long-dead dignitary. There were items of clothing and other bits and pieces that had actually belonged to Bert, together with framed documents of various kinds, all relating to his achievements and successes. There was no doubt at all that, in his time, Bert Hinkler had been a real celebrity, not just in Australia, but also in Great Britain (we discovered that he had been a long-time resident of Southampton), and in other parts of the world as well.

Pausing to look out across the gardens from of one of the upstairs windows I felt a sudden wave of sadness and a momentary shiver of something akin to fear. The inside of that house was so intimate and Bert Hinkler-ish. He and it had been so important once. Could it be possible that he simply didn't exist any more, and that hardly anybody really cared whether he ever had done or not? His name had meant nothing to me before arriving at the motel last night. I had vaguely assumed that he must be some kind of motel boss. I had been wrong, but what difference did it really make? All that fame and press coverage and excitement and sheer intensity of life had been more or less forgotten in England, where he had obviously been extremely well known at one time. I wondered how many Australians remained familiar with his name and exploits.

It suddenly occurred to me that I had still not solved the mystery of the house.

'Why,' I asked the lady who sat by the front door taking money, 'have you built a copy of an English house in an Australian town?'

'We haven't,' she replied.

'You haven't?'

'No, this isn't a copy of an English house, sir. This *is* an English house.'

'But how—?'

'This is the actual house that Bert Hinkler owned when he was living in England. The whole building was taken to pieces brick by brick, everything was numbered and recorded and packed up, and then it was all transported over to Australia and put together again exactly as it was in Southampton. Amazing, isn't it?'

I nodded. 'Yes, it is, quite amazing.'

I wandered outside after that and stood for a moment leaning on a fence in the bright Queensland sunshine, just staring at Bert Hinkler's Southampton house and indulging in a little fantasy. Imagine, I thought, if Bert were to be given a little holiday from wherever he was now—heaven, hopefully—and allowed to pay a brief visit to his old hometown of Bundaberg. He finds himself walking along the street, taking in all the old familiar sights and sounds that he once knew so well, when suddenly he comes to a dead stop.

'Cripes!' he exclaims, being an Australian, 'that looks just like my old house in England! What the heck is something like that doing here in Bundaberg?'

Slowly approaching the building he studies it in detail, becoming more and more puzzled as it dawns on him that this is not only *like* his old house. This *is* his old house. How could his Southampton residence possibly have got to Bundaberg, for goodness' sake? How could it? Some angel due for a rocket, no doubt, when the boss finds that the reality-reconstruction plans have been studied a little too carelessly.

I think that once he had learned what actually happened Bert would be really pleased, don't you? What an honour for him that the citizens of Bundaberg thought it worthwhile to take his house like some giant building kit, and carry it right across to the other side of the world, so that it could be rebuilt in the town that is proud to claim him as a son.

Of course, they were not able actually to resurrect Bert Hinkler, although I think that they would have done if they could. They had a jolly good try, didn't they? The following notes are about resurrection, which, for each of us, will be much more total and spectacular than Bert's. We shall be alive again, complete down to the last detail with the personalities that are unique to us, fully aware and able to recognize and communicate with each other. We shall not be in Bundaberg, beautiful though that town is, but in an even better place, where God himself will welcome us proudly as returned sons and daughters, and we shall take our rightful place as citizens of heaven.

I do hope Bert will be there.

Prayer

Father, we sometimes get a bit worried about the reality of resurrection and eternal life. Help us to hold as tightly to the words of Jesus as if we were clinging to his cloak in a crowd. Thank you for his costly and ultimate gift to us of life in heaven with you. Amen.

A change of landscape **John 20:1–4 (RSV)**

Now on the first day of the week Mary Magdalene came to the tomb early, while it was still dark, and saw that the stone had been taken away from the tomb. So she ran, and went to Simon Peter and the other disciple, the one whom Jesus loved, and said to them, 'They have taken the Lord out of the tomb, and we do not know where they have laid him.' Peter then came out with the other disciple, and they went toward the tomb. They both ran, but the other disciple outran Peter and reached the tomb first.

A friend of mine had a very frightening experience when he was a teenager. Walking home in the dark after a late party, he suddenly became aware that the landscape near his parents' house was 'all wrong'. A field that had been empty twelve hours earlier was now occupied by something that, on that cloudy starless night, appeared to be a castle-like building. Simon stood stock-still for a moment as his mind attempted in vain to accommodate this logical impossibility. Then, seized by scalp-prickling horror, he sprinted away to the safety of home, only to learn from his amused parents that the 'castle' was actually a huge marquee, erected for some event on the following day.

Mary's experience was probably worse. The stone was gone, the soldiers were gone and the body was gone. It was *all wrong*, and it must have shaken her up. Mysterious empty tombs on dark nights are the stuff that Hammer films are made of. No wonder she ran to where Peter and John were, gasping out as she arrived the quite reasonable hypothesis that someone had moved the body. What an impact her news made on the disciples!

Bleary-eyed and unwashed, the Steve Ovett and Sebastian Coe of the New Testament hitched their skirts up and gave it everything they'd got. On the final bend John overtook Peter and was first to arrive at the tomb, where, ironically after all that explosive effort, he stopped abruptly and was unable to bring himself actually to enter it. What a tumult of emotions, questions and speculations must have filled the mind and heart of the disciple whom Jesus loved.

A question

Is there anybody or anything in the world or the universe that would make me run like that?

Moments of truth

John 20:5–10 (RSV)

...stooping to look in, he saw the linen cloths lying there, but he did not go in. Then Simon Peter came, following him, and went into the tomb; he saw the linen cloths lying, and the napkin, which had been on his head, not lying with the linen cloths but rolled up in a place by itself. Then the other disciple, who reached the tomb first, also went in, and he saw and believed; for as yet they did not know the scripture, that he must rise from the dead.

One of the most significant moments in my life occurred on the top of a double-decker bus when I was about ten years old. That morning I had read the words 'Everyone is I' in some obscure book, and I was frowningly anxious to work out what it meant. As the bus arrived in Tunbridge Wells and stopped at a zebra crossing, I looked down and, seeing an elderly lady making her laborious way from one side of the road to the other, the truth suddenly hit me. That lady was as important to herself as I was to myself. I was not *the* star-player in the universe, and the rest of the world's population were not bit-players in my life. That recognition changed my perception fundamentally.

A much more famous moment of recognition happened in Israel when Malcolm Muggeridge, feeling cynical and sickened by commercialism and tourist exploitation of the (alleged) scene of Jesus' birth, gradually became aware of the way in which the faces of visiting pilgrims were quite transfigured by the idea that they were in the place where the great life began. Muggeridge saw a vital truth on that day and was deeply affected on a personal level.

Such moments of recognition impart knowledge that cannot be taught in normal ways and they change lives.

Here, in the empty tomb, Peter and John gaze with growing awareness at the way in which the grave clothes are lying in an undisturbed position, as though the body had melted quietly away. **In John's mind** at least the awe-inspiring truth chimed like heavenly bells. It *wasn't* all over. The story was *not* finished. Somewhere, somehow—Jesus was alive!

A question

Have we told others about the significant moments of recognition in our lives? Perhaps we think they weren't spiritual enough.

Blind grief

John 20:11–14 (RSV)

But Mary stood weeping outside the tomb, and as she wept she stooped to look into the tomb; and she saw two angels in white, sitting where the body of Jesus had lain, one at the head and one at the feet. They said to her, 'Woman, why are you weeping?' She said to them, 'Because they have taken away my Lord, and I do not know where they have laid him.' Saying this, she turned round and saw Jesus standing, but she did not know that it was Jesus.

Mary must have been pretty tough to withstand the traumas of this extraordinary day. When she got to the tomb, she experienced two encounters that my son would (with typical irreverence) describe as gob-smackers. The first was with the two angels.

When we read that Mary, still weeping, leaned down and saw two angels sitting in the tomb, then had a little chat with them, we tend to forget the drama and tension of the situation. This is partly due to the brevity with which the event is recorded, and partly to the dismal presentation of the scriptures that we have allowed and endured for generations. Public readings of the Bible have been conducted in tones of such sepulchral monotony for so long now that there is a corporate perception of biblical characters as two-dimensional, unemotional, cardboard cut-out figures who trot out their appointed lines in semi-anaesthetized voices. This distraught lady must have come very near to braining herself on the roof of the tomb when she saw these two strange figures who'd posted themselves at either end of the place where Jesus' body had lain. Did she know they were angels? I don't know, but such odd behaviour from human beings would have been no less alarming.

Perhaps the strength of grief overpowered fear, though. As soon as it became clear that these two beings knew nothing about the whereabouts of the body, Mary turned away to search elsewhere. How ironic that the angels asked their 'silly' question about why was she weeping because they could see Jesus standing behind her! Her sight was blurred by tears when she turned. She didn't recognize him.

A question

Do we grieve his absence even as he stands before us?

Getting excited

John 20:15–17 (RSV)

Jesus said to her, 'Woman, why are you weeping? Whom do you seek?' Supposing him to be the gardener, she said to him, 'Sir, if you have carried him away, tell me where you have laid him, and I will take him away.' Jesus said to her, 'Mary.' She turned and said to him in Hebrew, 'Rab-bo'ni!' (which means Teacher). Jesus said to her, 'Do not hold me, for I have not yet ascended to the Father, but go to my brethren and say to them, I am ascending to my Father and your Father, to my God and your God.'

I have seen films, pictures and mimes of this wonderful encounter, the second and most staggering of Mary's 'gob-smackers'. In most of these presentations Jesus is standing like some product of the taxidermist's art, stiffly gesturing away a remarkably restrained Mary who has attempted to touch him in an elegant, saint-like manner. If it *really* happened like that let's all give up and go and become frog-worshippers. G.K. Chesterton made the point that believers and non-believers alike have great problems about genuinely accepting the fact that 'he became man'. The divine ordinariness of Jesus should be one of our greatest comforts. Instead, it's a serious stumbling block to many, perhaps because it brings the reality of God so close that we are forced to respond from the heart, rather than from bits of our minds.

Do you really believe that Jesus was *not* smiling broadly when he asked Mary why she was crying and who she was looking for? Do you really think that Mary *didn't* throw herself at her beloved friend and master after he said her name in a way that was specially his? And do you not think he would have chucklingly retreated with both arms extended as he warned her that she must not touch him because he had not yet ascended to his Father ('not cooked yet' as a small friend put it)?

How we need some of this Mary-style excitement in the modern Church, the kind of excitement that follows *real* meetings with this *real* Jesus who is more down-to-earth than many of his followers.

Can you see her running and leaping, her eyes now wet with tears of joy, on her way to tell the disciples?

A prayer

We want to be excited, Lord.

Who needs who?

John 20:19–23 (RSV)

On the evening of that day, the first day of the week, the doors being shut where the disciples were, for fear of the Jews, Jesus came and stood among them and said to them, 'Peace be with you.' When he had said this, he showed them his hands and his side. Then the disciples were glad when they saw the Lord. Jesus said to them again, 'Peace be with you. As the Father has sent me, even so I send you.' And when he had said this, he breathed on them, and said to them, 'Receive the Holy Spirit. If you forgive the sins of any, they are forgiven, if you retain the sins of any, they are retained.'

Neither John's perception of the truth, nor Mary's account of that first sparkling meeting, seems to have inspired any courage in the disciples. Here they are on the evening of that same Sunday, securely locked in for fear of the Jewish authorities tracking them down, probably discussing the day's events over and over again, but unable to *do* anything without the direct leadership and guidance of Jesus.

A lot of prayer-groups, churches and fellowships are in the same position. I've belonged to some of them. I've led one or two of them. Personally, I think it's far better to wait for Jesus to come, than to fabricate or role-play religious activity that is not authorized or commissioned. It's interesting to note that Jesus sends the disciples as he has been sent by the Father. In other words, he is asking for the kind of love and obedience that characterized his own ministry—a tall order for most of us without the comfort and assistance of the Holy Spirit. William Barclay points out how, from this speech, we learn that Jesus needs the Church, and the Church needs Jesus. Our failing groups might do well to abandon religion and invite Jesus to stand in their midst.

Once again the drama of the moment is rather inadequately expressed by the writer's assertion that 'the disciples were glad when they saw the Lord'. I'm quite sure that their responses varied from stunned silence to wild, celebrated joy. These people were not stained-glass window types. Jesus was alive—anything was possible.

A question

Do we believe that Jesus needs us? Do we need him?

Staying honest

John 20:24–25 (RSV)

Now Thomas, one of the twelve, called the Twin, was not with them when Jesus came. So the other disciples told him, 'We have seen the Lord.' But he said to them, 'Unless I see in his hands the print of the nails, and place my finger in the mark of the nails, and place my hand in his side, I will not believe.'

I like the sound of Thomas. He may have been a bit of an Eeyore ('Let us also go, that we may die with him'), but he was honest and straightforward, and more than ready to commit himself when the evidence was clear. We could do with a few more like him in the Church today.

A friend of mine had to attend a foundation course run by a fellowship in the Midlands (attendance was compulsory for all prospective church members). The leader read out 1 John 3:6, and said it meant that anyone who became a Christian would stop sinning. My friend (a Christian for many years) interjected. 'You're not saying, are you, that Christians never sin? Because they do, don't they?'

Reproof, Christian forgiveness, humble disagreement and heavily veiled human annoyance met in the crinkly smile of the leader. 'If that's what the scripture says,' he replied, 'then that must be the truth, mustn't it?' 'Well, I sin,' said my friend, 'don't you? And anyway, it says later on in the same letter that if we *do* sin—' 'I think we'd better agree to differ, friend,' interrupted the leader, 'we'll talk about it afterwards, OK?'

They did—and what horrified my friend was that it wasn't just a matter of mistaken teaching.

'Between you and me,' said the leader, 'of course Christians sin, but I didn't want to mislead all those new Christians on the course.'

Maybe Thomas was at fault for going off to be solitary with his grief (I would have missed Jesus' first appearance as well), but he stuck to his guns when faced with the emotional intensity of the others' experience. He wasn't going to say anything he didn't actually believe, however much he wanted it to be true. I like him.

A prayer

Father, help us to be honest and loving like Thomas, and help those of us who get a bit solitary, to be part of the Church, for your sake. We don't want to miss anything good!

A message from the past **John 20:26–31 (RSV)**

Eight days later, his disciples were again in the house, and Thomas was with them. The doors were shut, but Jesus came and stood among them, and said, 'Peace be with you.' Then he said to Thomas, 'Put your finger here, and see my hands, and put out your hand, and place it in my side: do not be faithless, but believing.' Thomas answered him, 'My Lord and my God!' Jesus said to him, 'Have you believed because you have seen me? Blessed are those who have not seen and yet believe.' Now Jesus did many other signs in the presence of the disciples, which are not written in this book; but these are written that you may believe that Jesus is the Christ, the Son of God, and that believing you may have life in his name.

Eight days after his first appearances Jesus stood among his disciples again, a real, touchable man. But the Bible doesn't say that Thomas did touch him, and I doubt if he bothered. That man standing in front of him, the man who had been at the front of his mind for the last eight days, as the other disciples endlessly discussed recent events, was Jesus. He was alive.

'My Lord and my God!' Thomas was as direct and uncompromising in his new-found belief as he had been in his doubt. As I said, Thomas (and all the others present behind those locked doors) were lucky. They met the risen Jesus and knew that death was somehow defeated. But now Jesus speaks a message down through the passage of 2,000 years to those of us who were not able to be there at the time.

'Blessed are those who have not seen and yet believe.' That's us, folks! We can meet the risen Jesus in the Bible, in personal or corporate prayer, and in the lives of others, but (except for a minuscule minority) we cannot meet him face to face as the disciples did. Jesus says we are blessed if we believe in him without that benefit. Let's face it, however good we may be at debating, it is only our personal experience of the risen Jesus that will convince others of the truth.

A reflection

Sceptic: *Why did God create evil, then?*
Disciple: *I don't know, but Jesus came back to life...*

Working and waiting

John 21:1–3 (RSV)

After this Jesus revealed himself again to the disciples by the Sea of Tiberias; and he revealed himself in this way. Simon Peter, Thomas called the Twin, Nathanael of Cana in Galilee, the sons of Zebedee, and two others of his disciples were together. Simon Peter said to them, 'I am going fishing.' They said to him, 'We will go with you.' They went out and got into the boat, but that night they caught nothing.

'Blow this for a game of soldiers—I'm going fishing!' This may not be an exact rendering of the Greek text, but I suspect it sums up Peter's feelings and attitudes. How long was a volatile character like him going to put up with hiding behind locked doors and waiting for something to happen? Jesus had said he was sending the disciples out to forgive and retain sins, empowered by the Holy Spirit, but somehow the 'Go!' had not yet been said. Perhaps, also, Peter was secretly troubled by his triple denial. Did it disqualify him? Was he forgiven? Would it ever be brought up? Peter was neither the first nor the last man to seek refuge from his anxieties in a day's fishing. They spent the whole night in the boat, but caught nothing. I bet they enjoyed it, though. A spot of hard physical effort can be an excellent antidote to the poison of emotional or spiritual turmoil. (This applies particularly to overweight, sedentary writers whose only exercise is eating.)

Whatever else was happening in the hearts of these disciples as they toiled with their nets, they must have been filled with a constant, buzzing excitement, an excitement that sprung from the knowledge that Jesus could turn up at any moment, in any place. Perhaps he would come walking across the surface of the water just as he had done before. Perhaps this time, Peter would keep his footing, join his master and do a little dance of joy with him across the Sea of Tiberius.

The Christian life at its best is like that, isn't it? Jesus can enter any situation, transforming it, and you and me. As the dawn breaks, that is what is about to happen to Peter.

A question

Am I watching for him? Do I expect him?

Unconditional love **John 21:4–8 (RSV)**

Just as day was breaking, Jesus stood on the beach; yet the disciples did not know that it was Jesus. Jesus said to them, 'Children, have you any fish?' They answered him, 'No.' He said to them, 'Cast the net on the right side of the boat, and you will find some.' So they cast it, and now they were not able to haul it in, for the quantity of fish. That disciple whom Jesus loved said to Peter, 'It is the Lord!' When Simon Peter heard that it was the Lord, he put on his clothes, for he was stripped for work, and sprang into the sea. But the other disciples came in the boat, dragging the net full of fish, for they were not far from the land, but about a hundred yards off.

If you want to know what the Christian faith is really about, this incident will provide as good an answer as any. It is about the kind of spontaneous, non-religious, extravagant love and affection that has motivated true followers of Jesus for generations.

At first, in the half-light of dawn, the disciples failed to recognize Jesus. As far are they were concerned he was a stranger who shouted advice from the shore (quite a common occurrence apparently), and very good advice it turned out to be.

Then, as the sky lightened and visibility improved, John happened to look towards the shore as he paused from his efforts for a moment, and something about the silhouette and stance of the solitary figure on the beach seemed terribly familiar.

'It's the Lord!' he whispered to Peter. Seconds later he must have been rocking in the slipstream of his large piscatorial colleague, who had stayed only for as long as it took to throw some clothes on before leaping into the water and splashing his way towards Jesus. Thoroughly confused at that point about the meaning of Jesus' past ministry, uncertain about the present, totally ignorant of what the future might hold, and with the knotty tissue of those three denials still unresolved, Peter just wanted to be with the person he loved. God grant us that same unconditional desire to be with Jesus.

A prayer

Father, help us to recognize Jesus when he helps us with ordinary things. We want to love him as much as Peter did.

God in his own world John 23:9–14 (RSV)

When they got out on land, they saw a charcoal fire there, with fish lying on it, and bread. Jesus said to them, 'Bring some of the fish that you have just caught.' So Simon Peter went aboard and hauled the net ashore, full of large fish, a hundred and fifty-three of them; and although there were so many, the net was not torn. Jesus said to them, 'Come and have breakfast.' Now none of the disciples dared asked him, 'Who are you?' They knew it was the Lord. Jesus came and took the bread and gave it to them, and so with the fish. This was now the third time that Jesus was revealed to the disciples after he was raised from the dead.

I have already mentioned, in connection with Mary's first sight of her risen master, the divine ordinariness of Jesus. Here, in this little scene on the beach, the same quality is even more dramatically evident. How wonderful that God doesn't approach such moments in his own history as though he was an epic film producer. No stirring music, no cast of thousands, no apocalyptic visions in the sky. The risen Jesus—God himself, the glory of the universe—was cooking breakfast for his friends. Real and solid, he nudged the fire into more effective life and moved his head to avoid getting smoke in his eyes. Ordinary. Peaceful.

Like waking up after a nightmare, a real encounter with God nearly always feels like a blessedly reassuring return to the familiar and warm sensation of true reality. That's why it's so important to make it clear to non-believers that they are not being asked to give their hearts to some alien, far-away, irrelevant concept. They might be more willing to give their hearts to a God who knows how to get an open fire going without matches or paraffin. This is the world *he* made. He and it are parts of the same reality.

Do you feel ignorant sometimes when you read the Bible? I often do. That's why I had to find out what other writers thought about the significance of the 153 fish that were caught by the disciples, and I was amazed at the number of complex explanations that have been suggested over the years. Do you think they just enjoyed counting their big catch, do you? Is that a possible explanation? No—too ordinary, eh?

A final question

What is 'real life'?

It has to be said

John 21:15–19 (RSV)

When they had finished breakfast, Jesus said to Simon Peter, 'Simon, son of John, do you love me more than these?' He said to him, 'Yes, Lord, you know that I love you.' He said to him, 'Feed my lambs.' A second time he said to him. 'Simon, son of John, do you love me?' He said to him, 'Yes, Lord, you know that I love you.' He said to him. 'Tend my sheep.' He said to him the third time, 'Simon, son of John, do you love me?' Peter was grieved because he said to him the third time, 'Do you love me?' And he said to him, 'Lord, you know everything; you know that I love you.' Jesus said to him, 'Feed my sheep. Truly, truly, I say to you, when you were young, you girded yourself and walked where you would; but when you are old, you will stretch out your hands, and another will gird you and carry you where you do not wish to go.' (This he said to show by what death he was to glorify God). And after this he said to him. 'Follow me.'

A young friend phoned me to describe a visit she had made to her grandmother in Germany. The old lady is matriarchal, stubborn and full of strong opinions—a force to be reckoned with. My friend, Greta, is a considerable force in her own right, but on this particular occasion she wasn't feeling very sure about anything. Since her baby son had died she had been struggling back to some level of hopefulness. Grandmother had clearly decided that the process would be accelerated by a detailed analysis of Greta's faults, weaknesses and recent failures, and that she would be the one to do it. Greta listened to this barrage of criticism until she just couldn't take any more. 'Even if that's all true, Gran,' she said, 'why don't you say nice things as well? Why don't you tell me you love me? That's what I need to hear.' 'Tell you I love you?' said her grandmother. 'I don't need to tell you that, it goes without saying.' But it didn't. Love needs to be spoken and heard. Peter needed to express his love for Jesus. His words sealed the total commitment that was being asked of him if he was to follow his master to the death.

A thought

God needs to be told that he's loved.

Never mind him **John 21:20–end (RSV)**

Peter turned and saw following them the disciple whom Jesus loved... When Peter saw him, he said to Jesus, 'Lord, what about this man?' Jesus said to him, 'if it is my will that he remain until I come, what is that to you? Follow me!' The saying spread abroad among the brethren that this disciple was not to die: yet Jesus did not say to him that he was not to die, but, 'If it is my will that he remain until I come, what is that to you?' This is the disciple who is bearing witness to these things, and who has written these things: and we know that his testimony is true. But there are also many other things which Jesus did; were every one of them to be written, I suppose that the world itself could not contain the books that would be written.

It's a little wearying to see that misunderstandings in the Christian Church began as long ago as this. And we've been pretty consistent ever since, haven't we? How have we managed to get so confused and puzzled and divided on issues such as healing and tongues and denominationalism and communion and how to arrange the chairs?

There is, however, no misunderstanding at all about Jesus' response to Peter's question: 'Never mind him—I'll sort him out. You follow me.' Isn't it difficult to allow other people to be what they are without commenting or wanting to modify their behaviour? Jesus was quite clear about these two disciples. Peter was to be a shepherd to the followers of the Saviour, and John was to be a witness to the things that Jesus had done and said. Both of these tasks were essential and each was assigned to an individual specially chosen by God.

So much to be done, but so much power and guidance available if we are willing to follow. The final verse of the book emphasizes the limitless scope of Jesus' activity in our world.

A prayer

Father, help us to be humble enough to appreciate and value the work that others do for you. We need each other so much. Teach us how to make the Church strong.

Also by Adrian Plass

THE UNLOCKING

God's escape plan for frightened people

With great honesty, through this collection of readings, meditations and prayers, Adrian Plass gently dismantles our carefully constructed edifices of pretence and face-saving to reveal our true selves. But he never makes us feel small or devalued. Instead he shows that the love and power of God can unlock our frightened selves and lead us out into truth and freedom. Also available in an audio version read by the author himself (approx. 3 hours listening time).

'Touching honesty about his failings and vulnerability gives reality and depth'
Ministry

'A first-class book that aims to get to the heart of the matter. A book for Christians of all persuasions.'
Eric Thorn, *European Christian Bookstore Journal*

Book: 128pp, pb, ref 3510 9, £5.99
2 C96 cassettes, ref 3512 5, £7.99 (incl. VAT)

Available from your local Christian bookshop or, in case of difficulty, direct from BRF. For address, see page 350.

Also from BRF

NEW DAYLIGHT

Daily Bible Reading Notes

If you have enjoyed reading *When You Walk*, you may wish to know that Adrian Plass is a regular contributor to *New Daylight*, BRF's series of daily Bible reading notes. *New Daylight* is published three times a year, in January, May and September.

New Daylight can be obtained from your local Christian bookshop, or on subscription. Contact BRF at the address below for details. *New Daylight* is also available in a large print edition.

The Bible Reading Fellowship
Peter's Way, Sandy Lane West
Oxford OX4 5HG
Tel. 01865 748227 Fax. 01865 773150